SCIENCE IN SOCCER

SCIENCE
IN SOCCER:
TRANSLATING
THEORY INTO PRACTICE

Warren Gregson
and
Martin Littlewood

BLOOMSBURY SPORT
LONDON · OXFORD · NEW YORK · NEW DELHI · SYDNEY

BLOOMSBURY SPORT
Bloomsbury Publishing Plc
50 Bedford Square, London, WC1B 3DP, UK

BLOOMSBURY, BLOOMSBURY SPORT and the Diana logo are trademarks of
Bloomsbury Publishing Plc

First published in Great Britain 2018

A catalogue record for this book is available from the British Library

Library of Congress Cataloguing-in-Publication data has been applied for

ISBN: PB: 978-1-4081-7380-0; eBook: 978-1-4081-8254-3

2 4 6 8 10 9 7 5 3 1

Typeset in Minion Pro by Deanta Global Publishing Services, Chennai, India
Printed and bound in Great Britain by CPI Group UK Ltd, Croydon CR0 4SY

FSC
www.fsc.org
MIX
Paper from
responsible sources
FSC® C013604

To find out more about our authors and books visit www.bloomsbury.com and
sign up for our newsletters

CONTENTS

FOREWORD

Sir Alex Ferguson

*Board Member and former manager,
Manchester United FC*

Throughout the period of my career as a player, coach and manager, I have seen the game evolve and change in many dimensions, both on and off the field. The fundamentals of the game have not changed, of course, and should not change. Many developments have taken place off the field with significant commercial and financial changes within the clubs and within the industry, both in the UK and globally. If we leave aside the move to varying formations and styles of play introduced by generations of coaches, the biggest impact on the game has been the application of sports science in the preparation, performance and review of all aspects of the game from within. I have always adopted an open mind on any new method or initiative if I could be convinced of the direct and tangible benefit of such advances, and I had many such instances in my time as a manager and enjoyed the direct benefits of those projects in my work.

Sports science now permeates all aspects of professional football and has provided a platform to enable players to develop, maximise potential and even extend their playing career. Coaches have also been able to tap into new forms of data and feedback to enable them to make more informed and therefore more effective decisions in managing their squads to perform consistently at the highest level. The intensity of the game in the UK and the congested programme of games have placed new demands on managers and players. Without the scientific research and application of such knowledge by qualified professionals, the industry could not have reached such levels, which ultimately have made the game faster and more exciting for the fan in the stadium or at home.

The recruitment and utilisation of sports science staff and the associated technologies have themselves provided a competitive advantage within the industry, and clubs at the top end of the game invest heavily in this discipline to give them an edge in performing at their optimum.

This ground-breaking text has been a cornerstone of the birth of sports science within football in the UK and beyond. It is fitting that the book has been renewed and extended in the memory of the late Professor Reilly, with the contribution of industry leading experts to further support its value to the aspiring student.

Professor Reilly was a visionary with the intellect, drive and determination to establish and extend the possibilities of science in football. The contribution of his legacy is assured through the generations of students who now deliver at the highest level in the industry and have become experts in their own right. Personally, I owe him a great debt – over the years, as many as fourteen staff members of my team were educated, inspired and mentored by Professor Reilly. We have also had several partnership academic research projects, some of which are ongoing.

I trust that this text and the knowledge contained within will inspire you to learn, develop and deliver your contribution in the same way as many have before you.

FOREWORD

Stuart Baxter

Head National Team Coach, South Africa

Over the years, no one could accuse our great game of football as traditionally welcoming changes with open arms, especially in the home of football, Great Britain. From the organising bodies to individual coaches and players, new concepts, ideas and knowledge had always taken time to gain credence within our game. Being wary rather than experimental was an attitude that had seen us turn a blind eye to developments outside of our immediate circle for far too long. If we didn't understand it, we attacked it, in an effort to retain our comfort zone, albeit one of limited scope. Maurice Maeterlinck, who in 1911 won the Nobel prize in literature, wrote 'each progressive spirit is opposed by a thousand mediocre minds appointed to guard the past'. Doing what you are comfortable with is easier than challenging your comfort zone and boundaries, and having played for your country does not exclude you from the need to grow.

The truth is that experience, and even knowledge, alone is not enough, as some would lead us to believe, other qualities such as curiosity and desire to learn are also necessary and form the triple axis of a football coach. Having these characteristics means that nothing is left uninvestigated in the quest for excellence, and a willingness to develop knowledge is essential. Fortunately, football has had her pioneers, who have gradually oiled the wheels of change and encouraged a definite awakening in how we perceive our game and the coaching of it. This greater curiosity has been reflected on many levels but possibly most of all in the area of sports science. Nowadays, sports science has gradually become more accepted and better understood and the majority of coaches now enjoy the challenge of integrating the components of sports science programmes into their preparations. What began as a physical trainer has been replaced by a sports science unit at the top clubs, with a much wider remit for improving performance.

Why wouldn't all coaches want the benefits of a full sports science support system? Some coaches still do not 'have time for it'. Some tolerate some aspects due to pressure from their sporting director or chairman, but never really embrace it. Some coaches feel comfortable incorporating a limited amount into their schedule, but feel that it shouldn't 'interfere' too much. Is this solely the fault of the coach? Absolutely not. During coach education, it is vital that the benefits of sports science are presented in a way that is both interesting and attractive to the coach. He should see very clearly that this is about 'interact' and not 'interfere'. He has to be set on a path that is worth travelling along so that he is not intimidated by concepts that he doesn't know where to place.

The main hurdle to overcome is one of insecurity! The decision-making and control base of the coach may be perceived to be diluted but it is not diminished by delegating responsibilities. Quite the opposite – it demonstrates confidence and assuredness and the controlling technique just changes slightly. Having said that, we are still loath to utilise the full extent of weaponry that sports science makes available. On coaching courses we are introduced to strategies that seem attractive, yet still we do not 'dare' to imagine, design or discuss how we could integrate more elements into our total strategy, or how we can use these weapons in our fight for points and trophies. At this point, maybe we should remind ourselves that it is actually still our goal, and that this is not some sort of footballing cosmetic surgery to impress the chairman. If we examine the nations, teams and managers who have achieved either excellent, surprising or consistently good results, we will find that the ability to dovetail progressive and, at times, aggressive and innovative elements of their sports science support into their own tactical/technical/social vision will be apparent. Often, the over-achievers have created their edge by bridging that 'quality' gap with better mental strength, physical power, coaching techniques, recuperation strategies and social unity, and the consistent achievers do not miss a trick. As I said earlier, we were slow starting and that cost us dearly. We have learned and adapted but the wealth of knowledge and expertise at our fingertips is still (for some) a no-go area.

American football has long embraced the multiple coach system, accepting that everyone has their special strength when coaching. They have utilised physical coaches and psychologists with a head coach coordinating things through his expertise of both coaching and management. This, for me, is the basis for modern coaching thinking: the head coach doing as much or as little on-field work as he deems necessary, but, moreover, having the self-confidence to incorporate assets from the sports science programme into his vision for the development of the team. Physical preparations and loading controls, recuperation strategies, monitoring and scouting, game and training analysis and psychology support to aid the learning process are all woven into the fabric that is the head coach's blueprint for success – trusting and challenging the various units to create an effective and empowered environment. It will therefore be a vital quality of this modern coach to have an overview of his blueprint, delegating detail, but understanding the larger brushstrokes. This can only be achieved through better, more dynamic coach education and the coach's desire to leave no stone unturned to achieve optimal results with the assets at his disposal. This synergy will become more and more important. The inquisitive, analytical and searching mindset of the forward-thinking coach and his ability to layer greater efficiency into his preparations helps to create a more positive and meticulous culture around the team, where tactically, technically, physically, mentally and socially, nothing is left to chance.

Carlos Bilardo, the famous Argentinian national coach, said: 'If you don't understand your past, then the present will be confused and you can have no hope for the future.' Well, we know what we have gone through in sports science and the trailblazers whose footsteps we are following. The content of this book both reflects and recognises the work that they pioneered in their specific fields and the inspiration that they spread among others. We owe them. So, with the help of the knowledge contained in these pages, let's make the 'now' an exciting first step of a new era of possibilities. Who will be blazing the trail for others to follow into the future?

INTRODUCTION

Professional soccer has evolved considerably over the last decade, coinciding with marked developments in the approaches to player preparation. In years gone by, the support team available to the manager or head coach often comprised a single fitness coach, a doctor and a physiotherapist to cater for the wide array of requirements that we have now come to associate with the modern-day player. Today, many clubs continue to invest significantly in state-of-the-art training facilities alongside a vast array of experts in fields ranging from performance analysis and nutrition to strength and conditioning and data science. Like many other professions, advances in knowledge and expertise are also now routinely acquired through external collaboration with university research centres and industry pioneers, from both within and outside the football industry. Furthermore, many clubs are routinely engaged in their own in-house research and development programmes in order to try and obtain every conceivable competitive edge.

Previous texts have provided comprehensive overviews of the ways in which the various sub-disciplines of sports science, including physiology, psychology, biomechanics, performance analysis, sociology and coaching science, can be used to improve development and performance in soccer. While these texts provide valuable insights into the science which underpins performance of the modern-day player, much of what we know today concerning elite player performance has been gleaned from the knowledge and experience gained from practitioners working in the field (practice-informed knowledge and research) alongside those applied scientists undertaking contemporary research (research-informed practice). Indeed, in the modern-day game, it is the merging of these facets that will lead to the greatest developments across many of the areas important in the development of the modern player.

In this book, we bring together the knowledge and experience of leading practitioners and applied scientists from a range of disciplines. Each chapter will provide an insight into the process of how the different scientific disciplines are translated into practice with the goal of enhancing player performance. Practical advice and solutions for neophyte practitioners and coaches will be given alongside coverage of the challenges frequently faced in multi-disciplinary support. The text also presents a series of reflections from graduates who have successfully gained employment in the professional football industry, highlighting the knowledge, skills and experience required to successfully progress in the various professions.

The book is divided into four parts. The focus in Part One is on managing the high-performance environment, with a specific emphasis on the use of psychology with players and teams. In the first chapter, Littlewood, Richardson and Nesti discuss how the sports psychologist can assist with shaping a culture conducive to high-level performance. In Chapter 2, the focus shifts as Littlewood, Luthardt and Nesti discuss the operationalisation and integration of sports psychology within academy settings in England and Germany, as well as the reality of attempting to construct an authentic psychological development programme. In Chapter 3, Nesti considers how sports psychology can be used to enhance performance in the first-team environment, particularly looking at the type of approaches that can be adopted with players and staff in what is often a very challenging, ruthless and pressured setting.

Part Two of the text focuses on the use of physiology with players and teams in professional football. In Chapter 4, Strudwick and Iaia initially outline how scientific principles are applied to maximise the training and delivery of field-based sessions to elite players. In Chapter 5, Driscoll and English then discuss the important processes evident in successful injury prevention and rehabilitation programmes. In Chapter 6 Beato and Drust discuss the role of both laboratory and field-based performance assessments in modern-day clubs. Chapter 7 sees Gregson, Hawkins and Thorpe discuss approaches to monitoring player load and fatigue status and the essential components of successful systems. In Chapter 8, the final chapter of this section, Morton and Close discuss the nutritional requirements of elite players and provide insights into the requirements before, during and after training and match-play.

Part Three focuses on skill acquisition and performance analysis. In Chapter 9, Ford, Diggle, Sulley and Williams provide advice to those responsible for delivering skill acquisition support to players, and propose solutions. In Chapter 10, Carling, Lawlor and Wells provide an overview of the structure and processes that are essential for the delivery of high-level performance analysis solutions in modern clubs. In Part Four we present a series of case-study reflections from sports science graduates who have successfully gained employment in the professional football industry. Here the graduates outline their thoughts concerning the knowledge and key skills required to progress in the various disciplines within the game.

This book is dedicated to Professor Tom Reilly. Tom was a true pioneer in science and football – arguably the founding father. A number of the research themes, scientific committees and conferences which continue to impact the game today stem from his visionary leadership. He inspired many people – indeed, many of the contributors to this text – and paved the way for future generations of scientists and practitioners to continue to impact the game he loved. A truly great professional, but more importantly, a truly great man.

Martin Littlewood and Warren Gregson
Football Exchange, Research Institute for Sport & Exercise Sciences, Liverpool John Moores University, United Kingdom

PART ONE

PART ONE

CHAPTER 1

SHAPING THE PERFORMANCE CULTURE: THE ROLE OF THE PERFORMANCE DIRECTOR

Dr Martin Littlewood, Prof. David Richardson and Dr Mark Nesti

*Football Exchange, Research Institute for Sport &
Exercise Sciences, Liverpool John Moores University, UK*

INTRODUCTION

In this chapter we outline the sports psychologist's potential role as performance director within a professional football club. In doing so, we draw upon two of the authors' (Littlewood's and Nesti's) extensive applied engagement within the English Premier League (EPL), spanning more than 15 years. We have also worked alongside a number of performance directors and individuals who have held related positions in professional football, and feel that this blend of experience provides a real-world insight that further informs the chapter. As academics, we also believe that this level of applied engagement should be viewed against the existing research (as little as there is in this field) and theoretical perspectives. It is in this way, through a critical dialogue between the worlds of practice and theory, that understanding of this particular role can be developed.

More specifically, we attempt to consider how the sports psychologist can assist with shaping a culture conducive to high-level performance. In order to do this, we will argue that the sports psychologist needs first of all to understand the existing organisational culture. It is our belief that change, especially in this challenging environment, is best achieved through a process that involves attending to daily working practices and helping the broader culture to evolve. We will examine notions around culture – why it is important, and how it impacts performance in a range of elite sports settings. This will highlight the stark contrast in performance cultures between sports. In relation to professional football, we will argue that, due to a range of historical and traditional features, the dominant cultural norms and values are particularly unique. Given this, it is vital that the sports psychologist is fully cognisant of this characteristic. We suggest that failure to allow this to direct the nature of the role will likely result in the sports psychologist either being largely ineffective, or being removed from their post (Nesti, 2010; Chandler *et al.*, 2014, McDougall *et al.*, 2015).

SCIENTIFIC BASIS

Before we can explore how to go about shaping a culture conducive to high-level sport performance we need to consider culture more generally. Culture is one of the most popular yet most misunderstood concepts that surrounds current and historical discourse concerning the evolution of societies and social entities. It is a complex hybrid of the disciplines of social psychology, sociology and anthropology (Nesti *et al.*, 2012; Richardson *et al.*, 2013). Although each discipline may lay claim to a definitive definition, we must recognise that the origins of cultural studies lie primarily within a social and anthropological context. Culture in psychology has endured a rollercoaster ride of acceptance, rejection and acceptance through its early citations through the 18th and 19th centuries, to the more recent renaissance of interest in it as an academic concept. Typically, the complex mosaic that defines culture leads to an unwillingness to study, research and/or consult in such areas. Furthermore, given that we are all a product of our exposure to cultural influence, it is a topic that (most) people feel that they have some level of knowledge and/or expertise in. Edward Burnett Tylor (1832–1917), a British anthropologist is (sometimes) credited with the first definition of culture in anthropology. Through an ethnographic lens, Tylor equated culture and civilisation in what he described as a complex body of work that embraced 'knowledge, belief, art, morals, law, custom, and any other capabilities and habits acquired by man as a member of society' (Tylor, 1871/1920, p. 1). While it is beyond the scope of this chapter to document the historical turbulence surrounding the meaning and concept of culture (i.e. in social psychology, sociology and/or anthropology), we accept that human behaviour can be influenced by, and perhaps explained through, understanding the context of the social groups to which we are exposed and subsequently socialised in and through.

To make sense of the influence of culture in a sporting context (i.e. within a developmental and performance environment), it is perhaps useful to refine the components of culture that are relevant to shaping the performance environment. Culture is the transfer of behaviour that is non-genetic, but, rather, that occurs through the interactions that exist within and between groups of people, or members of a group or groups. Culture, regardless of whether it is facilitative or debilitative to athletic development or performance enhancement, is a durable entity that typically defines the environment within which we operate. The culture of an environment tends to reflect its history and traditions, which are subsequently passed down from one generation to another. Such history and tradition also provide a guide for what constitutes acceptable behaviour within the environment. Wilson (2001, p. 354) suggests that 'many aspects of culture are embodied in rules of various sorts; some are laws … which are backed by official punishment for deviation, others are social norms (e.g. about what clothes to wear), which are backed by social disapproval and rejection of deviates.' Such an appreciation of culture allows us to discriminate between culture (i.e. organisational or environmental culture) and society (or societal culture). Culture, in this sense, captures the collection of people, their history, traditions, practices, ideas and relationships that exist within their respective institutions and that are represented through a range of objects, artefacts, images, rules and behaviours. Given our acceptance that culture and organisational culture exist, we must also acknowledge that it does not necessarily therefore mean that culture is strategically manipulated, organised or structured. Indeed, culture may be present, but we cannot assume that it is a systemised entity.

In basic terms, culture has been referred to as the 'feeling or meaning of the organisation' or 'what the organisation stands for' (Wilson, 2001). Typically such rhetoric has been misinterpreted or misrepresented as a function of the mission, vision and values that, through strategic management practices, organisations have been encouraged to capture. Whilst such mission statements, visions and values may act as a starting point, or may offer an external, more visible marker as to what the organisation is supposed to be about, they tend to fail to capture the deeper, more meaningful, less visible and more complex constituents of an organisation's culture. Schein described culture in the following terms:

A pattern of basic assumptions, invented, discovered or developed by a given group as it learns to cope with its problems of external adaptation and internal integration – that has worked well enough to be considered valid and, therefore, to be taught to new members as the correct way to perceive, think and relate to those problems. (Schein, 1991, p. 9)

Most organisations possess groups of people who gravitate towards each other through shared interests or expertise, in the pursuit of a common goal, or as a consequence of the collective provision of a particular service or function within the organisation. The world of codified football and the football industry have been around for many years (since the late 19th century and the 1950s, respectively) and are therefore beset with a host of traditions, values and expectations. The fairly recent commodification of the football product (see Relvas *et al.*, 2010) has begun to (slowly) witness the emergence of club mission statements, or customer charters, that may allude to such traditions, values, expectations and behaviours.* Argyris and Schön (1978) (cited in Wilson, 2001) suggested that if such values are not based on prior cultural learning then they might be seen as 'espoused values', rather than real values – in other words, as this is what we say we do, rather than as this is what we actually do. For example, a football club may report a commitment to the development of (indigenous) homegrown players, yet their first team may be full of foreign players and therefore contrary to their value statement.

The last 15 years or so have witnessed the scientific evolution of football and growth in the number of support staff surrounding both the performance and the youth environments. This evolution has consequently resulted in a number of 'newer' groups being formed within the organisation (e.g. sports science support, including strength and conditioning; performance analysis; sports psychologists; nutritionists; academy staff; education and welfare), alongside the existing, more traditional groups, such as the first team management and the coaching, medical and physiotherapy staff. Football has been accused of possessing a fairly traditional and myopic approach to the development of performance. Moreover, football clubs have been traditionally seen as closed cultures (Parker, 2000) with a reluctance to open their doors to outsiders and/or non-football people. In this regard, football clubs may be considered a hostage to the perils of organisational socialisation, as traditions and practices get passed down from generation to generation. At the same time as they are part of the wider organisation, these newer, non-traditional, even alien entities have had to seek acceptance within, and by, the traditional groups. Furthermore, these newer groups with distinct pockets of expertise have the potential to develop distinctive roles, values and norms that may not be shared by the culture as a whole. For example, an exercise physiologist may be at odds with the coaching staff as to the intensity of the coaching session prior to, or after, a specific fitness session, or each of these 'experts' may be championing the virtues of their specific session or expertise in terms of enhancing the performance of the individual or the team. Indeed, while both experts may have a legitimate performance argument, the fact that another entity (or expert) can contradict or challenge the status of the coach is a relatively new experience for the football club, and one that requires managing.

The prospect of subcultures (i.e. those that either do align or don't with the existing culture) being present within the organisation is a significant managerial consideration. Our earlier work (see Relvas et al., 2010) identified the presence of distinctly different cultures in youth and elite football environments. In that study we reported on the cultural incongruence that exists between youth and first-team environments, each with their own distinct game and operational cultures, resulting in a clear disconnect between the youth environment and the

---

* While mission statements are slowly emerging for business-orientated football clubs, a number of clubs still define themselves by their club motto rather than by a mission, a vision or values.

first-team environment. While we referred to the potential cultural incongruence that existed between youth and professional environments among the 26 elite European football clubs (including clubs from Spain, England, Italy, France and Sweden), we also noted the presence of the business managers, general sports directors and sports directors within the operating structures of these clubs. Given the plethora of emerging departments associated with sport performance and performance enhancement, and the challenges that football clubs face in managing and coordinating the input of each area, it is no surprise that we have witnessed the growing presence and significance of these sporting or performance directors within the strategic apex of the football club.

The presence of sporting directors or performance directors is not peculiar to football. Indeed, in that respect, it could be argued that football is just beginning to catch up with other sports. For example, Sir Dave Brailsford was appointed as the performance director at British Cycling in 2003. He has been lauded as one of the most successful performance directors in British sport, if not the world. The world of high-performance cycling is characterised by a similar array of sport performance expertise, including sports psychologists, sports technicians, biomechanists, physiologists and coaches. We also recognise that managing the co-existence of the 'gifted' athlete alongside these experts is a critical component of the role of the performance director. Brailsford described himself as a conductor who orchestrates the strategic synthesis and direction of the team (inclusive of the support staff and the athletes) (see Richardson, 2011). While there is limited academic literature around the role of the performance director, the work of Richardson and Nesti with the Leaders in Sport organisation (see leadersinsport. com), which includes interviews with the likes of Dave Brailsford, Steve Peters, Damien Comolli, Dan Ashworth, Peter Vint and Gary Anderson, tends to depict the role as a strategic facilitator. Specifically, the role involves the harmonisation of science and coaching staff and athletes to encourage them to improve and progress for the betterment of the individual and/or the team.

TRANSLATING THEORY TO PRACTICE: DELIVERY AND PRACTITIONER CHALLENGES

We will now consider how practitioners can operate when they are positioned in this type of performance-director role in an organisational structure. It is not uncommon that a sports psychologist will often be expected to take on the role of helping to develop a culture that can sustain peak performance. As has been discussed already, culture is often something that is easier to feel and sense than to identify in precise terms. Nevertheless, it is recognised as having a very influential role in creating the best sporting environments in the world. Evidence for this can be found in the work of Gilson et al. (2001) that involved examining how several of the most successful sports clubs in the world created and sustained high-performance cultures. Although it appeared that no club employed sports psychologists specifically to take the lead on developing this vital aspect of organisational life, there was ample evidence that key staff were expected to assume this role alongside other more specific responsibilities. Only one football club, Bayern Munich, is included in the sample. However, there are many similarities between Bayern's approach to culture and that found in the other sports clubs discussed in the book. Arguably, one of the most important of these is that there is a clear recognition that culture can be actively influenced and shaped, and that to do this effectively, there needs to be agreement at all levels about what type of culture should prevail. In addition, it seems that all of these elite teams are in agreement about the fundamental elements that must be in place to create a high-performance culture. These include establishing a vision and long-term goals, building from the ground up, operating in a consistent way, and protecting the values, traditions and philosophy of the club. Or, expressed differently, remembering who you are and what you stand for, and finding ways to allow this to infuse the organisation's culture at all levels, and on all occasions.

We argue that sports psychologists operating inside professional football clubs are ideally placed to be cultural engineers. Their job is to help the culture evolve so that it can support high-level performance. They can do this by taking practical steps to grow and renew the culture, and ensure that this creates the conditions for optimal performance. The work of Gilmore and Gilson (2007), based on a longitudinal study of performance culture inside an English Premier League (EPL) club, revealed how the sports psychologist, with the support of key staff – including most importantly, the manager – was able to affect the culture to support sustained achievement. Gilmore and Gilson describe how this was carried out through a combination of tangible and less tangible activities and initiatives. We will consider some of these within the next section in this chapter. However, it is worth mentioning at this point that very few tasks carried out by the sports psychologist connect closely to the sports psychology literature on developing team cohesion (Carron *et al.*, 2002) or on team dynamics and leadership (Chelladurai and Saleh, 1980). Rather, most of what takes place seems closer to the accounts provided by researchers and others writing about business management (Hardy, 1996; Palmer and Hardy, 1999) and cultural change and leadership (Wilson, 2001). This should not really be a surprise since much of the sports psychology literature to date is based on non-professional sport environments, whereas the business-related accounts share much common ground with professional sports like football.

THE ROLE AND DOING THE JOB

In this section we will look at the role that a sports psychologist can adopt to impact the performance culture when working within a professional football club. Until recently, most literature and theory gave the impression that the sports psychologist would be involved solely in delivering mental skills training and educational workshops to individuals and groups of players. However, more recent accounts strongly suggest that the reality is somewhat different (Chandler *et al.*, 2014; McDougall *et al.*, 2015). Whether the sports psychologist anticipates it or not, there is evidence to support the idea that professional football clubs expect the sports psychologist to work alongside senior staff to facilitate culture change, at both academy and first-team levels. In terms of theory and research relating to this fact, there is as yet very little beyond the work of Gilmore and Gilson (2007), Nesti (2010) and Nesti and Littlewood (2011), and, from a more empirical perspective, Fletcher *et al.* (2011), although the latter work is not in the area of elite level Premier League football. One of the common features of this academic work is that each in different ways draws on theory and concepts from organisational psychology and business and management theory. The earlier work of Carron on group dynamics and cohesion and of Chelladurai on leadership in sport is not especially useful to guide the applied practice of the sports psychologist in this unique and challenging environment. However, an improvement on this work – theory from mainstream organisational psychology – can be criticised for being unable to capture and relate to the reality of the occupational practices and culture in professional football. Because of this situation, the sports psychologist may feel lacking in theoretical guidance and preparation for the role. Therefore, this means that they will very often experience the uncomfortable situation of having to carry out work without possessing the requisite underpinning theoretical knowledge. In other words, they may feel that they are operating beyond the limits of their professional training and knowledge base. However, to carry out the job usefully and effectively, such training and knowledge is a necessity. In our view, and in agreement with Gilbourne and Richardson (2006), it is in this type of demanding situation that the sports psychologists draw on their craft knowledge and skills to enable them to meet the needs of the environment and the demands of the job. Given that craft knowledge is derived from experience and from critical reflection on practice, the sports psychologist will need to develop their knowledge and skills continuously in this regard. One of the ways in which they can do so is by working closely with a professionally accredited supervisor, especially one who has carried out similar types of work within professional football. As more practitioners who have experienced these demands themselves emerge as supervisors, the level of support available to the sports psychologist delivering in professional football will expand accordingly. We would argue that this is a vital need given the distinctive set of demands placed upon individuals in these positions.

The role of the sports psychologist includes dealing with broader, longer-term projects and issues that form part of the club's existing performance culture. To impact on these, the sports psychologist will necessarily be involved in matters relating to club philosophy, traditions, identity, values and behaviours. By definition, this complex task is continuous; it is impossible to identify a precise starting point or moment of completion. It is a process, and yet one that will have clear and visible impact on every activity, no matter how minor. At the other end of the continuum, the sports psychologist must help the club to build structures, systems and procedures that impact on the daily working practices of both staff and players. This work, while being very tangible and concrete, is of huge importance in shaping the overall culture. The challenge is to create a connection between the micro and macro activity of the organisation. The specific task is to build organisational systems that are congruent with the broader culture. In its turn, the culture must be one that fosters the establishment of optimum organisational processes.

At a practical level, this involves a number of activities that we would expect a skilled and competent sports psychologist to engage in, ranging from writing job descriptions for staff and assisting with induction and recruitment, to mentoring staff and fostering continued professional development (CPD) opportunities. In addition, other powerful tools to enhance communication and stimulate development could include organising staff awaydays, building team identity with staff and players and pursuing greater cooperation with expertise in universities and businesses.

A vital task for the sports psychologist to deal with is to ensure that staff have up-to-date and accurate job descriptions. Within professional football it is crucial that staff are fully aware of their responsibilities and are clear about the roles of other staff within the organisation. Surprisingly, however, given the amount of financial investment in the sport, it is quite unusual for football staff and coaches to have detailed job descriptions that accurately outline the essential and desirable activities associated with their roles. Beyond being helpful to staff, this process is also a powerful mechanism enabling the sports psychologist to meet and interact with staff and develop relationships with them and a mutual understanding of each other's roles. More specifically, the process of developing job descriptions following communication with individual staff members can be empowering. It can also be used alongside a performance appraisal process that the sports psychologist can support. Staff are often keen to have more role clarity concerning the limits of their position and the expectations associated with their role, as traditionally the culture within professional football tends towards informality. In addition, the increasing range of specialist backroom staff and the greater complexity resulting from contemporary multidisciplinary approaches to player development, preparation and support have resulted in a more complex environment and potentially more difficulties with communication, role conflict, ambiguity and duplication.

The sports psychologist can also play an important role in establishing a more coherent and formal approach to staff recruitment. This can involve a number of tasks, such as writing job advertisements, organising interview protocols, establishing selection criteria and agreeing job descriptions. When new staff members are appointed, the sports psychologist can take a lead role in managing the induction process. When applied to both players and staff, this can be a very powerful way of transmitting the club's culture to newcomers and the expectations relating to their roles and responsibilities. A further task of the sports psychologist could be to provide a more systematic approach to CPD-related activity. Job descriptions and related performance appraisals could prove useful in determining the specific training and development needs of individuals and departments. Some of these needs may relate to recognised professional awards, while others may be more bespoke. Further to this, and given the academic background of sports psychologists, educational sessions for coaches and support staff could be delivered internally, addressing a variety of topics such as stress and coping, clinical issues and referral processes, and use of psychometrics and performance profiling.

Due to the highly volatile and uncertain performance environment in professional football, there is a need to help the staff and coaches keep their attention on future development and more medium-term matters. To facilitate this, the sports psychologist can organise an opportunity for staff to attend a formal day-long event away from the training ground or stadium. Facilitated by the sports psychologist and attended by all staff, including the first-team manager (or the academy director in a youth context), such a meeting would provide a space for staff to speak candidly and freely about significant issues that they are concerned with beyond their daily operational duties. The sports psychologist can shape the agenda to ensure that meaningful and open dialogue occurs within and between departments and individuals. This type of event can assist staff in understanding the roles and functions of other colleagues and how they can work more closely and effectively with each other. Nesti (2010) lists the specific topics that could typically be addressed as including: reviewing the performance phases during the season; periodisation; data analysis trends and benchmarking; academy-related issues; and inspirational presentations from external speakers. The format of the meetings should be developed alongside the staff to reflect their interest and concerns. By this means, increased participation and engagement should occur. It may also be useful to pre-organise in order to have specific sessions led by particular members of the staff or various departments.

It is important that the content of the discussions that take place during the meetings is recorded and disseminated appropriately to all staff who attended. This serves to remind them of action points that were agreed and of the follow-up that is required. This process is beneficial for some staff and helps to focus their attention on the immediate challenges of the workplace. It is not uncommon for the sports psychologist to facilitate between six and eight full-day meetings over the season to maximise their intended purpose. Moreover, these can be supplemented with more irregular and frequently occurring in-house meetings at the training ground to address more immediate short-term concerns. Ultimately, it is imperative that the sports psychologist has support from the manager and senior staff at the club to progress the focal points of the meetings. From our experience, this form of strategic practice can prove to be progressive for the club and staff, especially in strengthening the staff team, sustaining morale and enhancing practices.

A further role of the sports psychologist relates to working with staff and players to develop team identity and team spirit. From our experience, these are fundamental qualities attended to by managers and coaches in developing successful teams. Team-building activities can be useful when they place players and staff in demanding and occasionally extreme environments. Typical activities might include organising outdoor adventure programmes that expose individuals to experiences that they might well find uncomfortable. These sessions are planned to develop trust between individuals, and are carefully structured to place individuals in new and challenging situations. For example, activities that could be used to develop team spirit might include physically and mentally demanding tasks, such as training with the Army for several days, as well as less physical, more cultural activities, such as attending the theatre or visiting museums.

Thus far, we have attempted to outline the main functions of sports psychologists in shaping the performance culture through a variety of practical tasks. It is our belief, however, that this is not the only way that culture can be addressed. A more challenging and less visible role that the sports psychologist may adopt is to be a type of cultural architect. This requires them to have a firm grasp of the prevailing culture of professional football, including the way in which sports psychology is perceived within this. In drawing on the work of a small number of sports psychologists who have operated successfully within the EPL over a number of years, we argue that before cultural change can be achieved, it is imperative that the existing values, beliefs and identity of the club are fully understood. We contend that in the highly politically charged and sensitised environment of professional football, the sports psychologists' work will not be accepted unless they can demonstrate high-level contextual knowledge. This will help to develop credibility with key staff at the club and will provide a platform for the sports psychologist to initiate some form of cultural change. In our experience, this will invariably be a difficult process, one that will be subject to constant scrutiny, and at times its perceived value will be questioned.

Nesti (2010) has identified a number of key cultural markers that should be taken into consideration, based on his prolonged applied experience inside the EPL as well as on that of six other successful and highly experienced practitioners in professional football. Some of these key markers relate to confidentiality, time constraints, demystifying sports psychology, providing objective markers of practice and dealing with personally abrasive communication styles. However, even within these exceptionally demanding conditions, the sports psychologist must find a way to grow the culture in a way that is acceptable to the group, but which nevertheless is novel and needed. This can be carried out in a number of ways, depending upon the skills, knowledge base and personal qualities of the sports psychologist. It is also dependent on the nature of the engagement that they have with the club, key staff and the manager. In our experience, this type of work cannot be effectively carried out without the support of the manager or other key decision makers, such as the academy director.

SUMMARY

In summary, we believe that the role of the organisational sports psychologist, or performance director as referred to in a football context, is critically important in the modern-day football business. While the role and the specific activities outlined in this chapter are considered critical in shaping the performance culture, attempting to operationalise and implement such practices is not without its challenges. In that respect, the applied sports psychologist may have to deal with issues that are connected to individual staff (and player) resistance, financial constraints, time, broader organisational cultural factors, and ultimately performance and results of the first team. The constraints in an academy context are clearly not performance focused, yet there remain a number of challenges similar to those of the first-team world that the practitioner must navigate. As already noted, the role and key responsibilities of the organisational sports psychologist are (typically) not covered within professional training and development programmes (Chandler *et al.*, 2014), but they are very real in a club context. Indeed, we would go so far as to argue that if the practitioner is not able to deal effectively with these organisational-based challenges, then their presence and effectiveness will be increasingly questioned by club staff. We would contend therefore that effective practice in this area is connected not only to the professional and craft knowledge, skills and expertise of the individual, but also to the practitioner's own personal qualities.

In that respect, the recent research of Chandler *et al.* (2014) examined the views of sport physicians regarding the personal characteristics and qualities of applied sport psychologists that are deemed necessary for effective practice. The findings, from interviews with UK-based physicians and a Head of Medical Services, suggested that effective practice was fundamentally associated with the personal qualities and professionalism of the practitioner and with their ability to build trusting relationships, and also that similarities exist between psychologists and physicians (i.e. both should adopt a philosophical approach, and their caring nature will be reflected in their practice). The study emphasises the importance of understanding the person behind the practitioner. In addition, it notes how literature from counselling psychology and medical training may aid the development of practice, as well as of education and training, in sports psychology.

REFERENCES

Argyris, C. and Schön, D. *Organizational Learning: A Theory of Action Perspective* (Addison Wesley, 1978).

Carron, A.V., Bray, S.R. and Eys, M.A. 'Team Cohesion and Team Success in Sport', *Journal of Sports Sciences*, 20, no. 2 (2002), pp. 119–126.

Chandler, C., Eubank, M., Nesti, M. and Cable, T. 'Personal Qualities of Effective Sport Psychologists: A Sports Physician Perspective', *Physical Culture and Sport. Studies and Research*, 61, no. 1 (2014), pp. 28–38.

Chelladurai, P. and Saleh, S.D. 'Dimensions of Leader Behavior in Sports: Development of a Leadership Scale', *Journal of Sport Psychology*, 2 (1980), pp. 34–45.

Fletcher, D., Rumbold, J.L., Tester, R. and Coombes, M.S. 'Sport Psychologists' Experiences of Organizational Stressors', *The Sport Psychologist*, 25 (2011), pp. 363–381.

Gilbourne, D. and Richardson, D. 'Tales from the Field: Personal Reflections on the Provision of Psychological Support in Professional Soccer', *Psychology of Sport and Exercise*, 7 (2006), pp. 335–337.

Gilmore, S. and Gilson, C. 'Finding Form: Elite Sports and the Business of Change', *Journal of Organizational Change Management*, 20, no. 3 (2007), pp. 409–428.

Gilson, C., Pratt, M., Roberts, K. and Weymes, E. *Peak Performance: Business Lessons from the World's Top Sports Organizations* (HarperCollins Business, 2001).

Hardy, C. 'Understanding Power: Bringing about Strategic Change', *British Journal of Management*, 7, no. 1 (1996), pp. S3–S16.

McDougall, M., Nesti, M. and Richardson, D. 'The Challenges of Sport Psychology Delivery in Elite and Professional Sport: Reflections from Experienced Sport Psychologists', *Sport Psychologist*, 29 (2015), pp. 265–277.

Nesti, M. *Psychology in Football: Working with Elite and Professional Players* (Routledge, 2010).

Nesti, M. and Littlewood, M. 'Making Your Way in the Game: Boundary Situations in England's Professional Football World', in D. Gilbourne & M.B. Andersen (Eds.), *Critical Essays in Applied Sport Psychology* (Human Kinetics, 2011).

Nesti M, Littlewood M, O'Halloran L, Eubank M, Richardson D. 'Critical Moments in Elite Premiership Football: Who Do You Think You Are?', *Physical Culture and Sport. Studies and Research.*, vol. 56(1) (2012), pp.23-32.

Palmer, I. and Hardy, C. *Thinking About Management: Implications of Organizational Debates for Practice* (SAGE, 1999).

Parker, A. 'Training for "Glory", Schooling for "Failure"? English Professional Football, Traineeship and Educational Provision', *Journal of Education and Work*, 13 (2000), pp. 61–76.

Relvas, H., Littlewood, M., Nesti, M., Gilbourne, D. and Richardson, D. 'Organizational Structures and Working Practices in Elite European Professional Football Clubs: Understanding the Relationship between Youth and Professional Domains', *European Sport Management Quarterly*, 10, no. 2 (2010), pp. 165–187.

Richardson, D. 'No Magic Wand, Just a Baton'. Dave Richardson interviews David Brailsford, British Cycling Performance Director, 15 March 2011.

Richardson, D., Littlewood, M., Nesti, M. and Benstead, L. 'An Examination of the Migratory Transition of Elite Young European Soccer Players to the English Premier League', *Journal of Sports Sciences*, 30, no. 15 (2013), pp. 1605–1618.

Schein, E.H. 'What is Culture?' In P. Frost, L. Moore, M. Louis, C. Lundberg and J. Martin (Eds.), *Reframing Organizational Culture*, pp. 243–253 (SAGE, 1991).

Tylor, Edward. *Primitive Culture*, vol. 1 (J.P. Putnam's Sons, 1920 [1871]).

Wilson, A.M. 'Understanding Organisational Culture and the Implications for Corporate Marketing, *European Journal of Marketing*, 35 (2001), pp. 353–367. doi:10.1108/03090560110382066

DELIVERING APPLIED SPORTS PSYCHOLOGY SUPPORT IN PROFESSIONAL FOOTBALL ACADEMIES: ENGLISH PREMIER LEAGUE AND GERMAN BUNDESLIGA PERSPECTIVES

Dr Martin Littlewood, Dr Mark Nesti[1] and Christian Luthardt[2]

Football Exchange, Research Institute for Sport & Exercise Sciences, Liverpool John Moores University, UK[1], and Bayer 04 Leverkusen Football Club, Germany (2001–2017), FC Bayern München (2017–)[2]

INTRODUCTION

In this chapter we compare and contrast the experiences of three applied practitioners in terms of delivering applied sports psychology support in elite level academies in professional football. In doing so, our intention is to capture the reality of delivering within a variety of different club contexts while attempting to communicate to a number of different stakeholders. The chapter initially focuses on the historical context of psychology in football and its evolution over recent years, especially since the inception of certification systems in both the English Premier League (EPL) and the German Bundesliga (GB). In this regard, these changes have significantly enhanced the flow and presence inside professional clubs of practitioners who have a responsibility for the delivery of psychological aspects of player development. While this development is clearly positive for the discipline of applied sports psychology, we will discuss the unique social and cultural features of professional football that can make integrating a psychological support programme somewhat challenging. The chapter also addresses the divergent approaches that are typically adopted by applied sports psychologists when delivering support.

An important focus of the chapter is on the similarities and differences in delivering applied sports psychology within a number of clubs from two of the big five European leagues. We believe that this will help to demonstrate how important the national, local and club culture is to the effective delivery of this area of support inside clubs. Moreover, we believe that many of the issues described in this chapter are significant in the professional training and development of future applied sports psychologists in both England and Germany. Covering these issues will also help coaches and other practitioners to better understand how to integrate sports psychology into their practice with players. Fundamentally, we believe that this connected approach between the psychologist, the coach and others will ultimately determine the efficacy and perceived value of sports psychology. Our experiences of delivering inside clubs over 15 years suggest that this level of integration and synthesis remains an aspiration, rather than the reality. Nevertheless, we are convinced that without a joined-up approach to its delivery, applied sports psychology will continue to be the 'Cinderella' sports science discipline in the world of professional football.

THE SCIENTIFIC BASIS

The integration of sports psychologists in English professional football has traditionally been through the informal activity of managers and coaches responding to the performance needs of the team and individual players (Nesti, 2010). Typically, they have drawn upon their former experiences as players to allow them to deliver psychological principles. Sometimes unqualified consultants, brought in by the clubs to work on issues such as motivation, team cohesion, confidence and emotional control, have supported this. Although some of these individuals have provided a useful service, many others, through lack of qualifications, knowledge and skills, have been much less effective. It is our belief that the latter has contributed to the negative perceptions, attitudes and beliefs that many staff within professional football still hold with respect to the value and effectiveness of sports psychology provision (Pain and Harwood, 2004).

A number of organisations, including the Football Association (FA) within England, have responsibility for the education and professional training of coaches in the area of sports psychology. They do so by delivering psychological units within coaching qualifications and they usually involve workshops, seminars and follow-up study. Moreover, the FA launched an initiative to provide bespoke sports psychology qualifications aimed at existing coaches and others wishing to develop their understanding of psychological principles to inform their practice within professional football. This was delivered at five levels, and study took place over a designated time. Although there are merits to both of these approaches to education around sports psychology, there are also a number of drawbacks.

First, although the predominant focus on Mental Skills Training (MST) as the main approach to working with players in psychological areas can be useful at certain stages of development, the reality of players' experiences and journeys means that often much more than this is required to understand the person and their needs (Nesti and Littlewood, 2011; Cook *et al.*, 2014). As has been mentioned frequently in the sports psychology literature, MST is primarily a solutions-based approach aimed at symptoms (Corlett, 1996). In contrast, Corlett (1996) argued that athletes (players) sometimes need to accept the challenges and difficult emotions and anxiety that they will experience. In this regard, MST alone could actually be quite harmful, as it never fully encourages the person to confront and better understand the reason(s) underpinning the particular cognitions and emotions that they are experiencing. In addition, it is common to find that higher-level and more experienced players already possess excellent mental skills (Nesti, 2010). They have usually acquired these over many years of practice in their sport and implicitly through engagement with their peers and coaches. The MST approach can also be criticised for being superficial, in that it lacks theoretical depth and rigour (Nesti and Littlewood, 2010). It also fails to acknowledge the whole person; instead, the focus is on short-term immediate needs and interventions for the performer to use, such as self-talk, coping techniques, visualisation and goal setting. Although these techniques can be useful, much of what players must confront throughout the different phases of an academy journey is associated with broader issues around identity, relationships and non-performance issues (Manley *et al.*, 2012; Nesti *et al.*, 2012; Cook *et al.*, 2014), which themselves affect success and achievement. Regarding approaches to the provision of applied sports psychology support, we believe that the content and approach of professional training qualifications for practitioners in professional football need to better reflect the broader challenges that players experience throughout their journey within the game (Nesti and Littlewood, 2010; Nesti *et al.*, 2012). By doing so, we believe that the 'acceptance' of individuals within these roles and their general integration will be enhanced.

In 2011, a major new policy was introduced by the EPL to restructure and improve the quality of youth player development at academies across the professional leagues. Its vision was to increase the number and quality of home-grown players playing 'first team football at the highest level' (Premier League, 2011, p. 12). More specifically, it aimed to deliver an environment that promotes excellence and nurtures talent, and to systematically convert this talent into first-team football players. It suggested these aims would be met by providing a world-class support service for academy players. The academies of all professional clubs are audited by the Premier League to determine which category they will be awarded. This ranges from 1 for clubs that meet all requirements to 4 for those that only partially fill the criteria. This process is carried out every three years. Referred to as the *Elite Player Performance Plan* (EPPP), an element of it focuses on sports psychology provision. However, while the EPPP requires category 1 academies to appoint lead sports scientists, senior sports physiotherapists and match analysts, it states that academies have the option to appoint a sports psychologist, which is left at the discretion of the academy manager. Specifically, the EPPP demands that clubs ensure that all players receive sports psychology support at all stages of their progression. Clearly, this is a significant improvement on previous practices, but there still remains a dominant focus on MST and player profiling. For example, the EPPP includes 'focussing' and 'imaging' as part of the psychological delivery for under-17s to under-21s on a sports science programme at a category 1 academy. In addition, clubs do not have to appoint a full-time sports psychologist and can rely upon a mixed approach to provision. This can include delivery by coaches, education and welfare staff, as well as the use of part-time sports psychology consultants.

In contrast, within a German context, in 2014 the German Football League (DFL) and the German Football Association (DFB) decided to obligate every club in the German Bundesliga (Divisions 1 and 2) to employ a sports psychologist at least on a half-day basis. Employing a sports psychologist is therefore now considered a necessary condition for being licensed as a youth academy of a Bundesliga club. In addition, by employing a full-time sports psychologist, a club will receive extra credits in a certification process carried out by an independent company whose role is to evaluate all German youth academies. This certification process can result in the club receiving additional funds and being awarded an official certificate of excellence. The subject of sports psychology has also become an integral part of the curriculum of future professional and youth coaches. Without any doubt, these developments have been important steps towards the integration of psychological support into the world of elite youth football in Germany.

While sports psychology in German football is now officially considered to be an important part of youth development and German youth academies are now obligated to employ a sports psychologist at least part time, the reality of practice differs a lot from club to club, and the sports psychologists employed follow very different approaches in their work, with MST being the most common denominator. Sports psychology support is still supplied by practitioners with a wide range of professional backgrounds, including sports scientists, psychologists, pedagogues and so-called mental coaches, and a lot of academy directors and coaches continue to lack detailed knowledge about what constitutes a qualified and good sports psychologist. Due to the variety of professionals trying to access elite youth and professional football, the German FA and the German Football League have now introduced a task force and hold regular conferences in order to establish clear quality standards for the practitioners in the field. Although these measures will surely provide some important orientation for sports psychologists, coaches and academy directors, all practitioners will have to develop their own role within the context of their academy. The next section focuses on the topic of transitions and attempts to provide a concise overview of the challenges that players may experience during their journey through an academy environment.

The subject of player (athlete) transitions has received significant attention in the academic literature over recent years and has been defined as the 'occurrence of one or more specific events that brings about a change in assumptions about oneself, but also a social disequilibrium that goes beyond the ongoing changes of everyday life' (Wylleman et al., 2004, p. 8). Two types of transitions exist: normative, characterised by events that are predictable and expected to happen (e.g. transition from youth to senior environment); and non-normative, referring to those events that are unpredictable and unexpected (e.g. injuries or unexpected success) (Stambulova, 2000). Much of the research within this area has tended to concentrate on career termination or (normal) retirement (a normative transition) and the psychological difficulties associated with this readjustment process. While the focus of research has been dominated by the post-career phase, there is a requirement for applied practitioners and researchers to document the challenges associated with the journey during the context of the career. Indeed, Richardson, Relvas et al. (2013) suggest that individuals experiencing both 'career termination' and 'within career transitions' require considerable personal adjustment. More specifically, they adapted the Wylleman et al. (2004) model of athlete development to capture the role and importance of the 'environment' and 'culture' during a player's progression through a club's organisational structure (see Figure 1).

Athletic level	Academy Development	Post-Academy Developing Mastery	First team Mastery
Psychological level	Adolescence	Social insecurity and comparison	(young) Adulthood, Limelight, Stardom
Psycho-social level	Peers, parents, coach, sports psych. Ed and welfare	Partner, New Coach(es), Family	Manager, New coach(es)
Environmental and cultural level	Process orientated, Nurturing, Caring, Empathic	Uncompetitive, Lonely, Isolated, Uncertain, Stagnant	Outcome orientated, Ruthless, Masculine/ macho, Heightened competition Team
Nature of Support	Highly supportive	Bereft of social support	(Typically) crisis management, sophist

FIGURE 1 Socio-cultural model of athlete transition (adapted from Richardson et al., 2013)

In the context of a professional football club, it may be argued that a critical phase in a player's development and future progression occurs at the Under-23 level (see 'Post-Academy Developing Mastery' phase of Figure 1). However, the difference between the three phases of progression (Academy, Post-Academy and First Team), specifically at the environmental and cultural level, has not fully been explored in the literature. Richardson, Relvas *et al.* (2013) argue that the Post-Academy phase is possibly the most critical period for a young soccer player. They note that at that stage players have moved from a 'developmentally focused' environment within the academy to a phase where they are not yet ready for full engagement in the first-team environment, which is regarded as outcome orientated and ruthless, and in which higher levels of performance are expected. There are clearly different tactical, technical and physical demands that players will have to adapt to throughout the phases, and, in a sense, these might be described as visible expectations. The psychological demands, however, are somewhat invisible, and in that respect are harder to plan, execute and evaluate. Another layer of complexity within this area is connected to the unique cultures that exist between and within many professional football clubs. The beliefs, values and attitudes of each individual practitioner (predominantly the coach) will determine the type of environment that is created within a team and within each phase of development. Players may not necessarily commit time to understanding these features and the impact they may have upon their development. Additionally, we are aware that practitioners have a diverse range of views with respect to the type of psychological qualities that they feel are needed to succeed at a higher level in professional football (see Cook *et al.*, 2014). This is further evidence of the challenge faced by players aiming to transition effectively into the first-team world. Figure 2 provides further psychosocial context for the transition from Academy to post-Academy to first team.

Figure 2 has been developed from a range of connected research projects (see Nesti and Littlewood, 2011, Nesti *et al.*, 2012; Richardson, Relvas *et al.*, 2013) and from the applied practice experiences of Nesti and Littlewood. While not exhaustive, it aims to illustrate a range of psychosocial challenges that players may encounter during different phases of a club's structure in the pursuit of first-team status. The concept of social role relates to the changing occupational identities that players will possess as a function of the team they sign to and type of contract that they sign. For example, a player will typically be a full-time employee of the club from the age of 16 when signing a football scholarship/apprenticeship contract, while some players are also eligible to sign a professional contract on their 17th birthday. Terms such as 'Scholar', 'Apprentice' and 'Pro' are all occupational terms of reference that reflect the status and position of players in this particular social world. Dealing with the internal and external expectations and pressures associated with their position is central to players' lived experiences (Nesti, 2013). Players' movement through their football club's structure and teams may also lead to an increased level of social comparison with their peers. The enhanced quality

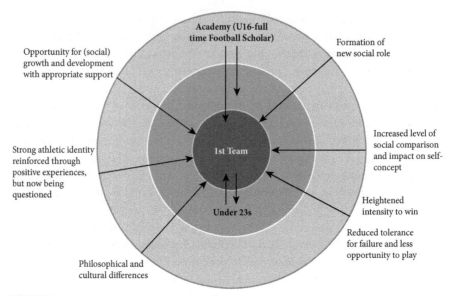

FIGURE 2 Challenges to player identity during the transition from youth to senior environments in elite-level professional football

and talent pool of players in a club's Under-18s and Under-23s teams may lead players to question their perceived value, self-worth and identity. Importantly here, this may be the very first time in a player's journey in a football academy that they are confronted with this type of challenge, as players typically reach this stage through continual selection and progression to the next age-group team.

We also know that philosophical and cultural features of the first-team environment are associated with the heightened intensity to win, with the subsequent reduced tolerance for failure and with less opportunity to play. These present players with new and uncomfortable challenges that are often associated with anxiety. Otherwise described from an existential perspective as normal anxiety (May, 1977), it accompanies these critical moments and occurs because of the ability the individual has to act freely and make decisions in a given situation (Nesti, 2004) without ever fully knowing the implications of their actions. Critical moments can provide an individual with the opportunity to develop and grow psychologically, as they encourage individuals to challenge their values and beliefs, and in that way to develop new meaning (Nesti *et al.*, 2012). We believe 'critical moments' may be a more appropriate description of the experiences of players within the academy and post-academy setting, as they describe those moments during which an individual must confront anxiety due to changes in their occupational status and identity (Nesti *et al.*, 2012). We believe that this is an under-developed area that requires considerably greater attention if we are to better prepare players for the radically different culture that awaits them at the first-team (Mastery) level.

Beyond the individual challenges faced by players, there are also organisational issues that can lead to heightened levels of stress. These types of stressors can relate to communication problems between coaches and players, time management concerns, poor planning of schedules, political infighting between departments, and a lack of clarity about daily procedures and practices. These and other sources of stress can overwhelm the young player and make a demanding experience even more fraught with difficulty. At first-team levels, players are more likely to be familiar with these organisational stressors and have better-developed coping strategies, although research carried out by Fletcher and Wagstaff et al (2009) found that even for elite-level athletes, organisational stressors were a serious problem. Faced with these types of stressors, young players may fail to perform their best and become demotivated and frustrated and experience negative anxiety. At first-team levels (as is highlighted in Chapter 4) it is more common to see sports psychologists and others take on the role of performance director, partly to ameliorate the effects of organisational stress on both the players and the coaching and broader support staff.

In this chapter so far we have attempted to describe the historical development of sports psychology in a UK and German context, and outlined the different approaches that applied sports psychologists draw upon to guide their practice. We have also outlined what we believe to be the contemporary challenges that players encounter during their development pathway through childhood, adolescence and young adulthood. Clearly there will be differences in terms of the 'actual' practices within clubs and the 'experiences' of players; nevertheless, the research evidence and applied experiences of the authors suggest that the issues described in Figures 1 and 2 are central to many players' lived experiences. We believe that any psychological development programme within a football context should pay close attention to issues of this nature, providing support that is organically developed and authentic to the actual club culture and working practices. The next section focuses on the translation of theory into practice and charts the delivery mechanisms and the challenges experienced by the authors.

TRANSLATING THEORY INTO PRACTICE: DELIVERY AND PRACTITIONER CHALLENGES

We will now consider the detail of the actual delivery mechanisms and methods of practice of all three authors within the context of the academy environment. The experience of delivering in Germany is that the creation of a full-time job for a sports psychologist often leads to a certain kind of pressure on the person who takes the job to justify their role and efficacy. This can actually jeopardise the successful integration of sports psychology support in the youth academy. The neophyte sports psychologist might feel pressured to produce short-term results and to demonstrate his or her value and application. It is therefore vital for the new sports psychologist to develop a clear understanding with decision makers, coaches, players and other relevant contact persons concerning his or her philosophy of practice, key role and responsibilities.

From the beginning, sports psychology support at Bayer 04 Leverkusen was focused on the development of people, both coaches and athletes, in order to enhance personal development, well-being and ultimately performance. The basic approach has evolved over a period of four years from a primary focus on the delivery of mental skills towards an approach that is very close to what Orlick and Friesen (2010) referred to as 'holistic sport psychology' and the belief that in 'developing the core individual, the athlete persona is thereby developed itself'. This has also included a shift in the practitioner's own focus in professional development from techniques, strategies and skills towards his or her own personality, and especially the personal qualities of authenticity and caring. In this respect the exercise of reflective practice, continued supervision and a systematic exchange with other practitioners have been of paramount importance. The understanding of the sport psychologist's role and responsibilities will have important consequences for all of the work that will be carried out and will impact its effectiveness and acceptance.

At Bayer 04 Leverkusen FC, this understanding was achieved in both a formal and an informal way. When sports psychology was introduced to the Bayer 04 academy, teams from the Under-15s to Under-19s were shown the benefits of sports psychology support during team activities that were designed to develop a dialogue on what the players could expect from a sports psychologist and how the support would be realised during the season. Players then were given the opportunity to discuss individually with the sports psychologist how they might benefit personally from working with them, an offer which was well received by the players. This was accompanied by a lot of informal conversations with coaches, support staff, players and decision makers from the youth academy, all of which deepened the sports psychologist's understanding of the environment he was going to work in. This approach was a fundamental part of the attempt to identify the needs of the different coaches and the age group they were coaching. The process of ongoing communication gradually led to the establishment of informal contracts of collaboration. Coaches would initially put an emphasis on the individual support of their players, on the observation of training sessions and matches by the sports psychologist to add his expertise to the insights of the coaching team, and, depending on existing challenges throughout the season, on team development activities.

While team activities and individual one-to-one meetings with players started to develop, the most important work took place in the workplace in a naturalistic approach – by being present on a daily basis, by accompanying teams to tournaments, and through frequent informal conversation with the coaches in the locker room, on the training ground or at the club's café. The initial phase was therefore characterised by learning from and together with the coaches, getting to know the club, its culture and people, and building trust with all relevant partners within that environment. The aim of this was to give everybody within the club the possibility of getting to know the sports psychologist as a person first and to build trust by allowing him to show the qualities of empathy, care, openness and genuineness. This process required the sports psychologist to be patient, to learn when and how to share his point of view and to actually be himself. As the coaches started to feel at ease with the presence of the sports psychologist and developed an understanding of him as a person and of his role, they slowly started to open up to him and use his support for their own development.

Instead of initially jumping straight into the delivery of a diverse range of team activities, coach education workshops or other services, in the second author's opinion it is essential for the sports psychologist to patiently get to know the existing culture and to recognise the needs and development areas of coaches, players and staff and how they can best offer a service that will be perceived as useful and of additional value. Getting to know the culture of the youth academy means listening closely to the language of players, coaches and staff. For example, practitioners may need to ask themselves the following questions: what are players and coaches talking about and how are they talking? Are they talking in the first person? Are they complaining, blaming and looking for excuses? Which behaviours are reinforced and which are punished within this culture? Which unwritten rules underlie the routines and behaviours of players and coaches? Who are the heroes of this culture? What characterises the relationships within the youth academy?

This process of reflective practice led the second author to offer a service that was focused on establishing more open communication through the creation of spaces for players and coaches that allowed them to identify their own development in the attempt to foster a stronger process-orientation and learning culture at the club. This included the introduction of feedback processes and field trips to other European youth academies as a way of creating more openness and establishing the youth academy as a place for learning and development for both players and coaches.

In the second author's experience at a German Bundesliga youth academy, the role of the sports psychologist evolved during six years. It became much more that of a facilitator and designer of contexts for learning, dialogue and development. This includes both collaborating with the coaches in the development of optimal learning contexts around and within the daily practice sessions, and creating team activities that reinforce dialogue, authentic learning and psychological growth. These team activities at Bayer 04 were created together with the respective team coaches, taking into account their ideas as well. These team activities for the Under-10s to Under-14s level were focused on the development of life skills; sport performance was not established as a priority here. Only from the Under-15s level up were aspects of performance addressed more explicitly. Coaches were invited to participate within these team activities, and step-by-step singular team activities started to develop into systematic programmes.

Over time, coaches became willing to give the sports psychologist adequate space and time within the daily practice sessions. This was not always easy for all of the coaches, but patience and continued dialogue were essential to create a more systematic way of working with all age groups and to have all of the coaching staff buy into the programme. Now, Bayer 04 are looking to take the next step in this development and are starting to reintegrate life skills training sessions and team activities into the everyday training environment and make sports psychology not a distinct training area, but something that is integrated into everything the players and coaches do. This will be the challenge for the coming years at Bayer 04. In arriving at this point, it is important to point out that the integration of support can only come when relationships have been built to a level where trust, acceptance and respect are core features of the relationship with the coach. Potrac *et al.* (2002) discussed the importance of generating respect and framed this concept around the notions of informational and legitimate power.

Additionally, the sports psychologist might be able to create spaces and contexts within which coaches and staff at the youth academy can focus on their own personal and professional development. Important in this regard is the generation of opportunities that are free of hierarchy, where listening, dialogue and team learning are fostered and actively promoted. At Bayer 04, the main goal of the sports psychologist was seen as being to reinforce dialogue and communication across the different age groups. With the support of the youth academy director, weekly round tables were organised with four to six coaches from different teams discussing important issues, such as motivation, learning, guided discovery and the promotion of responsibility. Within these round tables, the sports psychologist's role was that of a facilitator, reinforcing dialogue, listening and self-reflection.

The institutionalisation of feedback processes may be another useful task for the sports psychologist to focus on. Players, their parents and even the staff of a youth academy might sometimes be concerned about voicing their opinion, criticising or making suggestions. At Bayer 04, the sports psychologist is trying to help create an environment where everyone feels comfortable receiving and giving feedback. This process started with anonymous player feedback for all interested coaches and continued on to yearly parent surveys, where players and parents could share their experiences and their degree of satisfaction with various aspects of the club. Parents also had the possibility to suggest improvements and changes, and to point to difficulties and challenges they were facing. These feedback processes have been of great value to the club. However, they should in the long term become dispensable in a culture that allows and encourages that kind of feedback face to face on a daily basis.

The establishment of this kind of culture requires the sports psychologist to look beyond team activities, coach education and one-to-one counselling and focus instead on organisational and cultural aspects. It requires a deeper look at the organisational and cultural roots of individual and group behaviour within the working environment. This includes helping decision makers to become aware of the psychological effects of certain organisational procedures relating to salary, contract and recruitment policy, meetings and their structure, feedback processes, public communication and other issues. If the practitioner is allowed to have an impact at an organisational level, then sports psychology support has the chance of providing the youth academy with a real competitive advantage, and even of providing such an edge within a first-team environment.

Sports psychology support in a youth academy, in our opinion, should not be limited to having either a performance-enhancement focus or a caring and well-being focus. Instead, it should include both in its agenda in a well-balanced manner within different age groups, responding to the needs of players and coaches, while always working with the whole person. The sports psychologists in a youth academy should perceive themselves not as a distinct department, but as providing a transversal function, interacting with people from all areas and at all levels of the organisation. This should be done in an attempt to create an environment that reinforces development and learning. Seen in this way, sports psychology is both everywhere, in the sense that it is woven into the everyday experience of the players, and nowhere, in the sense that it has a strong focus on background activities and the facilitation of contexts.

Within this kind of approach, the sports psychologist will have to face different challenges. First, the professionalisation of elite youth football in Germany seems to have led to an obsession with measurement and performance analysis. As sports psychology in Germany is still dominated by sports science, many practitioners follow this development by using psychometric tests to measure the young athlete's motivation, personality and mental skills. Yet a lot of the work of the sports psychologist is not measurable, and it is of great importance that coaches and decision makers accept that fact and understand the sport psychologist's philosophy of practice and its value.

In contrast to the academy, the delivery of sports psychology support within the first team will largely depend on the support of the head coach/manager and the key decision makers of the club. An organisational type of role, although very important and useful, will only be possible where this role is welcomed and reinforced by the club. As in the youth academy environment, however, this role might emerge after the sports psychologist has become an established and accepted part of the first-team staff. If the club does not establish this type of role from the beginning, it might be best for the sports psychologist to discuss possibilities for improvement slowly, and in agreement with other staff members. These improvements might concern the integration of foreign players (Richardson *et al.*, 2013), the treatment of injured players, the facilitation of interdisciplinary communication and communication between players.

German Bundesliga clubs are still reluctant to employ full-time sports psychologists within their staff, yet more and more of the younger coaches are very open to sports psychology and have a clearer understanding of how they can benefit from the input of a sports psychologist. A big challenge in this respect is to overcome stereotypes and prejudices concerning the role of the psychologist. Here again, a lot of work has to be done to develop a clear understanding of the role and a coherent image of what sports psychology means within that context.

Importantly, it is essential that the role of a sports psychologist and the discipline are communicated in such a way that beneficiaries can see how they relate to the performance and well-being of players and staff.

In a very similar way to how the sports psychologist works in a youth academy, in a first-team setting a lot will depend on the personality of the sports psychologist and how they are able to fit into that environment; they also need to develop a clear understanding of their role, to meet the needs of players and coaches, and to offer something that represents additional value. While, in the second author's experience, the role of sports psychology within the first team initially was strongly and almost exclusively focused on the one-to-one counselling of first team players and coaching staff, the sports psychologist's role as an organisational psychologist involved in the development of a high-performance environment slowly evolved.

From an English perspective, there are a number of similarities with Christian's philosophy and approach in terms of explaining our experiences of delivering applied sports psychology support in an academy context. Prior to his or her commencement in any role, we believe that it is essential that the applied sports psychologist is able to understand the organisational culture of the environment, and at what point in the cultural life cycle the organisation and its people are positioned. In that sense, a life cycle typically consists of different phases (e.g. research and development, introduction, growth, maturity and decline), and the culture of a particular discipline and/or approach may be located within any of these. From our applied experiences, we have found that the presence and provision of psychological development programmes and individuals within club structures have been somewhat limited (see Pain and Harwood, 2004; Nesti and Littlewood, 2010). That being the case, the practitioner needs to focus on understanding the values, attitudes, beliefs and practices of individuals working in the environment prior to introducing any form of activity that constitutes psychological delivery. This may be classed as research and development in the cultural life cycle, and it has been described as the reconnaissance phase in action research (Winter, 1998). Nevertheless, the process is one that may determine the successful acceptance of the individual who enters the football club. This acceptance can be achieved by spending time within the environment and being present at a range of meetings (i.e. coaching, multi-disciplinary and phase specific) that occur in the weekly academy planner. This allows for an understanding of the nature of the dialogue that occurs between staff members, the types of challenges that are present in the organisation, and the approaches that are subsequently adopted. Moreover, it is our belief that an effective psychological support programme is one that is developed organically and authentically from the environment that one engages in. This results in a support programme that is truly bespoke and that will be more aligned to the values and working practices of the organisation.

The process described above may represent a somewhat idealist position with respect to the integration of the practitioner and development of a psychological programme. The reality in terms of its delivery may be that at times the practitioner will need to fit into an existing structure and philosophy, and into the particular phase of the cultural life cycle that the club is in. We contend that the organic development of a programme is one that practitioners should aspire to, yet we appreciate the complexities of time, resources and experience that are involved in achieving this. One of the primary functions of any psychological programme and/or form of service delivery is to enhance and support the knowledge and understanding of clients (athletes, coaches, staff) through different forms of applied engagement. An approach that may be utilised in this regard, and one that is common in youth sports settings, is an educational workshop-based approach across different age groups of players. This was an approach that the first author engaged in during his applied engagement at a Premier League football club. Figure 3 illustrates a psychological educational framework that was designed and implemented over a number of seasons within an academy context.

Topics	Academy Age Groups									
	U9	U10	U11	U12	U13	U14	U15/16	1st year	2nd year	3rd year
Reflection	X	X	X	X	X	X	X	X	X	X
Goalsetting	X	X	X	X	X	X	X	X	X	X
Communication		X	X	X	X	X	X	X	X	X
Imagery			X	X	X	X	X	X	X	X
Self talk				X	X	X	X	X	X	X
Coping skills					X	X	X	X	X	X
Reflection						X	X	X	X	X
Concentration						X	X	X	X	X
Lifestyle issues							X	X	X	X
Professionalism								X	X	X
Culture								X	X	X
Roles and responsibilities								X	X	X
Coach expectations								X	X	X
Player-coach dynamic								X	X	X
Loans										X

FIGURE 3 Sports psychology educational framework (U9s–U18s) within a professional football academy

The aim of the programme was to enhance knowledge and understanding of players across a number of different age groups and development phases with respect to a range of psychological topics. From Under-9s to Under-14s, players were exposed to 'traditional' mental skills training topics related to understanding their role, function and efficacy in a performance context. As players moved through later stages of adolescence and the transition to Under-15s/16s and beyond, they were introduced to occupation-specific topics that represented broader challenges and issues that exist in the full-time occupation of a football scholar. The aim of the programme was to make individuals who were making the transition to higher levels better informed and better prepared to deal with the many critical moments that are inevitable within the highly pressured occupation of a professional footballer.

The programme was co-created by the applied practitioner and a range of stakeholders from within the club structure. In terms of delivery, all sessions were led by the performance psychologist and, at times, co-delivered with the lead coach of the age group (subject to the relational dynamic that existed between practitioner and coach). To supplement the delivery of the educational programme, the applied practitioners employed at the club (author 1 in the academy; author 3 in the first team) interviewed a range of academy and first-team staff and players on a number of topics within the framework. These interviews were used to add rich context to the messages and to enhance the 'buy-in' value and credibility of the programme. At a conceptual level, this approach clearly resonates with the transition-based literature (Stambulova, 2000; Wylleman *et al.*, 2004; Pummel *et al.*, 2008; Morris *et al.*, 2015), serving to add rigour and ecological validity to the applied framework. Moreover, it specifically relates to the socio-cultural model of elite player development in professional soccer at academy, post-academy and first-team level that was produced by Richardson, Relvas *et al.* (2013). In that sense, our expectations were that individuals would be able to draw upon a range of short-term quick-fix techniques in times of adversity and challenge, yet also have the knowledge and understanding of other contextually relevant issues that may explain a particular situation and/or experience.

The approach to educational delivery can also be accompanied by one-to-one applied sports psychology support to players within the academy and post-academy phases of development. Drawing on a mixture of both cognitive-behavioural (Perna *et al.*, 1995) and existential counselling-based approaches (Nesti, 2007), all full-time players (aged 16–19) engaged in a minimum of three confidential support sessions throughout the season. The sessions provided all players with the space and opportunity to discuss and explore issues, experiences and critical moments that were connected to their current time at the club. Clearly, and perhaps as expected, discussions centred on specific performance-based issues such as selection, de-selection, injury and performance levels, and narrow psychological issues such as emotional control, confidence and anxiety. While some players remained focused around topics such as these, others would highlight broader psychosocial, environmental and cultural-based issues that they were finding difficult to understand and manage. Central to many such concerns was the relationship with the coach(es). Players would often talk about feedback (lack of, inconsistent), a perception of preferential treatment for other players, and the coach's personal style and behaviour towards situations within the training environment as the dominant sources of distress. It is perhaps these types of encounters that reveal the inadequacy of the mental skills training approach to the consulting experience, in the sense that players need to draw upon much more than a specific skill and/or technique to manage their daily encounters in the environment.

This type of approach has been described by Nesti in relation to sport (Nesti, 2004), from within first-team English Premier League environments (2010), and in terms of academy football (Nesti and Sulley, 2014). In this literature, he describes how a counselling approach grounded in humanistic, existential and other person-centred perspectives could work with players and coaches. Using dialogue and being guided by the players' concerns, confidential one-to-one sessions can be carried out that help the individual to understand and clarify the situation they are in, and consider the options available to them to address the challenges they face. Although rarely an easy task to do, this exercise can help the player (or member of staff) begin to take more responsibility for their own development, often leading to improvements in well-being and performance. Although this form of support can be made available to all, it is usually the case that older and more mature individuals benefit the most from it.

The experiences of the first author have evolved over the years and seen a shift from a player-centred approach of delivery to one that is staff centred and organisational. To explain the rationale for this, it is important to return to the notion of the cultural life cycle, whereby the presence of sports psychology in the environment had not existed for some years and therefore the discipline of psychology was not positioned in any distinct phase of the life cycle. In addition, the philosophy of the strategic decision maker, with respect to the nature of applied engagement, was strongly connected to the personal development of individuals in a way that directly impacted players and the performance environment. These factors shaped the philosophy, approach and key responsibilities within the role. One of the primary responsibilities was focused on working alongside existing practitioners within the environment to support their day-to-day activity in terms of player development from a psychosocial perspective.

This type of engagement is clearly different from the dominant role of the applied sports psychologists and demands a number of qualities and competencies from the practitioner. Foremost of these is the ability to develop and maintain professional working relationships that are built upon trust, respect and professionalism. Similar to the way in which the discipline of sports psychology is located within the cultural life cycle, we would contend that personal relationships are also connected to this same life cycle, in the sense that it takes time to cultivate people's trust and respect before they feel comfortable allowing you into their working space. Just as a sports psychologist may work with a client in times of discomfort, so too may the practitioner. They too must learn to feel comfortable in difficult and uncomfortable situations with respect to their perceived role and impact in the environment. The challenge of developing an organic and authentic approach to delivery is that much of the work of the practitioner is often 'behind the scenes' and not immediately visible for others to see. There are often no programmes, workshops or material available when the approach is focused on developing the person. This activity is extremely personal, and it takes time to understand how practice can be enhanced. Approaches here involve meaningful dialogue, observation of practice and challenging individuals to consider the rationale for their particular approach to player engagement and development. This latter aspect involves a personal exchange between the sports psychologist and individual and it cannot be expected to occur within a matter of days or weeks of the sports psychologist entering the environment. This is not to say that it cannot happen for some in a shorter time depending on the individual and the broader culture in which the practitioner operates, but our collective experiences of delivering and supervision would suggest that it takes time before individuals feel comfortable with this type of dialogue.

Examples of work within this type of coach-centred approach are specific to the individual with whom the sports psychologist is working. However, we have found that connecting the engagement to the coaching process (i.e. planning, implementation, review and evaluation) is very effective. The sports psychologist in this respect is able to work with and alongside the coach to better understand the aims and learning outcomes that the coach intends to achieve within the context of the coaching session. The work of Harwood (2008) and Harwood and Anderson (2015) has been a useful resource for promoting and aligning discussion of the psychological qualities that are important in player development. It represents a concise, focused framework that coaches can connect to the practice and match environment.

Further examples of practice in this area are: working with coaches on enhancing player (and parental) understanding of individual learning objectives (ILO); and enhancing the player-parent-coach triad. The work with the coaches was over a six-month period and involved developing an intervention with players (and parents) who were within the specialising stage of development. The intervention essentially focused on enhancing the player-coach-parent relationship by providing a greater level of parental involvement in the development and communication of the player's six-week individual learning objective (i.e. a mandatory EPPP condition for every registered player in an academy system). The coach invited the parents and player to attend a brief (10–15-minute) pre-ILO meeting in which the aim and rationale of the ILO was explained. Supporting footage from previous games was also utilised within this meeting to enhance the rationale for the ILO. The pre-ILO meeting offered both player and parents the opportunity to discuss any questions with the coach prior to commencement of the focused developmental activity. After the immediate training session, both player and parents would engage in an open debrief with the coach on the training activity. Following one week of individual development activity on the ILO, the player and parents would again be invited to a meeting to review the degree of progress in the ILO, and again this provided an opportunity to discuss any areas of concern.

The role of the sports psychologist in the project is to support the coach in the pedagogical principles associated with the process (i.e. feed-forward, feedback, communication). In addition, he or she can discuss the psychosocial benefits for players and parents in the project. Feedback from parents and players regarding the efficacy of the intervention suggested that it positively influenced the relational dynamic in the triad. The improved relationships were characterised by increased closeness, greater consistency of information, and enhanced involvement of parents in their son's development. We believe that this approach highlights the effectiveness of a coach-centred approach to applied sports psychology support, and it is an approach that we feel future practitioners should consider with respect to applied practice in an academy context.

We also believe that the applied sports psychologist can play an important role in supporting the development of a research culture inside the professional football club. The ability to add rigour, enhance the ecological validity of applied interventions, and evaluate the efficacy of practice underpins all scientific-led practice. The practitioner can work alongside heads of departments and phase leads to design applied methodologies to evaluate a range of questions relating to player development. Examples of this type of activity can relate to the player-parent-coach triad described above, to systematic observation and evaluation of coach feedback strategies and reviewing hybrid/full-time models of player development and their impact on player identity. Ultimately, this type of research activity is aimed at enhancing the players' (and parents') holistic personal and professional development within the academy context.

SUMMARY

There is clear recognition in both England and Germany that sports psychologists working in academy football should maintain a joint player well-being and performance focus. The recent academic debate about the need to choose between performance enhancement or welfare and well-being is rejected as unhelpful, and as being quite literally unreal. In many ways, it is the type of dualistic thinking that could only have emerged from the academic world where we so often see dichotomous propositions that do not stand up to scrutiny in the real world or real practice. As can be imagined, how someone views this philosophical argument has considerable implications for the training and education of sport psychologists.

In both the German and English accounts it appears that there is a recognition that the most effective way to carry out sports psychology work at academy levels is through the support of the coach. This is described above in a number of indirect and direct ways. First, we have argued that building a relationship with the coach is essential in order that the sport psychologist can deliver directly through him or her. This can be seen with MST, a form of support that is best delivered by coaches in an integrated way within their coaching role on and off the pitch. The task of the sports psychologist here seems more about educating and guiding the coach in the use of these skills and in explaining their underpinning theory when necessary. More radically, sports psychologists discuss how they now see their most important function as that of educating the coach in the principles of psychology *and* as being a type of development coach to the individual member of staff. The view is developing the self-awareness and self-knowledge of the coach (and other staff) as the key role for the sports psychologist to take on.

Certainly in the EPL example, there seems to be a recognition that education of parents about the culture of professional football is important in order to manage expectations and help them provide better support to their children to help them to be among the few who make the grade, or to be better prepared to face life beyond the game when they are released. This different approach may reflect the different views typically prevailing between the two countries and their approaches to football concerning the importance of cultural factors and education.

One of the clearest statements from this chapter concerns the need to build relationships and trust before deciding how to proceed. We have focused strongly on the need to do more than be seen as an expert source of information about sports psychology and performance enhancement. We see the work of a sports psychologist at this level as being as much about their own personal qualities as it is about the skills and knowledge they possess. The importance of personal qualities such as empathy, integrity and humility has been discussed by Chandler *et al.* (2016) in their research with elite-level and professional sports people. Very much in line with the arguments presented in this chapter, they point out that although sports psychologists should not be perceived as friends, the best practitioners do not approach their work in an impersonal and mechanical way. Instead, they draw on their theoretical knowledge and technical skills to deliver their services in a flexible and client-centred way, where, according to Ronkainen and Nesti, (2015), 'the person of the sports psychologist reaches out to meet the person of the player'. This type of personal engagement can take place formally or in more informal and ad hoc ways. According to the applied practitioners in this chapter, this naturalistic mode of communication is vital to ensure that player needs are met, and that sports psychology is not viewed as some strange pseudo-scientific enterprise, or as merely common sense dressed up in conceptual terminology!

There are three very important messages contained in the material presented here. One is that there needs to be far less use of mental skills training in this type of environment in the future. Sports psychology has been invited to the table rather later than most disciplines; it would be a travesty if it was rejected as a failure because it persisted with approaches that do not meet the needs of players and staff in this sport. Second, the training and education of sports psychologists should be much more orientated towards understanding the culture and organisational stress that exists in professional and academy-level football. It is also essential that those who have a responsibility to train, educate or supervise sports psychologists working in academy football have a deep appreciation and understanding of the demands faced by their supervisees and students (Cruikshank *et al.*, 2014; McDougall *et al.*, 2015). Finally, the type of work done by sports psychologists at academy levels should help players to prepare for the demands and challenges they will face at first-team professional levels. Using the perspectives, the approaches, and indeed the philosophy of practice that are advocated in this chapter for academy-level players will be most useful in helping them prepare to meet the challenges of the first-team environment. This is because taking a greater responsibility for one's own development as a player and a person is vital if one is to survive and succeed in elite-level professional football.

REFERENCES

Chandler, C., Eubank, M., Nesti, M., Tod, D. and Cable, T. 'Personal qualities of effective Sport Psychologists: Coping with organisational demands in high performance sport', *International Journal of Sport Psychology*, 47, (2016), pp. 297–317.

Cook, C., Crust, L., Littlewood, M., Nesti, M. and Allen-Collinson, J. '"What it Takes": Perceptions of Mental Toughness and its Development in an English Premier League Soccer Academy', *Qualitative Research in Sport, Exercise and Health*, 6, no. 3 (2014), pp. 329–347.

Corlett, J. 'Sophistry, Socrates, and Sport Psychology', *Sport Psychologist*, 10, no. 1 (1996), pp. 84–94.

Cruickshank, A., Eubank, M. and Nesti, M. 'Understanding High Performance Sport Environments: Impact for the Professional Training and Supervision of Sport Psychologists', *Sport & Exercise Psychology Review*, 10, no. 3 (2014), pp. 30–36.

Fletcher, D. and Wagstaff, C.R.D. 'Organizational Psychology in Elite Sport: Its Emergence, Application and Future', *Psychology of Sport and Exercise*, 10, no. 4 (2009), pp. 427–434.

Harwood, C. 'Developmental Consulting in a Professional Football Academy: The 5Cs Coaching Efficacy Program', *The Sport Psychologist*, 22 (2008), pp. 109–133.

Harwood, C. and Anderson, R. *Coaching Psychological Skills in Youth Football* (Bennion Kearny, 2015).

Manley, A., Palmer, C. and Roderick, M. 'Disciplinary Power, the Oligopticon and Rhizomatic Surveillance in Elite Sports Academies', *Surveillance & Society*, 10, nos 3/4 (2012), pp. 303–319.

May, R. *The Meaning of Anxiety* (Ronald Press, 1977).

McDougall, M., Nesti, M. and Richardson, D. 'The Challenges of Sport Psychology Delivery in Elite and Professional Sport: Reflections from Experienced Sport Psychologists', *The Sport Psychologist*, 29 (2015), pp. 265–277.

Morris, R., Tod, D. and Oliver, E. 'An Analysis of Organizational Structure and Transition Outcomes in the Youth-to-Senior Professional Soccer Transition', *Journal of Applied Sport Psychology*, 27, no. 2 (2015), pp. 216–234.

Nesti, M. *Existential Psychology and Sport: Theory and Application* (Routledge, 2004).

Nesti, M. 'Persons and Players', in J. Parry, S. Robinson, N.J. Watson and M. Nesti (Eds.), *Sport and Spirituality: An Introduction* (Routledge, 2007).

Nesti, M. *Psychology in Football: Working with Elite and Professional Players* (Routledge, 2010).

Nesti, M. 'Mental Preparation of Elite Players', in A. Mark Williams (Ed), *Science and Soccer: Developing Elite Performers*, 3rd edn, pp. 357–371 (Routledge, 2013).

Nesti, M. and Littlewood, M. 'Psychological Preparation and Development of Players in Premiership Football: Practical and Theoretical Perspectives,' in T. Reilly, A.M. Williams and B. Trust (Eds.), *International Research in Science and Soccer*, pp. 169–176 (Routledge, 2010).

Nesti, M. and Littlewood, M. 'Making Your Way in the Game: Boundary Situations in England's Professional Football World', in D. Gilbourne and M.B. Andersen (Eds.), *Critical Essays in Applied Sport Psychology* (Human Kinetics, 2011).

Nesti, M., Littlewood, M., O'Halloran, L., Eubank, M. and Richardson, D. 'Critical Moments in Elite Premiership Football: Who Do You Think You Are?' *Physical Culture and Sport. Studies and Research*, 56, no. 1 (2012), pp. 23–32.

Nesti, M. and Sulley, C. *Youth Development in Football: Lessons from the World's Best Academies* (Routledge, 2014).

Orlick, T. and Friesen, A. 'A Qualitative Analysis of Holistic Sport Psychology Consultants' Professional Philosophies', *The Sport Psychologist*, 24, no. 2 (2010), pp. 227–244.

Pain, M.A. and Harwood, C.G. 'Knowledge and Perceptions of Sport Psychology within English Soccer', *Journal of Sports Sciences*, 22, no. 9 (2004), pp. 813–826.

Perna, F., Neyer, M., Murphy, S.M., Ogilvie, B.C. and Murphy, A. 'Consultations with Sport Organisations: A Cognitive-Behavioural Model', in S.M. Murphy (Ed.), *Sport Psychology Interventions* (Human Kinetics, 1995).

Potrac, P., Jones, R. and Armour, K. '"It's All About Getting Respect": The Coaching Behaviours of an Expert English Soccer Coach', *Sport, Education and Society*, 7, no. 2 (2002), pp. 183–202.

Premier League *Elite Player Performance Plan* (2011).

Pummell, B., Harwood, C. and Lavallee, D. 'Jumping to the Next Level: A Qualitative Examination of Within-Career Transition in Adolescent Event Riders', *Psychology of Sport and Exercise*, 9 (2008), pp. 427–447.

Richardson, D., Littlewood, M., Nesti, M. and Benstead, L. 'An Examination of the Migratory Transition of Elite Young European Soccer Players to the English Premier League', *Journal of Sports Sciences*, 30, no. 15 (2013), pp. 1605–1618.

Richardson, D., Relvas, H. and Littlewood, M. 'Sociological and Cultural Influences on Player Development', in A. Mark Williams (Ed.), *Science and Soccer: Developing Elite Performers*, 3rd edn (Routledge, 2013).

Ronkainen, N.J. and Nesti, M. 'An Existential Approach to Sport Psychology: Theory and Applied Practice', *International Journal of Sport and Exercise Psychology* (2015). DOI: 10.1080/1612197X.2015.1055288

Stambulova, N. 'Athletes' Crises: A Developmental Perspective', *International Journal of Sport Psychology*, 31, no. 4 (2000), pp. 584–601.

Winter, Richard. 'Finding a Voice – Thinking with Others: A Conception of Action Research', *Educational Action Research*, 6, no. 1 (1998), pp. 53–68.

Wylleman. P., Alfermann, D. and Lavallee, D. 'Career Transitions in Sport: European Perspectives', *Psychology of Sport and Exercise*, 5, no. 1 (2004), pp. 7–20.

CHAPTER 3

SPORTS PSYCHOLOGY SUPPORT AT FIRST-TEAM LEVELS IN THE ENGLISH PREMIER LEAGUE

Dr Mark Nesti

Football Exchange, Research Institute for Sport & Exercise Sciences, Liverpool John Moores University, UK

INTRODUCTION

In this chapter I consider how sports psychology can be used to enhance performance in first-team environments in professional football. In particular, I look at the types of approaches that can be taken when working with players and staff to assist them to produce optimal performances in what is often a very challenging and pressured setting (Nesti and Littlewood, 2009). Although it is possible to do good work in professional football by using a mental-skills-based perspective alone, I will argue that at higher levels of performance a different approach is required to meet the needs of the individuals concerned. The reasons behind this view will be briefly touched upon in this chapter, using research evidence (e.g. Pain and Harwood, 2007) and, more importantly, my experiences during more than two decades of applied practice with professional football.

One of the most important explanations about the limitations of relying exclusively on teaching mental skills comes from the research of a number of sport psychologists over the past 30 years. For example, Gould (2002) and Ravizza (2002) have reported that most elite-level athletes already possess outstanding psychological skills, and are very well aware of the importance of good goal setting, visualisation strategies and relaxation techniques. Although their work is not derived from professional football environments, much of what they have found could arguably be applied to that setting.

Another very important and overlooked branch of psychology that can help to create the best climate for performance excellence in professional football is occupational or organisational psychology. A number of directors of performance and performance coaches currently hold positions in the English Premier League (EPL) or in other professional football teams in the UK. These individuals often draw on theory and research from organisational and business psychology in their work. I have written extensively on what this can involve in practice (Nesti, 2010), basing my work upon having worked alongside several of these people at various clubs, collaborating with them during their careers in the sport, as well as carrying out this function myself on a part-time basis at two EPL clubs. Although this book will not address this important role for the sports psychologist, anyone hoping to be successful as a sports psychologist in high-level professional football should be cognisant of this particular role, its function and how it can impact on culture and organisational processes.

So, what is the psychological approach that guides the work presented here? First of all, it may be more accurate to refer to it as a perspective rather than any particular or singular approach. This is because my applied practice is informed most fully by a number of closely related yet specific theories in psychology. The most important of these are to be found in counselling psychology and psychotherapy, and include humanistic, existential and other person-centred accounts and traditions. These are opposed to those schools in psychology, such as behaviourism, psychoanalysis and some strands of cognitive psychology, that see human behaviour as being determined and that reject the concept of free will.

In conclusion, the perspective discussed in this chapter could best be described as a type of personalistic sports psychology counselling. This will be examined in more detail in section 2 of the chapter, but it is more concerned with developing an individual's self-awareness (Friesen and Orlick, 2010) and self-knowledge (Corlett, 1996) through use of dialogue and encounters (Nesti, 2004). In this way, it could be argued that it bears much resemblance to the recent work of Stelter and Law (2010) in the new area of coaching psychology and sport performance.

This type of counselling approach is, however, quite different to most other approaches that are advocated in sports psychology applied to football, in that it is based on thousands of hours of applied experience with hundreds of professional footballers and their staff, and that is the justification for using it. That is not to criticise the value of research, since it is hoped that in the future empirical studies will be carried out into the effectiveness of counselling approaches in professional football. At present, however, the barriers to this are very considerable, and include difficulty of access into the traditionally closed world of professional football (Roderick, 2006), lack of awareness about these different perspectives in sports psychology, and the reluctance of many scientific journals to publish this type of material. Hopefully, this may change as the professional game becomes more accepting of the important role that sports psychologists can play at the very highest levels, and as sports psychology journals become more willing to embrace a broader range of perspectives and more individual forms of representation.

To conclude, then: the aim of this chapter is to suggest how a sports psychologist can work with elite-level professional footballers and their staff to provide an ethically sound performance-orientated support service. The material presented here draws on the one-to-one sports psychology counselling sessions carried out in five EPL clubs with first-team players and staff, and with coaches and professional footballers from many different countries and cultures.

SCIENTIFIC BASIS

The humanistic-existential approach in psychology is derived from a human science perspective which rests on a personalist philosophy (Nesti, 2011). It is based on a rejection of the dominant natural scientific conception that tends to view human behaviour in terms of cause-and-effect relationships of the type found in sciences like physics (Giorgi, 1970). This means that how it understands human beings is radically different from the traditional view in academic psychology in that it proposes that we have free will. Words like responsibility and agency, and even the notion of the self can only make sense from the perspective of such an approach to psychology.

The theoretical framework that guides my work most strongly is based on certain strands of existential psychology (Nesti, 2004) and positive psychology (Seligman and Csikszentmihalyi, 2000). These schools of psychology adopt a very particular view in relation to how the individual can be understood. They argue that humans are partly shaped and influenced by their genetic inheritance and environmental histories, and most importantly, also by the choices they make. To my mind, this seems closest to the common-sense view (which is most likely why it has not been well received in the world of academia!), in that it suggests that we have a large say in what or who we become. This has been seen in psychology as a fairly new theoretical development, though in reality, it can be traced back thousands of years to ancient Greece (Corlett, 1996) and to the writings of early philosophers in China and Asia.

In this sense this work is embedded in a scientific account that is little known to psychologists in the English-speaking world, and therefore also little known to sports psychologists from these cultures. Within other parts of Europe, however, there is a much greater level of awareness that psychology can be viewed as either a natural science or a phenomenological mode of enquiry with its roots in philosophy (Nesti, 2011).

In the past decade, some articles on sports psychology have begun to examine the limitations of relying exclusively on mental skills training-based approaches and on a de-personalised psychology (e.g. Fifer *et al.*, 2008). These applied sports psychologists argue that mental skills training is best delivered through coaches, or in situations where sports psychologists incorporate it into their counselling sessions with athletes.

RELEVANCE TO REAL-WORLD WORKING PRACTICES IN PROFESSIONAL FOOTBALL

One of the difficulties faced by sports psychologists entering the world of professional football lies in ensuring that they provide something that will be welcomed and appreciated by the staff and players. This is no easy task. Many in the game are suspicious of the roles they assume psychologists will adopt. For example, will the information they give them be used for team selection and for making recommendations as to which players to sell? Do sports psychologists only work with those with problems, and are they only for weak characters? Another concern is around the issue of mental health. This reflects a misunderstanding common in society as a whole and not just within professional sport. Confusion exists over the different levels of expertise and the functions of psychologists, psychiatrists and psychotherapists. This could even lead to fears that the sports psychologist will uncover serious mental health problems and psychiatric illness. In simple terms, this erroneous view can lead to an expectation that sports psychologists deal with serious clinical problems and focus on psychological health rather than on performance. These misconceptions are not restricted to those outside sports psychology, but rather are still prevalent in the profession itself (Nesti, 2004).

Within the sports psychology literature there continues to be strong disagreement about the role of sports psychologists, with some arguing that the focus should be exclusively on performance enhancement (Brady and Maynard, 2010), while others argue that concern should be centred on athlete well-being and care (Andersen, 2009). These views have been challenged by sports psychologists who have worked extensively with elite professional sports performers. For example, Nesti (2010) and Friesen and Orlick (2010) suggest that in reality, these arguments represent a false dichotomy. They point out that when working with highly committed athletes or professional footballers there must always be a focus on helping them to improve performance alongside providing care for the person behind the sports role. This dual perspective is not just ethically attractive – evidence from many studies and work in counselling psychology and psychotherapy confirm that it is essential to developing trust and a strong therapeutic alliance between the client and the psychologist (Harter, 2002). The fact that there is often some level of tension between the demands to support players' well-being and welfare and the requirement to assist with performance enhancement makes the job of applied sports psychologists very demanding. However, the solution to this challenge is surely not to pretend that we will be helping the person when we refuse to see them as sports performers, or when we ignore the fact that they are human beings like the rest of us! I would suggest that in elite professional football, the sports psychologist could be accused of operating unethically and will be less effective in their work if they provide a service exclusively focused on either a caring role or a performance-focused agenda.

More positively, in recent years much greater recognition has emerged about the importance of psychological factors in influencing success and in dealing with failure. Many managers, coaches and other staff are convinced that at the highest levels, it is ultimately the psychological elements which make the difference. Closer examination of the actual practices of these key staff in professional football reveals that many are highly skilled in their use of psychology and have a subtle appreciation of how psychological parameters can impact performance negatively or positively. Usually acquired through craft knowledge (Gilbourne and Richardson, 2006) and occasionally supplemented by formal courses taken during coaching qualifications or other continuing professional development (CPD) activity, there is a wealth of knowledge in elite-level professional clubs in relation to football psychology.

Given the reality that has been described above, it is imperative that the sports psychologist entering the world of professional football can offer something that is different, and adds value to that which already exists. It is not a matter of merely providing something unfamiliar. Rather, it is about ensuring that what the sports psychologist offers can meet the needs of the players and the staff they are working with. To fail to do this very quickly will lead to considerable problems. The sports psychologist will soon find his or her work being rejected, and will be increasingly marginalised and ignored. This will most likely lead to vilification of their role and a questioning of the usefulness of employing a sports psychologist. If this continues, the most likely outcome in the highly charged and intense environment found in and around first-team levels in elite professional football clubs is that the sports psychologist will lose their job! This is very different from the experience of those psychologists working in publicly funded programmes concerned with amateur sport, or at university levels. In professional football, especially at the top end, staff can and will be removed immediately if it is felt that their services are ineffective or not well received – and this could be due to opinions rather than because of any precise empirical evidence. Concepts like the currently fashionable idea of evidence-based practice are understood in a very different way in elite professional football. Sometimes they are interpreted in a very subtle and creative way, though often the reality is cruder than this, and decisions are made based more on feelings and perceptions than on hard data.

It is crucial, therefore, that the sports psychologist can provide something different to what coaches and others can offer. In practice, many managers and coaches are highly proficient in teaching players to incorporate mental skills into their preparation for games and match play. In my experience, elite-level professional football players have acquired a high level of skill in the use of pre-performance routines, visualisation, self-talk, arousal regulation and goal setting. These and other mental skills have been learned through discussion with and guidance from coaches, alongside peers, and sometimes through a process of self-learning. This final way of learning could be described as a form of trial and error, and it can easily be explained by considering the development pathway. In very simple terms, the demands placed on individual players as they progress through the ranks means that very few can emerge at the top level without having acquired a good level of competence in a wide range of mental skills. This is very different to the situation at lower levels, or with younger players and coaching staff (Pain and Harwood, 2007) and youth systems (Holt and Mitchell, 2006). Given this situation, it is of utmost importance that the sports psychologist is able to provide something that others in the club cannot deliver, that is beyond anything that the players and staff currently have access to.

A counselling sports psychology approach does not necessarily exclude the use of mental skills training where necessary or appropriate. Sometimes it may be that players, especially when facing a new and difficult challenge, have forgotten to use their mental skills as fully as usual. Or they may benefit from being introduced to a new psychological skill for them to use when required. The rationale for the counselling-based approach is that the most important psychological factors that players will inevitably face in their career cannot be adequately managed away, or controlled, through mental skills techniques.

The important psychological topics that will impact all players could be divided into those that the sports psychology literature has acknowledged, and those rarely touched upon. The terms discussed and researched most, albeit rarely in relation to elite professional football, are around the psychology of retirement (Grove *et al.*, 1997), injury (Sparkes, 2002) and organisational stressors (Fletcher and Wagstaff, 2009). The other list, which includes terms largely ignored in the literature, is comprised of matters that are more clearly related to professional sport, and to elite-level first-team football in particular.

This includes dealing with the anxiety associated with critical moments (Nesti and Littlewood, 2011). Such moments are continually faced during a professional football career, and relate typically to dealing with de-selection (Brown and Potrac, 2009), being sent on loan, being sold to other clubs, dealing with increased expectations, and moving to a new club. In terms of the psychology associated with these critical moments, there is likely to be considerable impact on a player's identity. At a deeper level these issues are about isolation, choice, responsibility and courage. The counselling sports psychology perspective advocated here provides a way of understanding the motivational problems that players will face, and the existential anxiety (Nesti, 2004) they must confront.

This approach makes it possible for a sports psychologist to address all of these different forms of psychological support within one eclectic and integrated model. Although at a theoretical level there is tension between the underlying scientific philosophies of each of these different approaches, it is possible to operate effectively where the psychologist is fully aware of this tension. Instead of arguing in favour of a cognitive, cognitive-behavioural or more humanistic-orientated form of practice, maybe sports psychologists should be prepared to adapt their applied models to fit the needs of the people they are working with. This will be most effective in cases where a sports psychologist is guided by an overarching philosophy (Lindsay et al., 2007) that sees the individual as a person who happens to play professional football. In basing his or her work on this person-centred perspective, the sports psychologist will be able to allow the client to lead the sessions to ensure that it is their needs that are met, rather than those dictated by a particular psychological theory.

CASE STUDIES

What follows are two semi-fictional vignettes based on delivering sports psychology to EPL first-team football players. Although some of the demands faced by this level of player differ from those lower down, there are many shared experiences that professional footballers will inevitably encounter across their career in their game. The approach taken is guided by personalist approaches in psychology, most notably those found in humanistic and existential perspectives.

The dialogue and questions are derived from a phenomenological approach (Dale, 1996; Nesti, 2011). When phenomenology is applied to psychological practice, questions are framed in terms of getting clients to provide detailed explanations and descriptions of experiences and phenomena. In order that this can be achieved, phenomenologists state that questions should be directed at *what* rather than *why*. This is in order to avoid the tendency to analyse, and come instead to rapid and sometimes easy-to-accept solutions. Analysis is also rejected because it can become associated with a focus on abstract concerns, and lead to a detached and impersonal level of dialogue between the sports psychologist and the player. The aim is to encourage the player to describe in as much detail as possible what they are facing, so that consideration of choices will be based on addressing the real problem rather than a vague account of the difficulty. This form of phenomenological interviewing requires the sports psychologist to allow room for spontaneity and flow in the dialogue. However, it must not be allowed to wander too far from the main concerns facing the player, and continual effort must be made to attempt to describe each challenge in full and rich detail.

Dealing with New Expectations

In this example, a young professional player is meeting the sports psychologist to discuss the challenge of recently being rewarded with an outing in the first team.

Vignette 1

Sports Psychologist (SP): What has it been like for you stepping up to the first team, especially after such a brief period of time here at the club and in the development squad?

Player (P): It has been very exciting and has also made me feel nervous at the same time. I have wanted this since I began playing, even from being 7 years old, but having hoped for this day for so long, it has been a bit of a shock for it to actually happen!

SP: What has this been like for those closest to you – your family, two brothers and dad in particular?

P: They have said great things and told me that they always knew I would make it, which has been lovely to hear. To be honest, deep down I don't really know what they think about what I have done, but I know it makes them feel very happy for me and very proud for themselves and our family.

SP: What do you think about what you have just achieved? How would you describe this and how does it make you feel?

P: To be honest I feel a bit confused you know, in my mind, when I try to understand what is happening to me. I am so very motivated at the moment, you know, I love coming in and practising on improving my skills and working hard on my core strength, which I know I need to do. The performances so far have been pretty good, and have left me feeling confident and really good about myself. Even my girlfriend said the other day that I seem a really different person. I wasn't sure how to take this at first and asked her did she mean more cocky and big time! I think what she really meant was that I seem so focused and determined and really on my game you know, sharp and alive. I don't think it will change me as a person because I know what's important, and would hate if others thought I had gone big time.

SP: OK, that is interesting to hear you say this. You have described how enthusiastic and motivated you have been feeling, but have you had to prepare differently before playing the matches and how have you managed to keep the right mentality during these really high-pressured games you have been playing in?

P: I have been really surprised to be honest that my routines have felt so normal at this new level that, to be honest, is a massive step up, even though I usually try to pretend it is not! I have kept to my way of preparing from the night before, although I've made some little changes because in the away games we now travel so much earlier to the hotel than I am used to. In matches I still will use lots of positive words to myself after I have made a mistake, and so far, this is helping me as much as it did this time last year when I was playing in front of 300 people instead of 35,000. I can't really believe that these things still work for me, but then maybe it is because I have been doing them so regularly for so long. You know, Jeff [senior academy coach] made those mental skills things always part of our training sessions, and encouraged us to use them when we could in matches as well.

SP: OK, that's a great and detailed account which really shows that you have been thinking hard about what you already have in your locker to help you do well at this new level for you. But let me just briefly change focus a little. What do you feel about yourself in relation to the fact that you are doing so well at this level, how do you think that others like the manager and senior coaching staff in particular see how you are fitting in?

P: I think, no that's not right, I *know* because of what they say to me and how they treat me, that they think I am really fully at home at this level and that as the boss said a couple of weeks ago, I look as though I've been at this stage all of my life. After he said that to me I went home and couldn't sleep that night!

SP: What did that make you feel like, what was this like for you?

P: I know it should have made me really confident and calm and buzzing really. But I couldn't believe what happened as it didn't make me feel like that at all!

SP: How did it affect you? What was this experience like then?

P: To be honest I felt like a real fraud! I mean I know I've been doing well and scoring and getting rave reviews and all that stuff, but deep within me, I don't know another way to put it, but I feel a bit edgy you know, not really comfortable at all. As each week has gone on and I have had the same type of great feedback, doing well and all that, I kind of feel that it's not really me, as if things are moving so fast that I'm getting left behind! I suppose that sounds a bit crazy really, but it's how I've been feeling a lot more these last few weeks. All I know is that it is beginning to worry me and I am not sleeping as well as before, and feel more drained than a few weeks back. I'm beginning to think differently about my matches and feel like I am waiting and expecting stuff to go wrong.

SP: What is it that you want to do about this? How can you do something about it realistically – that is, if you think you need to?

P: I know I must do something about it because I can't keep up at this level when people's expectations about me are always getting higher, and I don't see myself the way they do. I need to find a way to bring how I really see myself much closer to how others see me.

SP: So does that mean moving how you see yourself closer to how others see you, trying to dampen expectations around you, or just keep going like this for as long as you can?

P: I know one thing, I can't keep going like this because I know that I will break eventually and my performances could drop off a long way if I don't watch out. I know something must be done and that only I can do something about this. Maybe the best choice is to try and see if the gaffer can take some of the focus off me, and for me to take some time to catch my breath and have a chance to really look at what I have achieved – you know, in a more slow, steady and detailed kind of way, so that I can see that it is real, and is not something that has just happened with a lot of luck. I never for one moment imagined that doing so well, having waited all my life for this moment, would bring challenges that I couldn't even see!

Psychological Skills and Broader Life Concerns

Sometimes the sports psychologist will be called in by the coaching team or the manager to help improve a very specific psychological factor or mental skill in the player. However, the sports psychologist may discover that the player is facing challenges associated with their broader life and that these are also impacting on performance.

In the next case presented here, the player was struggling to deal with mistakes in competitive matches in particular. When he misplaced passes and mistimed his tackles he seemed to lose all confidence in himself, and often descended into a spiral of further mistakes and lost emotional control. This was also associated with a higher frequency of infringements and fouls. In order to address this, the first-team manager asked the sports psychologist to meet with the player.

Vignette 2

SP: I know that the manager has encouraged you to meet with me to do some work together and try to help with one or two very specific things. I know you know how I like to work and the importance of confidentiality, and making sure that you feel able to say anything you want to in this session. This is a little different because the coaching team are really keen for you to try something different to help your performance in competitive games. How do you feel about us working on this?

P: No, I'm really good with this. I have been thinking myself about arranging a slot to see you so I suppose I'm not surprised that they also want this to happen. After all, we're all after the same things, aren't we? It is really frustrating at times and I would like to try and break the cycle if I can.

SP: Tell me more about what is happening to you out there on the pitch. How does this feel for you at the moment?

P: It is really ugly! I have never had anything quite like this before, and playing at the back I have always thought of myself as being pretty good at dealing with adversity, you know, reacting to the things that can go wrong, or maybe I should say things that will definitely go wrong because it is not possible to play perfectly through an entire match.

SP: What exactly happens to you when you have made a mistake out there? What do you think about before, during and after? Can you think back to last week against Tottenham and describe what happens in these moments?

P: When I under-hit that back pass after only five minutes I couldn't believe it was going to be one of those days again for me. I have told myself all week after training that this was a great chance against a quality strike force to show what I could do. I was sure that I felt really confident, and in the changing room, before the buzzer went, I felt really calm. After the buzzer and when we went out into the tunnel all I could hear in my head was, *Don't cock up today early on or you're in for a torrid afternoon!*

SP: What did these words do to you? How were you thinking at that time?

P: To be absolutely honest, I was all over the place, dreading making a mistake, and all I could think about was hoping that I would get through at least the first half without some major problem. All I could really hear, which was getting louder as I awaited kick-off, was as though someone was standing at my shoulder telling me that I couldn't afford any mistakes because this could be the last time I play for a long time as I know that the fans and the papers will be on my case, and the manager will shout and react on the line every time something goes wrong.

SP: We have discussed before the use of something that's called positive self-talk which can be useful to reduce the effects of any negative feelings and words. When we first met together two years ago, I asked you about your mental skills and I looked at my notes last night to check some things before this meeting. At that time you mentioned that one of your strongest features was how you were able to constantly encourage the rest of the back four even when serious mistakes were made and that this positive language was something you'd used to prepare yourself before matches across your career. Do you think we will be able to deal with this challenge you are facing now by trying to replace all of this negativity with some positive self-talk and some positive images? That was something else you said was normally part of your pre-performance routines.

P: I'd love to say that it could be so easy but I have already tried repeatedly to be more planned you know, I suppose you would say systematic, and use my visualisation and positive language more of the time. However, for some reason this is not what has been happening. I don't feel that given how long I have been experiencing this problem now that these mental skills are enough to help me turn things around.

SP: What are things like away from the training ground in the rest of your life at the moment?

P: Funny that you should ask that because to be honest things are very different to how they usually are. You know me well enough that I like things to be nice and calm at home, so I can relax with the family and take my mind off professional football for a time at least. But this past three months something different has been happening. I suppose it has crept up on us, but me and my wife have been really struggling with the huge support that she has to give to her sick elderly parents. Their condition has got much worse recently and this puts a big strain on us – you know, time, energy and also from an emotional point of view.

SP: How much control do you have over what is happening to you in this situation, and what have you been feeling during this time?

P: To be honest I feel a bit guilty and selfish. What I mean is that I am not sharing the load properly and I leave my wife to do most of it, including looking after our two young children. That is not how I like to see myself, it's not what I'm about! My family are my rock, you know, it is really them that makes everything else make sense. I suppose I have been pretending to myself that I can somehow separate out what goes on in matches from the tough things we are dealing with in our outside lives. I am not sure what to do about it, and to be honest, I think I have put my head in the sand a bit over it all. I know some people seem able to get by like that, but not me. I always like to feel in control.

SP: And how much control do you feel you have at the moment?

P: Hardly any. It has never ever been like this for me that I can remember. This is new and I don't like this feeling. I know I can't perform to my best like this. Something has to give and at the moment it's my performance.

SP: What do you feel you could maybe do to help these matters?

P: I could help my wife more with this incredible burden, or try to forget about it more – after all, there are doctors and all sorts of other people able to help them. Maybe what I need to do is become a bit more selfish in a professional way you know, and make sure I focus properly on what I need to do. After all, my whole family and our life is based on me continuing to perform and do well as a professional player, so this is maybe where my energies should go.

SP: What do you think about those choices and how do they make you feel when you imagine yourself carrying them through?

P: It is OK to say these things and important for me to put them on the table. I think I have not been doing this lately, and talking about it now, I realise I should have done this before. There is only one option there that I could imagine doing, one that fits in to what I think is important, and that is to help my wife more fully and find a way to help her to cope. It's funny really because I waste lots of time sitting and worrying about what I am not doing, and thinking about how little I really do to help her, when I really should have been doing more rather than thinking more!

SP: These are difficult things that you are talking about, and you must not be too harsh with yourself, as after all, you're right in saying that if you don't perform it is not only you who will eventually suffer but those closest to you as well. I think you have been really courageous in describing what you really face and trying to come up with something practical that can help. This is not an easy thing to do.

P: Just thinking about what I have been saying has made me feel much better already, even though I know this is going to be tough to carry out. But it feels right to me, and that's very important. Because I can't act things, it's not what I'm like. At least this way I will be more of a help to others, and I think this in turn will help me to feel ready to begin to put my mistakes in some perspective and stop overreacting to things.

TRANSLATING THEORY INTO PRACTICE

Without doubt one of the most important issues facing the sports psychologist wishing to work in professional football surrounds the matter of confidentiality. There are a number of reasons for this. First, it is important to appreciate that in professional sport there is often considerable distrust of outsiders. There can be great reluctance to share information, especially with those who may have links with other competing organisations, teams or individuals. Many university researchers can attest to the fact that gaining access to elite-level professional footballers and staff is a difficult process. In professional football there exists a high degree of suspicion in relation to the motives of people outside the game. For example, there has traditionally been a reluctance to allow the media to see behind the scenes and enter fully into the lives of those involved in the game and witness the professional demands made of them. Second, confidentiality is an essential factor in promoting trusting relationships. It is of huge importance that players and staff can be confident that the matters discussed with the sports psychologist are not divulged within the club or externally. This will ensure that individuals are more likely to place all of their concerns on the table during a meeting. Strict confidentiality can assist the sports psychologist in reassuring the player or member of staff that there is no need to withhold any information during sessions. This can serve to enhance the sports psychology counselling dialogue and help ensure that all important matters can be examined during the sessions.

In my own counselling work with professional footballers and staff, I commence encounters by explaining how I practise, the mechanisms I use to record dialogue and any action identified, and exactly how important confidentiality is to my work. This is done by explaining that I am fully aware that should I break confidentiality, my relationship with this individual and anyone else I am working with at a particular club will be severely compromised. Indeed, I usually state this in more forceful terms by acknowledging that if I were to break confidentiality, I would be removed from my post, rejected by those I am working with, and be subject to censure by my professional body, the British Psychological Society. More positively, I explain that confidentiality will assist the process by giving the assurance that any topic relating to performance as a professional footballer can be considered in meetings. This is crucial given the holistic, personalist psychological approach that underpins my applied practice whereby the person is considered first and the professional footballer second. In other words, this approach, while acknowledging that the focus should be on performance enhancement, does not accept those views which tend to separate someone's professional identity from their personal one. In practical terms, this means that within an encounter it is possible to discuss matters relating to performance in competitive games as well as family difficulties associated with, for example, settling into a new country. These and many other matters can all be legitimately discussed within this theoretical approach since it is argued that our performance can be impacted by narrow sport-related issues and equally by broader social and personal concerns. And finally, it is important that the player is made aware that the only time confidentiality could be broken (beyond situations in which illegal or criminal acts and behaviours are brought into the discussion) is with the permission of the individual him or herself. I always emphasise that there may be, on very rare occasions, issues discussed that could be more easily and quickly resolved with the support of others such as coaches or the manager. However, it is made very clear that the decision to share any information ultimately rests with the player.

A further important aspect of the approach is that, as with humanistic and existential traditions in counselling psychology, sessions are self-directive. The accent is on the individual taking a lead and directing the dialogue. The sports psychologist's role is to help guide the direction of the dialogue and, most importantly, to ensure that clarification takes place. This often means that a more proactive and indeed provocative form of communication can be used at these moments. In this respect the approach is derived more from existential psychology than humanistic perspectives are, deeming it important to be ready to challenge the account provided by a player or staff member to ensure that they have examined the issue as fully, accurately and honestly as possible. This is a very important part of my practice, and it means that the encounter can sometimes involve moments of considerable tension, anxiety and even discomfort. This can happen when the individual has to search deeply into a topic that is personally important to him or her, and consider the choices that are possible as a result of this process.

KEY CONCEPTS

During a sports psychology encounter the focus is on gaining clarification of an issue or a number of issues to ensure that they are examined fully and carefully by the client. The next stage of the process is to encourage a consideration of the choices that they must select from in order to make progress. The role of the sports psychologist is to help the footballer or staff member to articulate these choices and assess how useful each could be in attempting to move forward. Facing choices inevitably brings anxiety. This type of anxiety has been described as existential anxiety (Nesti, 2004), in that it is the feeling of uncertainty we experience when faced with a number of competing choices. Existential psychologists accept that this may feel quite uncomfortable, but by no means do they mean it to be viewed as a negative phenomenon.

The sports psychologist's role is not to take over the responsibility for the professional footballer selecting a particular choice; rather, his or her job is to support and encourage the player to accept the need to consider their choices even where this brings an increase in existential anxiety. The rationale behind this is that, according to existential and other personalistic approaches in psychology, facing up to our freedom to choose and accepting personal responsibility for our decisions helps us to grow in self-knowledge and self-responsibility.

Those clients who refuse to examine their choices and attempt to avoid the need to make decisions are likely also to be less able to do so when facing future challenges. According to existential ideas, an individual who avoids the responsibility for choosing and hands it over to others, or who attempts to deny that they have any influence in what they choose, will become someone with a 'stunted person centre' (Buber, 1958, p. 25). In professional football, this could be a player who now merely follows orders and does as the group thinks, and whose decisions and future is out of their own hands. They may gain direction not from their own choices but from others, such as the manager, agents, coaches or family.

This describes the theoretical framework that I have used to inform my work with professional footballers and staff. The key words are *choice, responsibility, anxiety* and *courage.*

In one sense, it is possible to describe the work taking place here as aimed at assisting the individual to become more self-aware and to acquire greater self-knowledge. Self-awareness refers to the capacity to assess one's strengths and weaknesses in order to put in place a range of different activities to create further progress. Self-knowledge is about having a deeper understanding of oneself, an understanding that goes to the heart of the matter. Knowing who I really am means that I must reflect upon what is most important to me ultimately. This task, which is never-ending, relates to my values, beliefs and philosophy of life. It is possible to see how this type of work is essentially about the development of personal identity. Once again, some of the most important psychologists and psychotherapists (e.g. Maslow, 1968; May, 1977) have suggested that the development of greater self-knowledge and a more accurate idea about who we really are is vital for psychological health and improved performance.

Often the issues facing the professional footballer or staff in professional football concern motivation. Motivation can best be understood when it is separated into intrinsic and extrinsic components. Especially at higher levels of professional football, extrinsic motives in the form of rewards, status, public recognition and threats to career can be very significant. However, there is ample research evidence to support the theory originally proposed by Deci and Ryan (1985) that extrinsic rewards can, in some circumstances, undermine intrinsic motivation. Intrinsic motivation is related to the enjoyment associated with perceived competence and feelings of self-determination. When these are assailed by an excessive focus on extrinsic motives there can be considerable problems, especially when the extrinsic rewards are no longer forthcoming to the player.

Sometimes incorrectly referred to as self-motivation, intrinsic motivation is important because ultimately it is under the control of the individual themselves. This means that even when a player is receiving few rewards and having a difficult time, the presence of intrinsic motivation will help them to continue to work hard and focus on their goals. Good goal setting should always include a strong focus on process goals (Gould, 2002). These types of goals are closely related to intrinsic motivation in that they are in the individual's control and should relate to task-orientated matters, rather than to results and rewards, over which there is much less control.

Self-confidence and undermining of self-esteem can easily occur in such a performance- and results-orientated environment as professional football (Parker, 1995). Players can have their confidence undermined through their own performance failures and where coaches and others criticise them or drop them from the team for prolonged periods of time, for example. During these difficult phases, the sports psychologists may be able to assist with self-confidence and esteem through engaging in dialogue focusing on the player's past achievements. Especially for higher-level and very successful professionals, there is usually a vast store of previous examples of outstanding performance. This can be very powerful and effective where a player is prepared to reflect upon how this was achieved, and how this made them feel.

Finally, the sports psychologist may encounter matters relating more directly to emotional control and dealing with stress. This could be where a player is facing a new challenge as a result of moving up in terms of level, where they are returning from injury, or when they have high expectations placed upon them. In these and similar situations, the sports psychologist can use mental skills training in a targeted way to teach the player cognitive or cognitive-behavioural techniques to help manage the problem. Sometimes goal setting, positive self-talk, visualisation, relaxation strategies and other psychological skills can prove very useful in these situations.

CHALLENGES IN THE WORKING ENVIRONMENT

Working in professional football offers a number of challenges that are either less frequently met or do not exist at all in lower-level and amateur sport. The influence of money and one's media profile ensures that extrinsic motivation is a constant feature. Although most people in professional sport have high levels of intrinsic motivation for their sport, these motives must co-exist alongside the rewards and pressures associated with high achievement. Professional football is the most financially successful sport outside the major sporting franchises found in North America. Within a UK perspective, the recent multi-billion-pound media deals have ensured that the English Premier League is easily the wealthiest competition in world football. This brings great opportunities for increased investment in youth development, sports science staff, coach education and state-of-the-art facilities. It would be expected that more opportunities for sports psychologists to work at youth and first-team levels in professional football, at least within the English game, will follow.

Some of the specific challenges related to working as a sports psychologist in professional football are associated with the prevailing culture that exists. Roderick (2006) has described the traditional working-class culture that is still prevalent inside professional football clubs in Britain as one where an abrasive and macho environment is dominant. This culture has a tendency to regard new ideas and innovation with suspicion. Professional football also perceives itself as a traditional bastion of some of the very best values of industrial working-class culture. For example, communication tends to be direct and blunt, and all staff and players must demonstrate a strong work ethic. There is much talk about team work and common goals, and emphasis is placed on the importance of the group, team or club over the individual.

Less positively, this culture can often be seen as anti-education; those who are highly educated and speak in a more middle-class idiom are often viewed as outsiders, or even as threats to the culture. Within this milieu, psychology is sometimes seen as a support for those who are weak characters – players and staff who lack the mental strength to deal with adversity on their own. It is also often the case that psychology is denigrated for being a stereotypically feminine concern. This is because of a deep-seated prejudice which sees a concern with emotions and feelings as being for the most part the preserve of females.

The rate of change within elite professional football in particular is incredibly fast. Huge media interest, the global reach of the sport and the large amount of international investment have helped to bring about a culture of rapid change and volatility. There is often a high turnover of staff each season, especially of managers and senior coaches. This makes it much more difficult to generate strong relationships and trust, and it can damage the working relationships that the sports psychologist may have with other members of the support team and the players. Given how important the manager and senior coaching staff can be to the work of the sports psychologist, it is a significant challenge when a club can change key staff sometimes as many as three times across a season. This level of instability will affect all staff; however, for the sports psychologist, where confidentiality is such a crucial aspect of their work, it will present an even greater burden.

In this type of culture, the sports psychologist may find that he or she cannot survive after a change in manager and senior coaching team. Many sports psychologists who have worked in professional football have tended to tie themselves to the career path of a particular manager in an effort to enhance the effectiveness of their role and work. However, if the manager is removed from their post this can make things very much harder for the sports psychologist. The players and support staff will usually be aware of how important the manager's support is to the work of the sports psychologist and that without this high-level backing the psychologist will usually have a much harder time gaining access to the players.

Another major issue revolves around the high-profile hype and celebrity culture that often exists in the world of professional footballers. This will often make them reluctant to trust people easily and quickly. For sports scientists discussing sensitive performance data this can make matters very difficult. However, for the sports psychologist the problem is significantly greater. Particularly at high levels of performance where players usually have had an excellent range of mental skills, dialogue needs to be broad to allow the player to mention anything that they consider is impacting on their performance. As we have discussed, this could relate to narrow issues that take place in matches or at the training ground, or it could be related to broader life concerns. This more personal information that the sports psychologist may have access to would undoubtedly be highly valued in the world of media. There is an incredible appetite to hear about players' personal lives in quite a remarkable level of detail.

Although not all players and teams will experience relegation or threats of relegation in their careers, this is a very important factor that impacts the culture within professional football. Relegation can bring huge financial loss and result in the mass sale of players and the removal of staff. When a team is in the relegation zone in a league, or close to it, there can be a crushing level of anxiety, and communication between staff and players can break down. Although this provides the psychologist with an excellent opportunity to attempt to enhance communication and build bridges again, it is also something that can lead to the sports psychologist being considered irrelevant and a luxury.

Taken together, all of these cultural markers within professional football can easily create a climate of fear, mistrust and superficiality, as well as a demand for immediate results. Even more disruptive, this type of rapidly changing and fluctuating environment can generate a high degree of self-interest; players and staff begin to disengage from one another and begin to seek to protect their own positions and security, leading to a culture of negative anxiety. The sports psychologist will find it increasingly difficult to offer the support they feel is needed in a climate such as this.

Given the understandable demands for any scientific intervention to work quickly and with little difficulty, the sports psychologist may be surprised to hear some staff and players speak favourably about mental skills training. There is a desire to learn techniques such as those provided within neuro-linguistic programming that can assist the player after a relatively brief period, improving such important aspects as concentration, focus and dealing with negative emotions. This might mean initially that those sports psychologists who do not restrict themselves to mental skills training alone may be viewed as both too idealistic in their philosophy, and unable to meet immediate needs in such a ruthless and results-orientated culture.

In terms of the delivery of sports psychology support, there are a number of challenges to be met. There is often difficulty around gaining access to players and ensuring that meetings can take place at the optimum time for the individual. Psychology and sports psychology work are usually the last sessions to be protected in the weekly schedule, despite most within the game, especially at the highest levels, agreeing that psychological factors are very often the most important in determining performance. This paradox results from the fact that psychology is something that all have a responsibility for – not only the sports psychologist. It is also due to professional football culture most usually being orientated towards doing and action, rather than thinking and reflecting.

Psychology also suffers through comparison with the other sports science disciplines in professional football because of the problems around measurement and evaluation of outcomes. Although it is possible to keep good records identifying basic data around length of sessions, frequency and the general topics addressed, the confidentiality required makes it very difficult to provide much beyond this. This can lead to frustration on the part of other staff who feel that the sports psychologist should share their information more fully and, by not doing this, could be accused of operating very differently to the rest of the backroom team.

The sports psychologist will find that, beyond formal meetings, much of the expectation is that they will engage in informal and ad hoc sessions with players and staff. These can take place anywhere – within the training ground, or at locations where the individual feels comfortable and secure. Again, this is usually very different from the operating practices of other staff in the club, and it may be perceived as making the sports psychologist appear to be rather detached from the staff team.

Finally, in order to deliver a service according to the model described in this chapter, it is important for the sports psychologist to maintain some distance from the staff team and the players. They must not be perceived as a friend, but as a caring professional. Although this balance is difficult to achieve because of the considerable emphasis on developing a strong team spirit in professional football, it is a very important means of ensuring that the sports psychologist can operate effectively with all players and staff, no matter how much or little they like each of them as individuals.

SUMMARY

The sports psychologist working at first team level faces a number of challenges that are unique to this environment. It is usual to find, especially at the highest levels of the professional game, that most players already possess excellent mental skills. Without these skills, few could survive for long given the high expectations and performance pressure they face across a season. As has been discussed, this situation provides the sports psychologist with an opportunity to offer support that goes beyond mental skills training, and can include work that is more counselling based, focusing on both broader life issues and more narrow performance concerns. To carry out this work effectively will in most cases mean that the sports psychologist must have the support of key staff, especially the manager or head coach. They must also have the knowledge, skills and personal qualities to be able to offer something that complements the more informal support that usually already exists within high-quality environments. Acknowledging that very often there is considerable craft-based understanding around psychology, especially among coaches, will be essential if the sports psychologist hopes to build relationships, trust and professional respect. The wealthier clubs can have a highly skilled and competent workforce of between 30 and 60 or more performance staff at first team levels. This considerable resource, and the fact that most clubs have a large squad of players, will allow the sports psychologist ample opportunity to carry out their work. To do this successfully they must act with integrity, and offer to players and staff a confidential service focused on performance and well-being. And finally, the sports psychologist must possess the character and skills to try to engage in this work at all times, and most importantly during the inevitable crisis moments that are such a feature of this volatile and demanding professional sport culture.

REFERENCES

Andersen, M.B. 'Performance Enhancement as a Bad Start and a Dead End: A Parenthetical Comment on Mellalieu and Lane', *The Sport and Exercise Scientist*, 20 (2009), pp. 12–14.

Brady, A. and Maynard, I. 'At Elite Level the Role of the Sport Psychologist is Entirely about Performance Enhancement', *Sport and Exercise Psychology Review*, 6 (2010), pp. 59–66.

Brown, G. and Potrac, P. '"You've Not Made the Grade, Son": De-selection and Identity Disruption in Elite Level Youth Football', *Soccer and Society*, 10 (2009), pp. 143–159.

Buber, M. *I and Thou* (W. Kaufmann, Trans.) (Scribner's, 1958; original work published 1923).

Corlett, J. 'Sophistry, Socrates and Sport Psychology', *The Sport Psychologist*, 10 (1996), pp. 84–94.

Dale, G. 'Existential Phenomenology: Emphasising the Experience of the Athlete in Sport Psychology Research', *The Sport Psychologist*, 10 (1996), pp. 158–171.

Deci, E.L. and Ryan, R.M. *Intrinsic Motivation and Self-Determination in Human Behaviour* (Plenum Press, 1985).

Fifer, A., Henschen, K., Gould, D. and Ravizza, K. 'What Works When Working with Athletes', *The Sport Psychologist*, 22 (2008), pp. 356–377.

Fletcher, D. and Wagstaff, C.R.D. 'Organisational Psychology in Elite Sport: Its Emergence, Application and Future', *Psychology of Sport and Exercise*, 10 (2009), pp. 427–434.

Friesen, A. and Orlick, T. 'A Qualitative Analysis of Holistic Sport Psychology Consultants' Professional Philosophies', *The Sport Psychologist*, 24 (2010), pp. 227–244.

Gilbourne, D. and Richardson, D. 'Tales from the Field: Personal Reflections on the Provision of Psychological Support in Professional Soccer', *Psychology of Sport and Exercise*, 7 (2006), pp. 335–337.

Giorgi, A. *Psychology as a Human Science: A Phenomenologically Based Approach* (Harper & Row, 1970).

Gould, D. 'Sport Psychology in the New Millennium: The Psychology of Athletic Excellence and Beyond', *Journal of Applied Sport Psychology*, 14 (2002), pp. 137–139.

Grove, R.J., Lavallee, D. and Gordon, S. 'Coping with Retirement from Sport: The Influence of Athletic Identity', *Journal of Applied Sport Psychology*, 9 (1997), pp. 191–203.

Harter, S. 'Authenticity', in C.R. Synder and S.J. Lopez (Eds.), *Handbook of Counselling Psychology*, pp. 637–655 (SAGE, 2002).

Holt, N. and Mitchell, T. 'Talent Development in English Professional Soccer', *International Journal of Sport Psychology*, 37 (2006), pp. 77–98.

Lindsay, P., Breckon, J.D., Thomas, D. and Maynard, I. 'In Pursuit of Congruence: A Personal Reflection on Methods and Philosophy in Applied Practice', *The Sport Psychologist*, 21 (2007), pp. 335–352.

Maslow, A.H. *Toward a Psychology of Being* (Van Nostrand Reinhold Company, 1968).

May, R. *The Meaning of Anxiety* (Ronald Press, 1977).

Nesti, M. *Existential Psychology and Sport: Theory and Application* (Routledge, 2004).

Nesti, M. *Psychology and Professional Football: Working with Elite and Professional Players* (Routledge, 2010).

Nesti, M. 'Phenomenology and Sport Psychology: Back to Things Themselves', *Sport, Ethics and Philosophy*, 5, no. 3 (2011), pp. 285–296.

Nesti, M. and Littlewood, M. 'Psychological Preparation and Development of Players in Premiership Football: Practical and Theoretical Perspectives', in T. Riley., A.M. Williams and B. Drust (Eds.) *International Research in Science and Soccer*, pp. 169–176 (Routledge, 2009).

Nesti, M. and Littlewood, M. 'Making Your Way in the Game: Boundary Situations within the World of Professional Football', in D. Gilbourne and M. Andersen (Eds.), *Critical Essays in Sport Psychology* (Human Kinetics, 2011).

Pain, M. and Harwood, C. 'The Performance Environment of the England Youth Soccer Teams', *Journal of Sports Sciences*, 25 (2007), pp. 1307–1324.

Parker, A. '"Great Expectations: Grimness or Glamour?" The Football Apprentice in the 1990s', *The Sports Historian*, 15 (1995), pp. 107–126.

Ravizza, K. 'A Philosophical Construct: A Framework for Performance Enhancement', *International Journal of Sport Psychology*, 33 (2002), pp. 4–18.

Roderick, M. *The Work of Professional Football: A Labour of Love* (Routledge, 2006).

Seligman, M.E.P. and Csikszentmihalyi, M. 'Positive Psychology: An Introduction', *American Psychologist*, 55, no. 1 (2000), pp. 5–14.

Sparkes, A. *Telling Tales in Sport and Physical Activity: A Qualitative Journey* (Human Kinetics Press, 2002).

Stelter, R. and Law, H. 'Coaching – Narrative Collaborative Practice', *International Coaching Psychology Review*, 5, no. 2 (2010), pp. 152–164.

PART TWO

PART TWO

CHAPTER 4

PHYSICAL PREPARATION OF ELITE SOCCER PLAYERS

Dr Antony James Strudwick[1] and Dr F. Marcello Iaia[2]

Head of Performance, Football Association of Wales[1]
School of Exercise and Sport Sciences, Department of Biomedical Sciences for Health, Università degli studi di Milano and Head of Performance, FC Inter Milan[2]

INTRODUCTION

Throughout the past two decades there has been a movement towards systematic methods of preparing elite players for match-play. Contemporary coaches have been exposed to scientific approaches to preparing teams for competition. In general, teams that have adopted a strategic approach have been rewarded with success by gaining an advantage over competitors. While it has taken some time for the accumulation of scientific-based knowledge to be translated into a form that is usable by practitioners, there has been a major paradigm shift in elite soccer performance. This shift has facilitated better-informed practitioners working with teams, stronger links with scientific institutes and more coaches willing to accept the changing role of sports science in elite soccer. Greater efforts are now being made to compile scientific information and make it accessible to the soccer world. This chapter is a step in that direction.

The key objective of this chapter is to provide a comprehensive account of the parameters that impact upon the physical preparation of elite soccer players. In addition, it will provide guidelines on how to utilise scientific principles to maximise the training of elite soccer players and the delivery of field-based sessions to them. In the first section, a brief theoretical background about the importance of understanding the demands of the game and an overview of the different components of fitness training required will be given. The second section is mostly focused on applying the principles of conditioning, with a special insight into planning, training methods and sessions relevant to real working practices in professional soccer. The final section provides an insight into the issues involved in working with soccer players in an elite environment.

FITNESS TRAINING IN SOCCER

Although a variety of sports science disciplines will impact upon elite performance and player preparation, this chapter will focus specifically on the physiological aspects of performance planning and consider appropriate principles that should be incorporated into the training of elite soccer players.

The two major aims of fitness training in soccer are:

- to enable technical skills to be utilised throughout a match; and
- to allow the players to cope with game demands.

These aspects imply keeping players injury free and enhancing performance potential via the implementation of appropriate training, both on and off the field.

Many factors need to be considered when designing a programme, and such evaluations should encompass relevant experiences accumulated over the years together with applied research findings. A programme should not simply be imported, although the development of an appropriate training programme may stem from the results of others. Such a programme needs to be versatile, enabling it to be utilised as a model of training that can be easily applied to individuals with their own specific characteristics and goals.

The focus of field-based training from a fitness perspective is predominantly aimed at producing the appropriate stressors to ensure the energy systems of players adapt and are best equipped to withstand the competitive demands of the game. The approach is therefore to overload specific areas of physiology in isolation rather than stimulating every component within the same drill. In addition to physiological load, there is a mechanical load component that also needs to be taken into account in the construction of the training plan. The mechanical load imposed on players needs to be fully understood to make an appropriate assessment of the injury prevention impact of the total work completed. Where mechanical load is the focus, specific physiology may not be targeted, with drills involving many components. In these situations it is just as important to ensure that the necessary overload is achieved to ensure that players can withstand the mechanical stresses competitive matches impose on them.

Both of these requirements – energy system development and mechanical overload – require a thorough understanding of the demands of the game and of the limiting factors in terms of performance. These issues are addressed below; first, the match demands and its applications are considered, and this is followed by theoretical and practical training guidelines. Finally, issues surrounding planning are presented in a discussion of the combination of various types of training in the training week and the changing emphasis required through the various stages of the season.

MATCH DEMANDS AND PLAYER REQUIREMENTS: APPLICATIONS

The physiological demands on modern players are more complex than in many individual sports and these demands on players vary depending on level of performance, positional role and style of play incorporated by a team (Bradley et al., 2009; Di Salvo et al., 2009; Gregson et al., 2010). In elite men's soccer, top players may participate in approximately 220 training sessions and 60 competitive games over a season. This equates to 20 training sessions and 5.5 matches per month, yielding an average training/match ratio of 3.6 training sessions per match. However, these figures represent seasonal average values and there will be periods throughout the annual calendar where elite players are exposed to matches every 3.3 days over a five-game period. When one factors in the confounding variation in kick-off times, as well as travel commitments and international fixtures, it is evident that the demands on elite soccer players are intensive.

In order to cope with these increased demands, players must have the necessary physical resources to perform the high work rates and critical actions required during match-play. Higher levels of strength and power are now required at an elite level in order to be able to reproduce forceful bursts of energy and withstand the forces of physical impact. The observation that elite players perform 150–250 short, intense actions during a game indicates that the rate of anaerobic energy turnover is high during periods of match-play (Mohr et al., 2003). These activity patterns include maximal sprinting (30–40 times), turning (>700 times), tackling and jumping (30–40 times) as well as intense muscular bursts such as accelerations and decelerations (Bangsbo, 1993; Mohr et al., 2003; Bloomfield et al., 2007). All these efforts exacerbate the physiological strain imposed on players and contribute to high physical workloads during match-play, particularly during the most intensive blocks (see Table 1).

TABLE 1 Physical match demands on elite players

Parameters	Categories					
Velocity	Sprint (>25.2 km/h)	High-Speed Run (19.8–25.2 km/h)	Run (14.4–19.8 km/h)	Jog (7.2–14.4 km/h)	Walk (<7.2 km/h)	Total Distance
Average Match Distance	250 m	750	1,800	4,500	2,700	10,000
Very High Match Distance	550 m	900	2,000	5,500	3,000	12,000
Intense 5min Blocks	95 m	55	150	N/A	N/A	300

Source: STATS LLC (formerly Prozone)

Match analysis also suggests that the distance covered in high-speed running by elite players in the last 15 minutes of a game is 14–45% lower than in the first 15 minutes (Mohr *et al.*, 2003). According to Mohr *et al.* (2003), this finding supports the notion that fatigue occurs towards the end of the game for players who play the full 90 minutes. These effects are observed independent of position. Accordingly, in the 5 minutes following the most demanding 5-minute period of the game, the distance covered at high intensity is reduced by 6–12% compared with the game average. These findings suggest that at an elite level of play, players experience fatigue towards the end of the game, and temporarily following intense bursts.

CRITICAL AND INTENSE PHASES OF THE GAME: AN APPROPRIATE MODEL

With the use of the modern match analysis systems, a wide range of detailed information on a player's fitness performance is now available. However, how to interpret the information appropriately and the process by which such information is best utilised to effectively implement the training programme is not always clear. The majority of practitioners utilise match-analysis technology to gather information about the physiological strain imposed on players during match-play. Although this approach will yield an overview of the physiological strain during competition, much of the qualitative information during the most critical phases of the match will be overlooked. Moreover, while the total distance covered at various exercise intensities offers global measures of the physiological strain imposed on players, the most intense 5-minute blocks of match-play offer more detailed information that can be better used in the design of field-based conditioning drills. In addition, research has indicated a fairly high variability (20–30%) from game to game (Gregson *et al.*, 2010), suggesting large fluctuations in game demands. In this regard, situational factors such as the positional role, the level of the opponent, the result of the game and the tactical system played have been reported to markedly affect the amount of high-intensity work performed during a match (Bradley *et al.*, 2009).

Taken together, these various types of information provide sufficient evidence to suggest that global measures of match data are not always the optimal key performance indicators to utilise when designing conditioning programmes. A more appropriate model involves researching in depth the critical and more intense phases of the game. When applying a more sophisticated analytical approach, it emerges that individual physical profiles are varied and intermittent, with periods of very intense bouts followed by periods of low activity (see Figure 1).

Thus, a comprehensive quantification of the workload a player experiences during the most intense phases of the game is crucial for understanding the mechanisms taxed and the physiological demands imposed, and this, as a consequence, has practical implications for the subsequent creation of personalised training

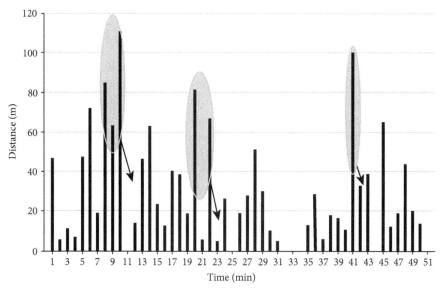

FIGURE 1 Pronounced reduction of work rate after the most intense phases

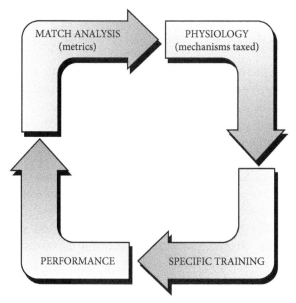

FIGURE 2 Examples of the use of match analysis for the planning of fitness training

programmes. Such an approach, besides being an effective and time-efficient strategy for maximising performance enhancement, has direct implications for injury prevention as it replicates the high-intensity periods, thereby exposing the players to the fatiguing actions occurring in the game. Before planning fitness training, the individual specific game requirements need to be clearly understood, and data from match analysis aid such understanding (see Figure 2).

APPLYING THE PRINCIPLES OF CONDITIONING

With the demands of contemporary soccer, there is a clear requirement for players to condition themselves and appropriately prepare the necessary energy systems to enable optimal performance. Practically speaking, fitness training is multifactorial and can be divided into a number of components, which reflect the physical demands of the game. For clarity, it is important that a common language is utilised and the physiological systems targeted by the various training categories fully understood. Some terminology has been used extensively and is known; however, various other training philosophy descriptors have been introduced over recent years to assist in the translation of physiological terminology into a language that enables a better transition of theory into practice by coaches.

However, by having an outline of the physiological pathways, there is less chance of ambiguity in discussions between support staff and coaches, as a clear picture of the training aims can be adequately presented. Table 2 identifies and summarises the key training categories of field-based conditioning methods that can be utilised with elite players.

Training Approach to Field

Many components need to be incorporated into a training programme. These include a full range of activities, such as activation modalities, injury prevention strategies, individual and team preparation (technical and tactical), match rehearsal and recovery strategies, in addition to the more obvious 'training session'. The design of the programme should be based on individual training philosophy and specificity to match performance per se.

The necessary isolation of match performance components and control of workload intensity is achieved by a series of activities conducted within the training session. Training effects do not occur by coincidence. Not all training sessions automatically result in the appropriate physiological and performance adaptations. The specific activities that are performed place specific demands upon the body, resulting in structural and physiological changes. Moreover, it is not feasible or desirable to target every mechanism to the same degree. Clearly, a decision needs to be made to prioritise the system(s) subsequently becoming the cornerstone of a team's field-based conditioning philosophy. This is fundamentally a decision by the coach and the sports scientist, and it forms a critical element of the training process.

Thus, where possible, specific physiological systems understood to be limiting factors to performance should be stimulated, rather than performing holistic training whereby many mechanisms are taxed to lesser degrees. As a consequence, during field-based conditioning, it is paramount that training load, consisting of

TABLE 2 The main categories of field-based conditioning and their methodology

Training category	Aim	Main physiological stimulus/ mechanism	Training protocol Exercise intensity	Rep duration	No. reps	Work: rest	Training Mode General	Soccer-specific
Aerobic low	Recovery from intense sessions/ matches	Aerobic peripheral	Light 7–11 km/h, <75% HRmax	10–30 min	2–3	1:0.1	Bike Jog	Shape Passing routine
Aerobic moderate	Exercise for prolonged periods	Aerobic peripheral	Moderate 11–14km/h, 75–85% HRmax	10–30 min	2–8	1:0.2	Straight, shuttle and multidirectional runs	7v7 to 10v10
Aerobic high	Perform repeated high-intensity work	Aerobic central/ peripheral – Anaerobic	High 15–20km/h, >85–90% HRmax	1–4 min	4–10	1:1 1:0.5	Straight, shuttle and multidirectional runs	3v3 to 6v6, 7v7 to 10v10 specific rules, big pitch area
Speed endurance maintenance	Sustain, tolerate and recover from very high-intensity work	Anaerobic lactic capacity – Aerobic central/ peripheral	Very high/near maximal (>VO$_2$ max speed)	15–90 s	3–12	1:1 – 1:3	Straight, shuttle and multidirectional runs	1v1 to 2v2 Individual soccer-specific drills

(Continued)

TABLE 2 (Continued)

Training category	Aim	Training protocol					Training Mode	
		Main physiological stimulus/mechanism	Exercise intensity	Rep duration	No. reps	Work: rest	General	Soccer-specific
Speed endurance production	Produce power rapidly and continuously, perform maximal runs more frequently	Anaerobic lactic power	Maximal/near maximal	10–40 s	4–12	>1:5	Straight, shuttle and multi-directional runs	Individual soccer-specific drills
Repeated sprint	Recover and perform repeated sprints	Anaerobic/aerobic	Maximal/near maximal	<10 s	4–25	1:3 – 1:5	Straight, shuttle and multidirectional runs	Finishing and skill drills
Speed	React and produce powerful actions and maximum sprinting speed	Anaerobic alactic/neural	Maximal	<10 s	4–20	1:10	Straight, shuttle and multi-directional runs	Position-specific drills

training intensity and duration, is appropriate for the intended physiological and performance adaptations.

All training sessions should incorporate elements of muscular activation and warming up to facilitate the appropriate recruitment of muscle fibres associated with the correct sequencing and timing of soccer-specific activities. Speed preparation should follow, with adequate recovery time between repetitions and sets to allow continual energy resynthesis. Subsequent stimulation of the aerobic and anaerobic systems should then be performed via specific drills with the ball involving changes of speed, direction and specific movement patterns typical of those performed during match-play. Appropriate recovery activities should be incorporated at the end of each training session that are principally based upon adequate rest/sleep and relevant nutrition and hydration strategies. The application of a variety of other modalities may also confer some advantage (refer to section below on the increasing role of recovery after training and competition).

Small-Sided Games

In recent years there has been a shift towards using soccer-specific activities (small-sided games/drills) in the preparation of elite players (Little and Williams, 2006; Hill-Haas et al., 2011). The rationale behind utilising this training mode for conditioning is to facilitate simultaneous physical and technical development with the twinned advantage of enhanced player motivation and greater transfer to match-specific fitness. Therefore, when possible, practitioners should utilise small-sided games and/or position-specific drills containing tactical/technical components associated with the demands of elite match-play.

The variable nature of movement in conditioned games and drills means that control over intensity is potentially less precise. Nonetheless, with detailed planning and knowledge, practices with a moderate number of players or imposed high-intensity activities appear to be optimal for physiological development as they consistently produce suitable work intensities (Rampinini et al., 2007; Kelly and Drust, 2009; Hill-Haas et al., 2011). A method to control the intensity during small-sided games is by manipulating variables such as field dimension and number of players involved, as well as by introducing specific rules (Bangsbo, 2008). For example, it has generally been found that larger pitches produce greater intensities, presumably because players cover greater distances and play is more open on the larger pitches. While coaches do use small-sided games with the specific intention of fitness training, few monitor the physical components taxed within each drill. Knowledge of work rates with certain drills, together with the fact that they are consistent, means that these can be applied properly to produce optimal fitness development.

Appropriate monitoring methods enable the identification of the physical demands of drills that may well impose specific technical/tactical demands on players while at the same time training desired components of physiology. This allows the staff to be better informed and to select more appropriate conditioning drills dependent on individual player needs and also to take into account their recent physical and physiological training and match loads.

Knowledge of workloads and their consistency during each of the training drills mean that two of the most important training principles can be applied during field-based conditioning – namely, progression and periodisation. Progression refers to gradually increasing the training load over time as fitness gains are incurred. Periodisation can be defined as a logical, phasic method of manipulating training variables in order to increase the potential for achieving specific performance goals.

Thus, in summary, small-sided games and/or position-specific drills containing technical/tactical elements associated with match-play have the potential to produce greater benefits as they allow simultaneous physical and technical development.

Insights into Planning – Weekly, Monthly and Annual Structures

When planning fitness training for elite players, the annual cycle should be divided into three stages: Off-season, preparation and in-season. The latter may be further divided into competition and peaking/maintenance. These phases have specific goals and require different levels of training variation. The use of a planned training programme can allow for tighter control of training variables, superior performance adaptations and generally better performance at the appropriate time.

Preparation Phase

This phase consists of moderate/high-volume, low-intensity training and is used as foundation training. The preparation phase is designed to increase exercise endurance, positively alter body composition and increase tissue size and tensile strength, anatomical balance resulting in a lower injury potential; it can also be used to increase basic strength. The preparation phase should be used to increase soccer-specific fitness, and is typically divided into general and specific parts. This process should enable players to become match fit prior to competition.

A guiding principle for all planning is that the programme of physiological preparation should develop from general to specific requirements and should be coupled with the development of training duration towards and including specific intensity requirements (Maille, 1999). The practitioner must also allow for adequate rest and regeneration. The preparation phase should concentrate on the following four important aspects:

1. improving high-intensity exercise endurance;
2. changing body composition, especially increasing muscle mass;
3. decreasing injury potential; and
4. increasing power.

TABLE 3 Outline of field-based conditioning priorities over six-week pre-season period

Weeks 1 and 2	Weeks 3 and 4	Weeks 5 and 6
General Endurance	Specific Endurance	Specific Endurance
7v7 to 10v10	3v3 to 6v6	1v1 to 2v2/sprints
Moderate- and high-intensity aerobic runs	Aerobic high-intensity and speed endurance runs	Repeated sprints and pure sprints
Quantity – Quality	⟶	

The length of time spent in this phase, however, is often limited due to the schedule of pre-season matches imposed, which now requires travelling worldwide to service sponsors and sell the club brand. However, an outline can still be useful in the coaching process, working on a pre-season period of typically 5–7 weeks. The first 10 days/two weeks encompass soccer activities from the start, with extensive endurance/aerobic moderate-intensity drills being the dominant training category. During the second part, 3–4 weeks prior to the start of the season, players frequently perform aerobic high-intensity and anaerobic interval sessions, with some quality sprint training as the overall volume decreases. The later portion of the preparation phase includes a lower volume of training with an emphasis on high-intensity exercise. It is the combination of all the training formats discussed and a steady progression in game exposure that is critical in developing soccer-specific fitness. Table 3 is a pre-season schematic that shows the relationship between the various types of training utilised throughout this period.

In-Season Phase

This phase is used to maintain optimal performance levels throughout the playing season. The training load should not be drastically reduced at the expense of training intensity during this phase; the management of the training intensity is the key, as high-intensity exercise remains a critical component for maintenance or further enhancement of training-induced adaptations. It is fundamental that elite players continue to develop the ability to repeatedly perform high-intensity exercise during the season. This can be achieved by conducting frequent sessions of aerobic high-intensity and speed, and, based on the players' individual needs, also speed endurance training specific to the physical, movement, technical and tactical demands of the game.

The key principle during the in-season phase is to ensure a balance is reached between training/match load and adequate rest and recovery. Because elite soccer players are expected to perform 40–60 times over a 42-week period, continued high-intensity and high-volume training over extended periods of time may contribute to potentially long-term debilitating effects associated with overtraining and increased occurrence of injury events.

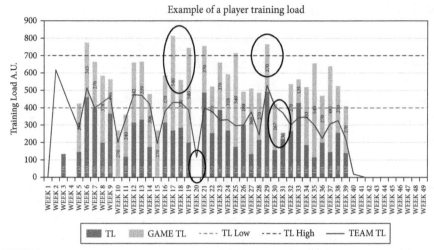

FIGURE 3 The balance of work throughout the in-season phase necessitates the inclusion of peaking/maintenance periods where adequate attention is placed on rest and regeneration

Thus, player performance parameters, together with actual physiological stress imposed on the athletes, need to be carefully monitored, and supplementary recovery sessions as well as reduction in the amount of training should be considered for players during heavy fixture periods. This concept of 'undulating periodisation', where changes to the training programme in terms of volume, intensity and frequency occur, also assists in maximising physiological adaptations and performance maintenance throughout the playing season. Figure 3 provides an example of the load profile throughout the competitive season for an elite player where the total amount of training was significantly reduced in two periods.

For squad players who do not play regularly, training load must be sufficient to cope with the physical requirements of a match. Pronounced mismatches between the demands of match-play compared with training, together with abrupt and severe increases in workload (due from switching from non-play to regular play), may enhance the risk of injury occurrence. Non-regular players therefore need to perform additional field-based high-intensity training or to engage in practice matches during such periods of non-play.

Weekly Planning

The training stimulus plays a key role in the adaptation of each individual player. To optimise training adaptation and reduce injury risk, it is important that players are exposed to different stimuli on a day-to-day basis, thus avoiding monotony or staleness. The inclusion of low-intensity and recovery together with high-intensity sessions will help achieve this, and therefore each training week should be carefully planned.

In practice, the number and type of games as well as the current fitness status of the players dictate the weekly planning, which often varies. Thus, it is logical that there exists flexibility in the programme, and different weekly templates are tailored to the team and the players' specific requirements, instead of using a single standard weekly programme. However, it is also beneficial to have some generic guidelines that are taken into account when creating a training plan that helps in directing the coaching process. Generally we are faced with two scenarios: one game per week and two games per week.

One Game Per Week

In this situation a decision needs to be made on whether players are brought into training to perform a recovery session the day after a game. There is a balancing act between keeping a mental freshness among the squad while also allowing them to have some quality time with their families, and ensuring that a competitive focus is maintained during difficult phases of the season. Experience is key in making these types of decisions, together with knowledge of the wellness status of the squad. In this example, assume a day off is provided for the players, the recovery session being of greater importance when there are two games per week.

Forty-eight hours after the game is probably the most critical time as the muscle soreness tends to be at its highest level and the recovery status is different from player to player. Thus there are players who can perform moderate exercise, others who are ready even for high-intensity sessions and those who at times require a second day of recovery. The third and the fourth day after the game are usually the most demanding ones, with sessions of aerobic high-intensity, strength and anaerobic training performed. The decision as to whether to include speed endurance or repeated sprints as part of the conditioning work will depend on the position-specific and individual needs of players. Two days prior to the next game there is a taper down in volume (and sometimes also in intensity, with a 'light load day' implemented), but there are frequent situations when players carry out either individual-based conditioning or surrogates of high-quality field-based fitness work. For the non-playing squad, the programme is the same, with the exception of the first two days, when additional high-intensity and/or individual-specific work is performed. Table 4 shows an example of a weekly template for both the playing and the non-playing squad.

Two Games Per Week

When two games per week are played it becomes more difficult to perform physical training in addition to the games as the vast majority of the time is dedicated to recovering; the day after the game, the playing squad carries out a recovery session which consists mainly of bike exercise, foam rolling, stretching, upper body strength training, deep pool water immersion, ice bath/contrast bathing and

TABLE 4 Planning: one game per week

	Sunday	*Monday*	*Tuesday*	*Wednesday*	*Thursday*	*Friday*	*Saturday*
Playing squad	REST or Recovery	Aerobic Moderate	Aerobic High	Anaerobic	Technical/ Tactical – individual	Quick feet/ agility	GAME
Non-playing squad	Individual training	Aerobic Moderate	Aerobic High	Anaerobic	Technical/ Tactical	Quick feet/ agility – individual training	REST

TABLE 5 Planning: two games per week

	Sunday	*Monday*	*Tuesday*	*Wednesday*	*Thursday*	*Friday*	*Saturday*
Playing squad	Recovery	Quick feet – aerobic moderate/high	GAME	Recovery	Aerobic moderate/ high – individual training	Quick feet/ agility	GAME
Non-playing squad	Individual training	Quick feet – aerobic moderate/high	REST	Anaerobic	Aerobic high	Quick feet/ agility – individual training	REST

massage. However, in situations when there are three or more days between a game and the following one, there is the possibility to perform some fitness work, usually consisting of aerobic high-intensity training, but often also individualised anaerobic-specific sessions can be carried out. For the non-playing squad, the day after a game is the crucial conditioning day as if there is a persistent lack of intensity in the session, players could conceivably detrain. Hence, training usually consists of additional high-intensity conditioning work through small-sided games or individualised drills. An example of how a typical week with two games is structured is presented in Table 5.

Off-Season

Following the competitive in-season phase, both physiological and psychological recovery are necessary. Thus, recovery from the in-season phase should take the form of 'active rest' (AR), in which the volume is kept low and the intensity of training is low to moderate. For some players, it may be beneficial for them to participate in some other sport, but at a recreational level. The exact length of time for the AR phase depends upon many different factors, including training status, injury history and age. The positive effects can include diminished fatigue, injury rehabilitation and psychological recovery.

Working with Elite Soccer Players

An elite soccer player attempting to reach the highest level requires a systematic approach to all areas of performance management. Such an approach can be achieved by identifying the critical component parts of the coaching process and the relationships between the sub-processes. There are several critical components that impact on player performance management, and these are discussed throughout the book. Although many of the components overlap, future success in soccer will be achieved by providing appropriate soccer-specific scientific support models. Clearly, the application of such models has a self-evident part to play in improving elite performance. Important features of these models, such as data management, performance profiling, devising training programmes, monitoring performance, establishing preparation for competition, and sport specific analysis, are informed by sports science knowledge.

KEY MESSAGE

It is imperative that a systematic performance management model is established when working with elite soccer players. Such a model will help shape and drive the coaching process.

The Increasing Importance of Analytics

At an elite level of playing soccer, an enormous amount of data is now generated about a team's performance on a constant basis. Some coaches now have first-hand experience of how to use 'sports analytics' to improve player and team performance. In the future, high-performing soccer teams (those that substantially outperform their competitors over the long term) will turn to analytics as a competitive strategy. While technology on its own cannot turn a soccer organisation into a high performer, time and effort focused on developing robust analytical processes has great potential.

Analytics refers to the extensive use of data, statistical and quantitative analysis, explanatory and predictive models, and fact-based management to drive decisions and actions (Davenport and Harris, 2007). The analytics may be input for human decisions or may drive fully automated decisions. Analytics are a subset of what has come to be called 'business intelligence', a set of technologies and processes that use data to understand and analyse performance. It must be stressed that analytics and intuitive decision-making need not represent two diametrically opposed paradigms.

The key deliverable of the analytics process will be an increasing emphasis on using data to make better decisions. In short, the sports world is tapping into the power of analytics. Business people have long borrowed insights from sports about teamwork and leadership. But data, especially in the form of statistics about players and teams, has traditionally only been fodder for sports commentaries or office chat. Only recently has hard data begun to transform the management of professional sports. In fact, some sports executives now have much to teach businesses about how to profitably capture and analyse data. These professionals have first-hand experience of how the intelligent use of analytics can improve asset acquisition and management, talent management, operational performance, and even injury prediction.

KEY MESSAGE

A critical concept in the process of data collection is distinguishing between which information/data is important and which is not. Data gathering for the sake of gathering data can be very expensive and futile unless it is used to drive action during the coaching process. While technology on its own cannot guarantee success at an elite level, time and effort focused on developing robust analytical processes has great potential.

Increasing Role of Recovery after Training and Competition

Training and competition will culminate in a certain level of fatigue, which temporarily reduces individuals' functional capacity. During the subsequent rest period, the biochemical stores should not only be replenished, they should actually exceed normal levels. This process of overcompensation should be considered as the foundation of all functional increases in athletic efficiency. The principle of recovery relates to the encouragement of adaptive processes after the presentation of the stimulus. If there is sufficient recovery before the next workload, the underlying system or fuel store stressed during training can improve its capacity to cope with the next stressor. Appropriate recovery results in the restoration of physiological and psychological processes, so that the player can compete or train again at an appropriate level. When working with elite players, it is imperative that a systematic recovery protocol is followed that is consistent and flexible.

KEY MESSAGE

Recovery from training and competition is complex, involves numerous factors and is typically dependent on the nature of the exercise performed and any other outside stressors that the player may be exposed to. Performance is affected by numerous factors, and for adequate recovery to take place, such factors as training/competition, nutrition, psychological stress, lifestyle, health and the environment should be considered.

Systematic Monitoring of Work Rates

A continual system of monitoring is essential to ensure that the correct decisions are made with regard to individual player requirements. Research has revealed that stress associated with multiple competitions and training causes fatigue and often temporarily impairs players' performance (Andersson *et al.*, 2008). Furthermore, elevated workload over extended periods of time may contribute to potentially long-term debilitating effects associated with overtraining and increased occurrence of injury events (Nimmo and Ekblom, 2007). Therefore player performance parameters, together with physiological and subjective ratings, need to be carefully monitored throughout the training programme.

A continual system of monitoring is essential in elite soccer to ensure that all players perform the required volume, intensity and frequency of training. Training load should be prescribed individually on the basis of the players' physical condition and movement requirements, as well as the technical and tactical requirements of match-play; however, daily adjustments should be made depending on the health and physiological and subjective status of each player.

KEY MESSAGE

Careful planning, implementation and monitoring allow for the optimisation of the training process, maximising a player's potential and reducing the risk of injury occurrence, detraining and/or overtraining.

Performance Analysis

The analysis of soccer performance can be undertaken at several different levels. For example, at the physiological level of analysis, information may focus upon the performance of the cardiovascular system, or yield information concerning the efficiency of the energy systems during the same performance. Although each level of analysis differs from the others in the theoretical basis from which its enquiries are generated, one critical element remains invariant: they all converge upon one behavioural outcome that has meaning within the context of the sport performance under examination (McGarry and Franks, 1994). Quantitative analysis describes the performance at this behavioural level of analysis. It involves the objective evaluation of a player's performance during match-play.

Analysis of soccer performance usually infers that there is some inherent organisation and predictability within the competitive situation. There is also the assumption that the events being analysed have a certain amount of structure and follow one another in a sequential manner. Moreover, if these assumptions were false, then one should expect that anything and everything is possible.

KEY MESSAGE

Since the events of soccer have a certain amount of organisation, identification of those patterns of play that yield favourable profits will provide the coach with valuable information concerning match strategy.

Injury Prevention

In the preparation of elite athletes, practitioners have a responsibility to implement a comprehensive and planned training programme that allows for gym-based injury-prevention strategies. The athlete has to be trained in such a way that the body will be prepared for optimum response to the physical demands of competition. Strength training has been increasingly employed in the holistic management of contemporary soccer players. In simple terms, strength training involves increasing the ability of the athlete to apply force. The ultimate objectives of strength training are to develop the capacity to reproduce forceful bursts of energy and to withstand the forces of physical impact, landing and deceleration.

KEY MESSAGE

Following specific screening protocols for local muscles, as well as joints and lower back/pelvis, preventative gym-based programmes in the form of core stability, balance, proprioception, muscular strength and power should be implemented to address the increasing issues of muscle strains in contemporary elite soccer.

Multi-Disciplinary Interaction

There is no doubt that successful soccer performance is multi-disciplinary in nature. Coaches and athletes need to be aware of the physiological, biomechanical, psychological, nutritional, medical and other issues that can impact on competition. When all these factors come together and work as an integrated system, excellence in high-performance soccer is possible. Coaching is above all about problem solving. Coaches who are trained to think critically about all aspects of performance and how they interact and influence each other will be rewarded with success by gaining an advantage over competitors.

KEY MESSAGE

While the concept of soccer science being comprised of various disciplines makes sense, there are traditional, cultural and historical barriers to the multi-disciplinary model which must be overcome if it is to make a real impact on soccer performance.

THE ROLE OF THE COACH

In many circumstances coaches may operate without the benefit of specialist support personnel. In these conditions, it is imperative that modern coaches act as applied soccer scientists who keep abreast of contemporary research and are capable of applying a multi-disciplinary understanding to their practice. It is further recommended that as part of the coaching process, modern coaches seek additional expertise when pulling together the support services around athlete management. Indeed, a number of academic institutions around the world now provide programmes specifically designed to support applied coaches with the offer of work placements and similar internships.

Preparing players for elite competition involves the coach, the athlete and a number of sports medicine and sports science practitioners. Each needs to appreciate the significance and complementary nature of one another's roles if the performance of the athlete is to be maximised. Modern coaches need to have sufficient knowledge and understanding of soccer science principles, and of how to use these principles in a coordinated manner. Moreover, coaches working at the elite level need to be familiar with the significant contributions that sports scientists, biomechanists, psychologists, sports medicine practitioners and nutritionists can offer. Without such knowledge, they will be unable to make critical decisions that impact on the holistic performance of athletes.

KEY MESSAGE

Contemporary coaches should be trained and educated to think and work in a multi-disciplinary environment. Coaching is above all about problem solving. Therefore, it is critical that coaches appreciate the vital role of specialist support personnel.

It is the role of the coach to drive the coaching process and assimilate information to maximise the training programme. While each arrangement will be different and distinctive and based on the particular organisational and cultural setting, the overall implementation of the process is the responsibility of the coach, although inevitably it may involve a significant group of other personnel too.

THE ROLE OF THE SOCCER SCIENTIST

If the role of the coach is to assimilate information and drive the coaching process, then it is the role of the soccer scientist to monitor, record and deliver performance insights. In line with this interpretation, sports science has been underdelivered in elite soccer for the past few decades due to the inability of practitioners to effectively collect data and present it in a format that can easily be translated by coaches. Just as modern coaches need to be familiar with the significant contributions that sports science can offer, so too soccer scientists need to be familiar with the specific demands of soccer and the appropriate methods of communicating with athletes and coaches.

KEY MESSAGE

Soccer scientists should provide information for subsequent action by both coach and athlete. In order to achieve this, the athlete, the coach and the soccer scientist should be conversant with the procedures involved. Engagement of all parties is critical to improving performance.

The systematic assessment of an athlete's performance is not simply a means of collecting large amounts of sophisticated data. Quite clearly, the soccer scientist must have the capacity to translate this data into meaningful and relevant soccer-specific information and advice. A balance must therefore be achieved between monitoring, testing and performance prescription.

In order for the soccer scientist to operate successfully within the coaching process, the following principles must be considered:

1. The soccer scientist needs to have an appreciation of the demands of soccer. This will include technical and tactical considerations as well as scientific principles.
2. The soccer scientist must recognise the key areas associated with successful soccer performance.
3. This information needs to be translated into soccer-specific conditioning components.
4. The soccer scientist must consider why and when assessments are carried out and the most appropriate form of assessment (i.e. laboratory or field based) to be used.
5. The soccer scientist must have the capacity to translate data into meaningful and relevant soccer-specific information and advice.

Finally, the current education and development programmes for soccer science professionals have the potential to narrow their focus into one area of sports science. At the elite level, where teams have the financial resources to employ experts in one particular field of sports science, this is appropriate. However, in most cases, sporting organisations do not have the capacity to employ experts in only one area of one discipline of sports science. Therefore, modern soccer science practitioners should be comfortable with all areas of sports science and have the capacity to educate coaches and athletes in biomechanical, physiological, psychological and peripheral areas of sports science. A multidisciplinary approach to high-performance soccer is required, accepting the limitations inherent in a single-discipline approach.

SUMMARY

This chapter has considered the key issues that impact upon the physical preparation of elite soccer players. Contemporary match-play is physically demanding and players require elevated fitness levels to cope with these energy demands. For this reason, practitioners need to have an enhanced appreciation of the processes that are involved in the holistic management of elite players.

At the elite level of soccer, the next decade will see improved coach education, enhanced sports science knowledge and better player management. Moreover, elite soccer teams will move towards existing in high-performance environments where the development of systematic performance models and increased accountability are commonplace. Innovations in player preparation are more challenging by the year and expectations continue to rise. Therefore, player preparation has to be sharper and better informed. Taken together, these factors call for superior sports science support models and deeper insights into issues relating to the management of elite performance.

CHAPTER 5

PREVENTION WITHIN TREATMENT AND REHABILITATION

Dr Bryan English[1] and Glen Driscoll[2]

Head of Medical and Science Department,
Middlesbrough Football and Athletic Club, UK[1]
Head of Performance, Celtic Football Club, UK[2]

PREVENTION

Injury prevention and associated screening strategies in professional football clubs tend to evolve and undergo transitional changes dependent on the staff, and even management, in any given place or time and can often be affected by the responses and demands of the players. Medical and science departments in football therefore often need to show great resilience and adaptability to adopt the very best injury prevention strategies and service for the players. The incentive to strive for and deliver the most successful prophylactic care and thus prevent injury is essential – benefiting the player, the manager and the club – in such a competitive and financially driven industry.

Injury prevention is difficult to measure within a small number of people and over a short period of time, as the only measure is the percentage of injury recurrence (which is multifactorial). Generalised injury prevention programmes involving the whole team, often taking place pre-training, can practically allow clubs with limited staff to deliver circuit-based exercises where players rotate between proprioception, strength, core stability and neuromuscular control stations. However, in practice, these non-specific programmes can be potentially unpopular with the players, who often become uninterested in the generic nature of the programme, and the resultant quality of the work is then poor.

The incorporation of activation exercises as part of the warm-up for training is being more frequently utilised in football, although they are generally designed to prepare players and prevent issues solely for the session ahead rather than tackling the individual predisposing risk factors based on injury history or any strength deficits each individual player may have.

The practice of injury prevention is also one of the most important areas that needs to be supported by evidence-based practice. On a practical level at a football club, no one can see when an injury has been prevented – they only see when an injury hasn't been prevented. As a result, it is a more efficient process to drive forward with those injuries which, on evidence, are most preventable with interventions that are scientifically proven to reduce the risk of injury.

INJURY PREVENTION MATRIX

On consideration of the practical implications of adopting injury prevention in the football environment, the best solution was the creation of the injury matrix (Table 1). This attempted to prioritise both screening tests and injury prevention interventions to improve player compliance in the system as a whole. The injury matrix scores a number of criteria related to the most commonly injured structures to focus and prioritise both screening procedures and injury prevention interventions. By targeting the most commonly injured structures, the scoring system will make the prioritisation of these areas more formal. It will also give guidance to the frequency and content of the regularly used screening procedures. For example, a player with no history of groin problems and found to have no issues on screening may only need to provide the adductor squeeze screening test once a month, whereas a player with both a history of groin problems and a weakness in that region may be expected to provide a groin squeeze score 2–3 times a week, during strength programmes when they feel warm and can see it as part of their individualised programme. Here, a more objective and target-driven gym culture at the club can enable the vast majority of injury prevention-based interventions to be targeted and delivered as part of the player's individual programmes and strength programmes.

Following completion of the screening and matrix each player will be issued with:

1. A summary including recommendations for targeted strength work with strength and conditioning coach.
2. An individualised screening plan.
3. An individualised injury prevention programme of exercises to be completed on days when strength exercises aren't suitable, and supervised where possible by issuing physiotherapist (see Appendix).
4. A plan for more formal review.

TABLE 1 Evidence-based injury prevention guidelines for soccer (C. Morgan, 2010, Liverpool FC)

Injury Prevention Matrix – Scoring (time + type + screen)

Injury Type	Preventable (hamstring, ankle inversion)	3	Time	Within past 6 months	3	Screen Findings	Specific to injury	3
	Soft tissue (muscle, ligament)	2		6–12 months	2		Indirectly related to injury	2
	Significant (off > 4 weeks)	1		12–18 months	1		Finding	1
	Recurrent (>1 in last 2 seasons)	1		18+ months	0		Nil found	0

Key Injuries	History – diagnosis/dates	Screening – significant findings related to injury
A		
B		
C		
D		
Other Injuries		Other screening findings
E		
F		
G		

Injury Prevention Strategy

Matrix Priorities: #6 or more = high priority; #5–6 = action required; #3 or less = monitor

Injury	Matrix Score (0–9)	Intervention (details separately): specific physio-led and strength programme aims	Date for review
A			
B			
C			
D			

SCREENING

A number of weekly screening measures can be taken by the physiotherapists over the course of the season to flag potential risk of injury. Two-day post-game adductor squeezes and weight-bearing dorsiflexion lunge scores collected from the whole squad, along with hamstring strength scores from those players with a previous history of hamstring injury, can provide early indications of potential problems in those areas, or show secondary issues, before players mention any symptoms. Other simple and non-exhaustive tests such as athlete self-report measures (ASRM) and functional tests, such as jump protocols using portable force platforms, may also serve to indicate predisposing fatigue in relation to injury (Thorpe *et al.*, 2017; also refer to Part Two, Chapter 7 for a more detailed review). This information, in combination with the intrinsic and extrinsic fitness status of the player, can highlight the potential injury risks before the player presents symptoms. The extrinsic loading of training and recovery strategies is covered in other chapters, but it is important to state that the biggest bang for the buck in terms of preventing injury is related to the appropriate extrinsic conditioning, loading and recovery of players in training between matches. Even the most holistic and comprehensive intrinsic prevention programmes designed by science and medical departments cannot affect the prevalence of injury as much as the manager or coach on the training field. Real-time GPS targets and thresholds for individuals in training can be set up by the science team to help guide the coach away from training errors. Those thresholds can only be derived from the conscientious trend analysis of injury (aetiology) in relation to training and games (see Part Two, Chapters 4 and 7 for a more detailed review).

As compliance with the screening procedures can be poor, in particular if players do not see or understand an outcome, it is important from a practical level that any information that is taken will be efficiently used, and will ultimately affect decisions relating to the modification of training or further individualising recovery or prevention strategies, such as in the injury matrix. Players are screened in July, often when they have just returned from a period of relative inactivity. The season then has two natural points at which the squad could be considered relatively settled for the next few months – namely, just after the transfer windows. Therefore up-to-date matrixes along with screening plans for each player should be reviewed (by way of full screens) by the middle of September and the middle of February each year (see Table 2), while new signings should be screened, matrixed and issued with an injury prevention programme within one week of signing. Prevention of injury also involves good recovery strategies (nutrition, rest, sleep) and the avoidance of over- and under-exercise and illness.

Injury prevention is a great challenge and needs to be implemented within the appropriate stages of rehabilitation to set up a practical and achievable routine that can be maintained once the player has returned to training. This provides the opportunity to instill in players the required compliance and to educate them in such a way as to drive home the importance of continued prevention. For example, from a passive treatment perspective, an ankle returning from chondral (articular cartilage) pathology in a player may require assessment on several occasions to check the range of movement of the joint and to comply with work to increase that range (if it is found to be quietly decreasing). So although asymptomatic, the work on range may prevent other issues such as a calf muscle tear from occurring.

REHABILITATION

Rehabilitation: 'To restore to useful life, as through therapy and education. To restore to good condition, operation or capacity.' (*Oxford English Dictionary*)

Rehabilitation is easy to do badly and difficult to do well. A technically excellent operative procedure can be undermined by poor rehabilitation and an average procedure can be complemented by expert rehabilitation.

Rehabilitation is carried out by a variety of specialists, and the closer they work as a team, the more successful is the end result. Rehabilitation is not the focus of just one practitioner. It may be mainly carried out by one practitioner, but the construction, judgment and case management of the process needs to have input from several professionals with differing areas of training and expertise. These include the coaches or the goalkeeping coach, but also nutritionists, the fitness coach, the strength and conditioning coach, the sports scientist, the psychologist, the podiatrist, as well as the doctors, physiotherapists and sports science support team. However, someone needs to take responsibility for the whole process, and the most appropriate person within a large medical team would be the physician with training and expertise within this field.

There are many ways to rehabilitate a medical problem. In relation to orthopaedics, such functional rehabilitation can be divided into seven categories:

1. Decrease pain and swelling.
2. Achieve full range of movement and flexibility.
3. Achieve full power and endurance.
4. Achieve top levels of proprioception and coordination.
5. Achieve previous levels of skill and agility.
6. Return to full training.
7. Return to play.

It is important to follow some form of structure in rehabilitation. Structure that is preferably, but not essentially, backed with some form of science/evidence gives the patient as well as the rehabilitation team confidence and reassurance that all is going to be well. Education of the staff and the patient through the process is important as each patient brings their own challenge. Previous history, expectations, operative success, time availability for rehabilitation (prior to necessity of return to work) will together lead to a case-by-case personal rehabilitation plan rather than a heavy protocol-based prescription. Constant review of the success/failure of the rehabilitation process is healthy to avoid following a path that may lead to failure. For this reason, measurements such as range of movement of a joint, heart response to exercise, maximal speed, ability to decelerate and many others can be taken to demonstrate to the rehabilitation team and the patient that progress is being made. Return to full training can be a target-setting criterion to provide a focus for motivation and standard setting for those carrying out the assessments and treatments.

Assessment of the rehabilitation phases can encompass state-of-the-art scientific evaluation such as high-speed video analysis, accelerometers and GPS data. However, it can also be done by using a stopwatch and some sticks in the ground! In other words, the process should be creative and imaginative for the practitioner, as well as enjoyable, possible and affordable for the patient. Return to Play (RTP) criteria are, nonetheless, enhanced by having the objective (GPS) information from match and training data as it tells us what the player's capacity is (in matches) and what we are asking the players to return to in training. The demands of the first training session the player is returning to and the tactical demands of the player's position also need to be factored in. For example, the demands on a centre back are significantly different from those on a full back – almost like those from two different sports, you could argue – and so the rehabilitation and injury prevention staff need to be aware if their player (a centre back) is about to be returned into a position that demands a greater capacity (full back) at such a vulnerable time post rehabilitation. If, for example, the injury this player is returning from is a hamstring, there could be added cost and fatigue due to the extra high-intensity distance being demanded of them (potentially tactically), leading to a risk of re-injury. Rehabilitation is required to get players fit for their safe return to training. Training, then, needs to get the player fit and available for matches. The length of time a player needs to train for is dependent on the duration of their injury, their conditioning pre-injury (which may be the aetiological factor that was involved in causing the injury in the first place) and their current physical status.

Here we make a small apology to the reader that this part of the text is not illustrated. This is because we believe that rehabilitation is a functional process and as such, is best demonstrated by video. Still images lead to misconceptions, which is why we would prefer the study of the written word.

1. Decrease the pain and swelling
After an injury or an operation, the main focus is to keep swelling to a minimum, and by doing so, one would hope that the pain will also be minimised. Pain and

swelling will prevent any progress towards Phase 2. There are many methods to alleviate swelling; however, compression, cooling and elevation appear to be the mainstays of treatment. 'Decreased function' should also be included in that list as early lack of swelling and pain can lead to complacency, and the patient then starts to 'try it out'. The importance of rest and recovery, even if just for 48 hours, depending on the case, can be very productive. The patient should be educated as to why this is important. If the surgery has been elective, then hopefully steps will have been made by the patient to create a support network to assist in this phase when at home (as returning home as soon as possible is beneficial to all) (van den Bekerom *et al.*, 2012; Waterman *et al*, 2012). Gentle active resisted muscle activation is possible at this stage – and, indeed, this can be induced by electrical activation – to avoid the muscle-damaging effect of pain and swelling.

Aquatic therapy is an excellent modality to ease swelling and pain because of the compressive effect of water and the beneficial effect of minimal movement in deep water (Eyestone *et al.*, 1993; Bushman *et al.*, 1997). Naturally there may be anxiety with regard to wound protection; however, such anxiety should be allayed by expertise in wound protection and management, and aquatic therapy in these circumstances should not be contraindicated as there is no evidence to indicate that well-maintained pool chemistry should cause a problem (especially when the wound can be covered with a waterproof dressing) (Pool Water Treatment Advisory Group, 2009; Villalta and Peiris, 2012). Analgesia has its place at this stage, decreasing inflammation and allowing the patient to become more mobile and, importantly, to adopt as normal a gait as possible as early as possible.

Manual therapy/effleurage is a useful way to make the patient feel that he or she is being looked after (don't underestimate the power of this), and gentle passive mobilisation will start to produce less fear in the patient that movement will cause pain. The manual therapist will get a feeling of the degree of swelling of the injured area, as well as of its warmth and range, and of the reactivity of the contractile tissues. This hands-on knowledge is valuable in determining progression or regression in this initial crucial phase. Wound breakdown, bleeding and infection are issues that can easily be avoided by experienced professionals with care and diligence. An over-zealous rehabilitation team or an over-ambitious and impatient patient can disturb the healing phase at this stage and send the plan completely off course. Leadership and guidance is a priority here to support those responsible for the success or failure of rehabilitation. Good communication between all parties will hopefully see the patient through Phase 1 as soon as possible without fear and with a positive expectation of Phase 2 (which naturally overlaps with Phase 1 on a case-by-case basis).

Can Phase 1 be measured? Yes – swelling can be measured by daily measurement of limb girth, and pain can be measured by many methods, including the visual analogue scale.

2. Achieve full range of movement and flexibility

The range of movement of the joints and contractile tissues involved (proximal and distal to the injury) should be mobilised as soon as possible. Fear and pain should not stand in the way unless there is a specific reason to restrict movement. Increased range can be encouraged by passive and active movements of the joints and soft tissues. Both passive and active movements should be observed, documented and, where possible, measured with reproducibility. Methods for measurements should be standardised and discussed by the rehabilitation team to encourage good inter-measurer reliability, while recognising that intra-tester testing may be ideal. Knowledge of range of movement pre-injury is beneficial, which is why annual musculoskeletal screening/profiling is beneficial in sport. However, the contralateral limb is also a good comparison, with obvious assumptions being made about pre-injury symmetry.

The patient is often anxious in this phase and needs to be made aware that increasing range is not often a pain-free process. Warming up the joint (using applied heat or exercise) prior to end of range movement can help. Cradling of the joint in experienced hands can provide reassurance during the passive movement phase. Active movements can be encouraged with the use of aquatic therapy along with many other tools, such as static cycling. Daily measurement can provide a visual for the medical team and the patient, with goal setting providing a target. Such measurements also act as a guide as to whether the mobilisation is being overdone (resulting in increased swelling and decreased range of movement, especially first thing in the morning).

Can Phase 2 range of movement be measured? Yes, goniometers are still a useful tool to measure range of movement of a joint, while recognising that the range may be restricted due to swelling, tight soft tissues, pain, bone etc. Flexibility is less easy to measure as such measurements tend to be more global than local. Ability to touch one's toes with extended knees (to use a rather clumsy example) covers movements of the spine, sacroiliac joints, hip, knee and ankle, along with associated ligament, tendon, muscle, fascia and neurovascular structures. However, this should not deter the medical team from addressing all these structures in order to obtain full range of movement. The use of passive and active stretches, manual therapy, active resisted techniques (hold, contract, stretch) and techniques to decrease hypertonic tissue (heat, electrical therapy) can all be considered part of the arsenal to create as much range as possible (van der Wees *et al.*, 2006). Can Phase 2 flexibility be measured? Yes – a knee-to-wall test, for example, can demonstrate flexibility of the calf muscle and/or the deep flexors of the foot and ankle as well as range of movement of the ankle. It would be up to the practitioner to determine whether this restriction is due to lack of range or lack of flexibility. Such tests can be arranged for any joint and they can be combined with 'range' assessment.

The importance of experience in this phase cannot be overstated. It is vital to achieve good range early (extension post anterior cruciate surgery, for example) with sympathy for the restriction and information provided from the tissues during the treatment process. Careful mobilisation may indicate that the joint is just not ready for the range, that there is too much swelling or too much pain, or, indeed, that there has been a defective surgical procedure. When dealing with living human tissue, one can 'listen' to the structure rather than just mobilising and forcing the restriction. This phase, like many of the others, can be very individual. Some joints will respond well and one can accelerate through the process. Others will react and will need more patience. Therefore progression should be the target and goal setting should not be hastened by unrealistic time schedules. Occasionally 'rest' for 48 hours can allow the joint to settle and be followed by a much more productive phase.

3. Achieve full power and endurance

The overlap between Phase 1 and 2 is marked. However, there is little overlap between Phases 2 and 3 because progress in Phase 3 is limited and even switched off. For example, vastus medialis switches off with a knee effusion and, in the author's opinion, tibialis posterior switches off with an ankle effusion (Palmieri et al., 2004; Kulig et al., 2011). One cannot get the power back in these areas and exercise them to the full until Phases 1 and 2 have been completed. In contrast, early stages of Phase 4 can be introduced in the mid stages of Phase 3.

Power is an expression by the muscle of full physiological function and it is one of the most easily measured of the modalities (using weights, scales, dynamometers or isokinetic machines, to name a few methods). The progress can easily be recorded showing the whole range from maximal effort or exercise to fatigue ('Can you do 10 lunges?' for example) using either scientific laboratory-based assessment or field testing of functional movement patterns.

Can power be measured in Phase 3? Yes – exercise is the key in this phase. Isometric and isotonic exercise are cheap and easy to do as self-management processes, and can be done with the joint isolated (for example, knee extension while sitting) or, if preferred, using the whole kinetic chain (the standing jump, for example). These movements can be measured and they are repeatable and reliable (Hölmich et al., 1999; Hölmich et al., 2004; Verrall et al., 2005; Crow et al, 2009; Engebretsen et al., 2010). Can endurance be measured in Phase 3? Yes – repeated calf raises to fatigue can be measured; however, quality of movement needs to be supervised. Repeated concentric loading at a certain speed can be accurately measured with an isokinetic machine. These tests can measure isolated endurance.

Whole body endurance is also important at this stage and this can be measured with lactate testing on treadmill running, for example (or by devising another exercise for a multidirectional athlete). Lactate testing involves sequential blood samples, measuring the increase in body lactate as a response to increasing exercise. The less fit an individual is, the sooner his or her blood lactate rises. A less invasive way to measure fitness can be by field testing and by judging heat-rate response to a submaximal exercise (such as the yo-yo test). Whole body endurance work can be wrongly ignored in Phase 3, more due to fear on the part of the practitioner than anything else. After passing Phase 2, the patient should not be viewed as a fragile being who is going to break down. The injured area can still be respected while the body performs heavy cardiovascular work.

The heart can be worked hard in the water, for example. There are numerous ways to exercise in deep water to produce a significant cardiorespiratory challenge. The big muscle groups can be challenged with power repetitions to produce/reinforce range, power and flexibility. The exercises can be entertaining to aid compliance, and the practitioner should ideally be sufficiently physically fit to be able to join in and demonstrate such work to the patient (with intermittent breaks doing such things as playing head tennis in the water for recovery). A higher state of monitoring can involve the wearing of a heart-rate monitor throughout the working day to produce an estimate of cardiovascular 'work done'. GPS is crucial for the integration of a returning player into a training session. Doing so three days before a game will result in completely different demands on the player than if he or she returned to training the day before a match, across all variables – including distance covered, peak speed, high-intensity distance and high accelerations and decelerations.

4. Achieve top levels of proprioception and coordination

This is arguably the most important rehabilitation phase, yet, in the author's opinion, Phase 4 is easily dismissed by the improving athlete who is eager to get to Phase 5 and beyond. Phase 4 requires concentration and discipline from the practitioner and the patient. However, the practitioner who understands human nature may wish to drop in aspects of Phase 5 to provide a taste of things to come when Phase 4 has been successfully mastered.

This phase also allows the artistry and imagination of the practitioner to flourish. It can be rewarding to find a variety of ways to use the disciplines of balance, proprioception and coordination to enable the patient to master body control. Movements that test and train proprioception and coordination need to be diverse, challenging, entertaining and relevant to the person's future activity (as this helps with compliance). There are many examples of how to do this work. A simple one is the hop and hold test, which brings to the patient's attention their deficiencies, highlighting asymmetry by means of this basic movement (and therefore enabling them to understand that Phase 5 is not possible without being able to control function in Phase 4 first). This test can be progressed onto different surfaces, such as sand or a trampoline. The complexity of the test can be heightened by asking the patient to catch a ball after landing, in the 'hold' phase (Narducci et al., 2011; Thomée et al., 2011). The aim here is to safely increase the complexity of the work that is being done by the body, time and time again. The execution of the work has to be good otherwise the patient may be learning abnormal movement patterns that will be difficult to undo at a later stage. If the body learns highly complex tasks and performs these well, then the introduction of Phase 5 will take place safely.

Can proprioception and coordination be measured? Yes – balancing and hop and hold tests can be visualised and videoed. The amount of sway can be measured on force platforms, as can the quality of foot strike and the propulsive force (if one wishes to take such measurements into the biomechanics laboratory). Revisiting Phase 4 with the new challenge of different surfaces such as sand and the trampoline can lead to a higher level of function and can increase the challenge for the patient and player (Pinnington *et al.*, 2005; Kvist, 2006; Kidgell *et al.*, 2007; Aragão *et al.*, 2011; Binnie *et al.*, 2012).

5. Achieve previous levels of skill and agility

Phase 5 is the exciting phase as the patient starts to feel as though he or she is nearly there. So it is a very positive phase, but also a dangerous one. There are some important skills left to learn. The patient/player may now be under pressure to return to full activity as they are now seen to be functioning at a high level.

The player needs to get back to work. For example, following an injury to the ankle syndesmosis, and after progressing though the previous rehabilitation phases, the player now has:

a. no ankle swelling or pain and good range of movement;
b. good power of the calf, deep flexors, peroneals and thigh/buttock musculature. The yo-yo test shows good cardiovascular endurance compared with previous testing;
c. basic proprioception and coordination in the water and on sand, trampoline and grass shows symmetry.

So what does the player do now?

a. He performs tasks relating to his sport, such as kicking, jumping, twisting, sprinting, tackling.
b. He performs these tasks with increasing load, such as a heavier ball, greater speed of movement, tighter angle of movement, and involving contact from other players or trainers.
c. He repeats these tasks hundreds of times with precise execution and quality of movement to start to match the demands of full training.

By the time the patient leaves this phase, the rehabilitation team will know that the demands of full training have been met, and that there will be no dramatic increase in demand when they do return to training. If the player is working with a rehabilitation programme of quality, then this phase may cross over daily with Phase 6. The player is allowed to take part in some, but not all, parts of training. This will help rehabilitation, with mutual understanding between those involved in the process, and it will be tailored to the individual needs of the player/patient.

Can Phase 5 be measured? Yes, it can, and many of these methods of measurement are discussed in Phase 6. One can measure the speed and movement of the individual. The quality of movement and agility can be seen on video or measured with accelerometers in the field. The accuracy of kicking a moving ball can be seen and felt by the rehabilitator. Although some of the skills related to work may be difficult to measure, there is a type of visual analogue scale (VAS) for this form of work. The rehabilitator/trainer may mention, for example, that the quality of short ball striking is 10 out of 10 though the long ball striking is 8 out of 10 for power and 6 out of 10 for accuracy.

6. Return to full training

Return to training criteria can be set in the initial stages of rehabilitation. Such criteria may take several forms. For example, in a 75-year-old bowls player recovering from an ankle arthroscopy, they may involve:

a. maximal ankle range in comparison with 'normal side' or acceptable range;
b. no swelling or pain;
c. ability to walk up and down stairs pain free;
d. ability to get out of a chair using both legs (separately);
e. ability to perform crown green bowling for an hour;
f. an understanding of self-management strategies.

Another example could be a professional football player recovering from the same operation, for whom the criteria might be:

a. maximal joint range in comparison with the other side/pre-injury range;
b. no pain or swelling;
c. maximal isotonic/isokinetic power of lower leg musculature;
d. maximal jump test in comparison with previous measures (compare left with right);
e. ability to perform hop and hold test with maximal proprioception/agility;
f. reach pre-injury levels in terms of number and quality of maximal accelerations and decelerations, comparing right side with left;
g. ability to cope with striking a ball and endurance work on the grass for up to time spent in normal training session;
h. have an understanding that self-management work is accepted and will be complied with.

The above are just two brief, return-to-training criteria lists that may form part of the thought process involved in deciding when a patient is ready to return to their sport, without support but with the knowledge that compliance with self-management strategies will be high. Unrealistic/unreasonable demands are counterproductive and may lead to frustration and disappointment. Realistic goal setting is the aim. A visual display/chart can be used (similar to a visual analogue scale) to show how far down the line towards the target the patient has progressed over the previous days or weeks.

Can Phase 6 be measured? Yes – technology offers a multitude of support methods to assess function of human movement. Scales, cameras, dynamometers, accelerometers, global positioning satellite systems, heart-rate monitors and stopwatches are all pieces of equipment that can be used to measure the most basic of human movements up to the most dynamic movements. These measurements are reproducible and can be collected and digitised to create a library of functional analysis. The process of collecting the data and their application are dependent upon the interest and education level of the clinician. Reams of meaningless and difficult-to-apply data can cause a great loss of time and money. Data that are easy to apply can prevent a 'nearly healed' injury from being over- or under-exposed in the rehabilitation process.

7. Return to play

Return to play (RTP) is multifactorial, not only from the individual patient's perspective, but also from that of the decision makers. In team sports, the people involved in the decision to RTP can be the doctor (clinical evaluation shows the patient is continuing to improve with increased load and increased demands of training), the scientist (satisfied with the performance-related data), the fitness coach (satisfied that the player has completed enough skill- and agility-related activity) and the coach (satisfied that the player has had enough time training to meet the requirements of the next game). Other stakeholders in the world of professional sport are also involved in the decision, such as the player's agent and the directors of the club. However, the most important stakeholder is the player, who needs to feel that he/she is ready, and this can cover a plethora of psychological as well as physical issues. Return to Play check-lists can be designed to ensure that all clinical and functional criteria, specific to each individual injury, have been achieved before the player is allowed to return back into training. Table 2 shows an example of a hamstring injury RTP template used at Celtic FC.

From a medical point of view, a successful return to play means that there will be no recurrence of the injury, and there will also be a secondary desire that the performance of the player is as good as, and possibly better than, it was before the injury (with the exception of certain aspects of the game that can only be achieved by playing the game or performing the sport in a competitive environment). Return to play can involve reassurance from the support/rehabilitation staff that 'everything will be okay', which involves education concerning the success of the progress to date. Psychological reassurance throughout all stages of the rehabilitation process should not be undervalued.

There may be occasions when a player's load can be managed to enable him to play. For example, management of a player suffering from recurrent achillodynia may be done by removing him from the training group the day after a game.

TABLE 2 Example hamstring injury RTP template from Celtic FC

		Clinical Assessment
Hamstring Length Tests		
SLR	Pain	Nil / tight
	Range	90 degrees / L=R / normal
AKE	Pain	Nil / tight
	Range	L=R / 160 degrees+ / normal
Slump	Pain	Nil / posterior hamstring only
	Range	L=R / normal
Hamstring Strength Tests		
Isometric testing @	Pain	Nil
	Strength	L=R
	Pain	Nil
	Strength	L=R
	Pain	Nil
	Strength	L=R
Isometric hamstring contraction in end range hip flex/knee ext position		
Short Bridge	Pain	Pain free
	Reps	10+
Long Bridge	Pain	Nil

(Continued)

TABLE 2 (Continued)

	Functional Assessment			Isokinetic Dynamometry
Nordics	Reps	Reps		5+
				4
Repeat Mechanism of injury	Pool — kicking	Gym — keiser kick-outs	On pitch — passing	
SL RDL (L/R)	Hop for distance (bilateral difference <10%)			
Yes/no	Left — Right	Left — Right	High Box step ups (bilateral difference <10%) — Right	
	Yes/No		Yes/No	
		Biodex Test		
Functional ratio (HAMSecc: Quadsconc)	Right / Left	30/240 (>0.98)		90/90 (>1.3)
Plateau of eccentric peak torque 60°/s	Left/Right	Yes/No	Peak torque	
Plateau of eccentric peak torque 90°/s	Left/Right	Yes/No	Peak torque	

Functional Hamstring Tests

GPS

GPS/Training Markers

	Total Distance		High Speed Distance		No. Accels		% Training and Match Max speed	
	Target	Actual	Target	Actual	Target	Actual	Target	Actual
Return to training – has player reached loads relative to those of training in terms of								

	Peak Training speed		Peak Match speed		Maximal Acceleration		Fatigued HS (>60 min)	
	Target	Actual	Target	Actual	Target	Actual	Target	Actual
RETURN TO PLAY Training session equivalent to 60 mins of a game with following markers hit								

STRENGTH
TD (5000m), Av Sp (75), TRIMP (<250), Ex/min (3.2), DSL (<250) and Max accels/decels (12, 12): 4762, 73.1, 310, 4.8, 98, 12, 3

Date:

RESISTANCE
TD (6500m), HID (450m), Av Sp (85), TRIMP (<250) and Ex/min (3.2): 5622, 380, 80.3, 256, 3.7

Date:

SPEED
TD (5500m), Av Sp (70), TRIMP (150-175), Ex/min (2.2), Max Acc (8-12): 5033, 78.6, 208, 3.3, 0

Date:

Completion of specific training sessions

PROGNOSIS

Days unavailable is = or > than original RTP prediction – yes/no

The player's own recovery day may be in the water, and on the second day of recovery the loading (that can be measured as stated before, using heart rate and GPS) can be restricted to whatever percentage the prevention team views as appropriate. The use of these modalities in rehabilitation is in its infancy and their reliability depends on the positioning of satellites around the world. In areas of reliable coverage current devices are thought to be up to 15 per cent inaccurate. Such loading data should be viewed artistically at this stage, but possibly this will become more defined in the future so that 'true loading' can be matched with cause and effect (Nielsen *et al.*, 2012).

CONSTRAINTS AND LIMITATIONS OF PREVENTING INJURY IN FOOTBALL

We have already mentioned how compliance and commitment from the player towards injury prevention affects the success of any injury prevention strategies. We have also touched on the lack of reward and objective markers determining that success – in other words, you will never know if an injury has been prevented or not, but will definitely know if an injury hasn't been prevented – making this an area of sports medicine that often seems like a thankless task.

Perhaps the greatest problem for the medical team, however, is that even the greatest intrinsic injury prevention programmes can be overridden by extrinsic training errors. These errors are detailed in other chapters of this book, but from my experience they include allowing a player (and his hamstrings) to perform at over 80% of his cadence in high-intensity running [leading to negative work by his hamstrings (Schache, *et al.*, 2010)] within two days of the next match, and not allowing enough recovery time (48 hours) after a match before applying equivalent loading of this same tissue.

No medic or physiotherapist has never injured a player. Yet there is nothing more despairing for the resident medical departments than a new management, and hence training strategy, that is brought into the club and consequently undermines the player's chances of remaining injury free. However, from the outside it is often the medical team that gets criticised, while the manager or coach simply talks of bad luck in the face of similar questioning. Increasing the intrinsic robustness of the player can help, but only within reason, and in the modern game, all football clubs worth their salt will have structured prevention programmes – yet the injury trends from club to club are varied, so the question is whether these intrinsic programmes are just the 'one percenters' in the context of the training and recovery strategies enforced by the coach or manager.

However, we must acknowledge (rather simplistically) that the ideal in football should be to 'win with no injuries', but second best is 'winning with injuries' rather than 'not winning with no injuries'. So even with a combined understanding of extrinsic and training causes of injury, the medical and science team have to accept that, for example, an erroneous spaced tactical session that doesn't protect the players may, from a physical or injury prevention perspective, tactically and psychologically better prepare them to win the game. In this sense, the resident medical department has to be supportive of the manager. It is a complex situation, and those on the outside of the inner workings of a football club who criticise medical and science departments show a lack of understanding of such grey areas – and of the ongoing weekly or daily conflict between winning and preventing injury – that all clubs have. This conflict can also occur between the science (fitness) department and the medical department if the latter staff feel the cost of injury is too high and is related to the fitness strategies being performed.

The art is often in how this information (depicting the potential for injury) is presented to the manager, coach or fitness coach in terms of the costs and benefits, as it requires skill, patience and ultimately a relationship with the manager, or at least trust from him that the information is being passed on for the good of the club and the players. It is for the manager to weigh it all up and ultimately decide whether the cost (of injury) outweighs the benefits (of performance). Global training methodologies, as performed by modern managers such as José Mourinho, Brendan Rodgers and Paul Clement, are the best, as they take into account all holistic variables and are manager or coach led.

In this sense, 'head of injury prevention' is ultimately the manager…

SUMMARY

Injury prevention and rehabilitation is easy to do badly and difficult to do well. Many people are involved in the process and they need to act as a team to support the patient with good communication and good team play (which supports the process). There should be a nominated head of the rehabilitation team, and the case manager in these circumstances should be the physician. The main practitioner carrying out the rehab (dependent therefore on the stage of the process) should not be the case manager as this person is not capable of critically evaluating the success or failure of their own treatment. The case manager may most appropriately be the patient's physician. Players or clubs without physicians may try to find a shortcut to this process; however, the danger then is that the failure of rehabilitation will result in the player seeking other expertise that may be detrimental to his/her recovery.

The case manager needs to evaluate the patient on a regular basis and be involved in the decision making throughout the rehabilitation. The case manager shares information within the team and makes the decision as to when to progress or when to arrest treatment. The whole process can be satisfying to all concerned when dealing with motivated and enthusiastic patients. Measuring the process is achievable and gives credibility and backup to the initial hypothesis of the individual's rehabilitation programme. Rehabilitation involves creativity with science and art, with the end result being the ultimate achievement of the patient returning to a normal life or excelling with the rehabilitation team's support (depending on the nature of the individual and the injury).

REFERENCES

Aragão, F.A., Karamanidis, K., Vaz, M.A. and Arampatzis, A. 'Mini-Trampoline Exercise Related to Mechanisms of Dynamic Stability Improves the Ability to Regain Balance in Elderly', *Journal of Electromyography and Kinesiology*, 21, no. 3 (June 2011), 512–518.

Binnie, M.J., Peeling, P., Pinnington, H., Landers, G. and Dawson, B. 'Effect of Training Surface on Acute Physiological Responses Following Interval Training', *Journal of Strength Conditioning Research*, 26 June 2012.

Bushman, B.A., Flynn, M.G., Andrea, F.F., Lambert, C.P., Taylor, M.S. and Braun, W.A. 'Effect of 4 Weeks of Deep Water Run Training on Running Performance', *Medicine and Science in Sports and Exercise*, 29, no. 5 (1997), pp. 694–699.

Crow, J.F., Pearce, A.J., Veale, J.P., VanderWesthuizen, D., Coburn, P.T. and Pizzari, T. 'Hip Adductor Muscle Strength is Reduced Preceding and During the Onset of Groin Pain in Elite Junior Australian Football Players', *Journal of Science and Medicine in Sport*, 13, no. 2 (2009), pp. 202–204.

Engebretsen, A.H., Myklebust, G., Holme, I., Engebretsen, L. and Bahr, R. 'Intrinsic Risk Factors for Groin Injuries Among Male Soccer Players: A Prospective Cohort Study', *American Journal of Sports Medicine*, 38, no. 10 (2010), pp. 2051–2057.

Eyestone, E.D., Fellingham, G., George, J. and Fisher, A.G. 'Effect of Water Running and Cycling on Maximum Oxygen Consumption and 2-mile Run Performance', *American Journal of Sports Medicine*, 21, no, 1 (1993), pp. 41–44.

Hölmich, P., Hölmich, L.R. and Bjerg, A.M. 'Clinical Examination of Athletes with Groin Pain: An Intraobserver and Interobserver Reliability Study', *British Journal of Sports Medicine*, 38 (2004), pp. 446–451.

Hölmich, P., Uhrskou, P., Ulniths, L., Kanstrup, I.L., Nielsen, M.B., Bjerg, A.M. and Krogsgaard, K. 'Effectiveness of Active Physical Training as a Treatment for Long-Standing Adductor-Related Groin Pain in Athletes: Randomised Trial', *The Lancet*, 353 (1999), pp. 439–443.

Kidgell, D.J., Horvath, D.M., Jackson, B.M. and Seymour, P.J. 'Effect of Six Weeks of Dura Disc and Mini-Trampoline Balance Training on Postural Sway in Athletes with Functional Ankle Instability', *Journal of Strength Conditioning Research*, 21, no. 2 (May 2007), 466–469.

Kulig, K., Popovich, J.M., Noceti-Dewit, L.M., Reischl, S.F. and Kim, D. 'Women with Posterior Tibial Tendon Dysfunction Have Diminished Ankle and Hip Muscle Performance', *Journal of Orthopaedic and Sports Physical Therapy*, 41, no. 9 (September 2011), pp. 687–694.

Kvist, J. 'Sagittal Plane Knee Motion in the ACL-Deficient Knee During Body Weight Shift Exercises on Different Support Surfaces', *Journal of Orthopaedic Sports Physical Therapy*, 36, no. 12 (December 2006), pp. 954–962.

Narducci, E., Waltz, A., Gorski, K., Leppia, L. and Donaldson, M. 'The Clinical Utility of Functional Performance Tests Within One Year of Post ACL Reconstruction: A Systematic Review', *International Journal of Sports Physical Therapy*, 6, no. 4 (December 2011), pp. 333–342.

Nielsen, R.O., Cederholm, P., Buist, I., Sørensen, H., Lind, M. and Rasmussen, S. 'Can GPS Be Used to Detect Deleterious Progression in Training Volume Among Runners?' *Journal of Strength Conditioning Research*, 17 September 2012.

Palmieri, R.M., Ingersoll, C.D., Hoffman, M.A., Cordova, M.L., Porter, D.A., Edwards, J.E., Babington, J.P., Krause, B.A. and Stone, M.B. 'Arthrogenic Muscle Response to a Simulated Ankle Joint Effusion', *British Journal of Sports Medicine*, 38, no. 1 (February 2004), pp. 26–33.

Pinnington, Hugh, C., Lloyd, David G., Besier, Thor F. and Dawson, Brian. 'Kinematic and Electromyography Analysis of Submaximal Differences Running on a Firm Surface Compared with Soft, Dry Sand', *European Journal of Applied Physiology*, 94 (2005), pp. 242–253.

Pool Water Treatment Advisory Group *Swimming Pool Water: Treatment and Quality Standards for Pools and Spas*, 2nd edn (2009).

Schache A.G., Kim H.J., Morgan D.L., Pandy M.G. 'Hamstring muscle forces prior to and immediately following an acute sprinting-related muscle strain injury', *Gait Posture*, 2010 May 32:1:136-40.

Thomeé, R., Kaplan, Y., Kvist, J., Myklebust, G., Risberg, M.A., Theisen, D., Tsepis, E., Werner, S., Wondrasch, B. and Witvrouw, E. 'Muscle Strength and Hop Performance Criteria Prior to Return to Sports after ACL Reconstruction', *Journal of Knee Surgery, Sports Traumatology, Arthroscopy*, 19, no. 11 (November 2011), pp. 1798–1805.

Thorpe R.T., Atkinson G., Drust B., Gregson W. 'Monitoring Fatigue Status in Elite Team-Sport Athletes: Implications for Practice', *International Journal Sports Physiology and Performance*. 2017 Apr;12(Suppl 2):S227-S234.

van den Bekerom, M.P., Struijs, P.A., Blankevoort, L., Welling, L., Van Dijk, C.N. and Kerkhoffs, G.M. 'What is the Evidence for Rest, Ice, Compression, and Elevation Therapy in the Treatment of Ankle Sprains in Adults?' *Journal of Athletic Training*, 47, no. 4 (2012), pp. 435–443.

van der Wees, P.J., Lenssen, A.F., Hendriks, E.J., Stomp, D.J., Dekker, J. and de Bie, R.A. 'Effectiveness of Exercise Therapy and Manual Mobilisation in Ankle Sprain and Functional Instability: A Systematic Review', *Australian Journal of Physiotherapy*, 52, no. 1 (2006), pp. 27–37.

Verrall, G.M., Slavotinek, J.P., Barnes, P.G. and Fon, G.T. 'Description of Pain Provocation Tests Used for the Diagnosis of Sports-Related Chronic Groin Pain: Relationship of Tests to Defined Clinical (Pain and Tenderness) and MRI (Pubic Bone Marrow Oedema) Criteria', *Scandinavian Journal of Medicine and Science in Sports*, 15, no. 1 (2005), pp. 36–42.

Villalta, E.M. and Peiris, C.L. 'Early Aquatic Physical Therapy Improves Function and Does Not Increase Risk of Wound-related Adverse Events for Adults Post Orthopedic Surgery: A Systematic Review and Meta-analysis', *Archives of Physical Medical and Rehabilitation*, 6 August 2012.

Waterman, B., Walker, J.J., Swaims, C., Shortt, M., Todd, M.S., Machen, S.M. and Owens, B.D. 'The Efficacy of Combined Cryotherapy and Compression Compared with Cryotherapy Alone Following Anterior Cruciate Ligament Reconstruction', *Journal of Knee Surgery*, 25, no. 2 (May 2012), pp. 155–160.

CHAPTER 6

FITNESS ASSESSMENT IN FOOTBALL

Dr Marco Beato[1] and Prof. Barry Drust[2]

School of Science, Technology and Engineering, University of Suffolk, Ipswich, United Kingdom[1]
Football Exchange, Research Institute for Sport & Exercise Sciences, Liverpool John Moores University, UK[2]

THE PHYSICAL DEMANDS OF FOOTBALL

Football is the world's most popular sport and is played in almost every nation at the professional level (Reilly and Williams, 2003). It is a game where physical fitness and technical and tactical skills play a fundamental role in the success of the match (Hoff *et al.*, 2002). From a physiological perspective, football is characterised by an intermittent aerobic-anaerobic energetic model. This is a consequence of the need to utilise different pathways for energy provision to support low- and high-intensity actions as well as being due to the recovery requirements in the short rest periods. Professional players cover a distance between 10 and 13 kilometres during the match, with high-intensity running (HIR) considered a crucial element of physical football performance. This HIR distance accounts for around 8–12% of the total distance performed, which equates to values of around 900 metres for HIR distance and 250–300 metres for sprint running. These values are, however, influenced by several factors – most importantly, playing position (Di Salvo *et al.*, 2009). For example, midfielders perform more HIR than central defenders, while forward and midfield players (especially those in wide positions) have a greater sprinting distance than defenders.

The aerobic energy system is highly stressed during the game and as such is thought to be the dominant energy pathway used. Previous research has reported a mean heart rate (HR) of around 85% of maximum during games, a value that is equivalent to an oxygen uptake of around 70–75% of VO_2max. An international top-class player performs approximately 1,350 activities during a game, with a change in activity every 4–6 seconds (Mohr et al., 2005). Many of these activities are high-intensity actions and include sport-specific movements such as changes of direction, short shuttle runs, sprints, jumps, tackles and technical actions (ball contacts). Anaerobic energy metabolism is important for such actions and therefore makes a contribution to the overall energy demand (Zamparo et al., 2015). These intense actions also require players to possess sufficient range of motion and flexibility in their joints and muscles. These parameters are considered necessary basic components for high performance as range of motion and flexibility seem be associated with improved movement (Overmoyer and Reiser, 2015). Muscle and joint flexibility can also be associated with the belief that this reduces injury risk. Strength is another fitness factor related to the prevention of injury. Strong and powerful muscles, especially in the lower limbs, have also been related to the performance of specific match actions such as kicking, jumping and sprinting. As such, strength and power capabilities are also essential in order to meet the demands of the game.

THE IMPORTANCE OF FITNESS FOR MATCH PERFORMANCE: FATIGUE DURING MATCH-PLAY

A large body of research has analysed changes in the activity levels of players during matches (Reilly et al., 2008). Generally, these studies observe that a player's performance decreases towards the end of the game. For example, the distance covered in the first half of the match is usually between 5% and 10% greater than that covered in the second half. A player's ability to perform sprints and high-intensity activities is also decreased (when the second half is compared with the first half) (Mohr et al., 2005; Krustrup et al., 2006). Such activities are also seen to decrease temporarily following periods of the game that have required individuals to complete high amounts of HIR. Both these decreases in ability to complete running activities may relate to fatigue that is physiological in origin. Fatigue also has a negative association with passing precision and so can affect the technical output produced by the team (Iaia et al., 2009). While the specific fatigue mechanisms responsible for these reductions in activity remain unclear, interventions to limit their impact on the physical and technical performance of players have been suggested. These include the completion of well-structured training programmes, nutritional interventions and appropriate pacing of effort (Reilly *et al.*, 2008).

THE TRAINING DEMANDS OF FOOTBALL

Training the physiological capabilities of footballers represents an important strategy to improve performance. The diverse physical demands associated with football would imply that players need a diverse range of physical attributes (endurance, speed, strength, etc.) as opposed to a single more specific physical capacity as is associated with a lot of other sports. This is supported by the available research that illustrates that football players often demonstrate mean values in physiological tests across a range of several fitness parameters rather than exceptional values in any one fitness component. The training requirements of players are therefore varied and necessitate the inclusion of a number of different types of physical training stimuli to provide a basis for meeting the demands of the sport. As such, training needs can be divided into three main categories: aerobic, strength and speed (anaerobic).

Irrespective of the type of training completed, periodisation is the framework that guides the training process. Periodisation is the purposeful sequencing of different training units so that the player can attain the desired physiological state and hence obtain their planned results (Issurin, 2010). In traditional periodisation training theory seasonal programmes are subdivided into smaller periods (cycles) that have specific purposes. These are termed macrocycles, mesocycles and microcycles. Ensuring the correct interaction between training load and recovery represents the key driver for the planning and development of the training activity within each of these phases as the correct dose of stimuli and recovery ensures the increase in physical performance (Vanrenterghem *et al.*, 2017). In football, traditional periodisation theory is difficult to apply and so may not be the most practical approach used for training management during the season. This is a consequence of the high number of games played by most teams and the impact that this has on the potential opportunities to train in a systematic way. But while the traditional concept of periodisation may not be suitable for completely guiding the training prescription of players, it has relevance for the development of strategies to evaluate the physical capacities of players. Approaches for the evaluation of players' physical capabilities are required for the monitoring of both the acute responses to a given training stimulus and the adaptations that are associated with long-term exposure to training sessions. As such, periodisation may provide a suitable framework for the scheduling of testing sessions to assess the impact of both single training sessions and more systematic training programmes.

For more on systematic training methods, we invite the reader to consult Chapter 4 (Physical Preparation of Elite Soccer Players).

MONITORING THE PHYSIOLOGICAL ADAPTATIONS TO TRAINING: EVALUATING THE ACUTE EXERCISE STIMULUS

Long-term adaptations will not be achieved without the correct exercise stimulus being systematically completed by players on a daily basis (i.e. without a periodised training programme). This makes an understanding of the evaluation of the acute exercise response relevant to this chapter. In recent years, evaluation of the training stimulus has become an important challenge for the applied practitioner. As a consequence, a large number of research papers have been published in peer-reviewed journals (Akubat *et al.*, 2014). Acute monitoring represents a daily evaluation strategy that takes into account the players' completed activities and the individual physiological responses that occur as a consequence of this exercise. Acute training monitoring has two important components that are categorised as internal and external load. External load is defined as the exercise prescribed to the player – for example, the weight lifted, the distance covered, the number of jumps, accelerations and sprints that have occurred. The internal load, on the other hand, is the individual response that the player makes to this completed set of activities. The internal load is therefore typically indicated by such physiological variables as heart rate (HR) and subjective ratings of perceived exertion (RPE) (i.e. psychological load). Although the external load is typically seen as an important determinant of an individual's adaptations, the individual fitness improvements that a player makes are better linked to the internal load.

Training load is evaluated by the combination of volume x intensity. Volume is representative of the total amount of exercise (e.g. training time), while intensity is the level of effort associated with the exercise. RPE and HR are two of the most common indicators of intensity. The HR approach is based on the linear relationship that exists between HR and VO_2max during steady-state exercise. Lactate samples can also be used to evaluate the internal load. Its concentration is frequently thought to represent the involvement of anaerobic metabolism. However, the intermittent nature of football will influence the production, release and removal of lactate, and so the use of this parameter is not recommended. In recent years, the use of global positioning systems (GPS) in team sports has rapidly increased. GPS data provide in-depth information on activity profiles of athletes, including objective measures such as the total distance and distances covered within specific speed categories. The number of accelerations and decelerations can also be measured, though the measurement error associated with such parameters is high. Akubat (*et al.*, 2014) has suggested that in football, an integrated ratio can be more useful than external or internal load alone. This approach may be the best way to estimate the correct training load during football training.

The balanced use of the methods mentioned above (acute monitoring as GPS, RPE, HR and tests) provides valuable help in the management of recovery strategies, prevention of fatigue and planning of workloads. Daily monitoring by acute evaluations has the aim of understanding the daily physical status of the players. Questionnaires (e.g. muscle soreness, mood state, sleep quality) and physiological-functional tests (e.g. presence of illness, fatigue) are frequently used for this purpose in football practice. Tests should be easy to implement in practical settings and take minimal time out of the programme; however, these evaluations should be both valid and reliable. For more information on this topic, we invite the reader to consult Chapter 7 (Monitoring Player Load and Fatigue Status).

THE NEED FOR PHYSIOLOGICAL TESTS: PROBLEMS OF USING MATCH ACTIVITIES AS AN INDICATOR OF PERFORMANCE

The best marker of an athlete's physical performance capabilities is provided by the feats that they can produce in the actual competitive event that they undertake. This approach is difficult to utilise in football due to the nature of performance in competitive games. Contemporary semi-automatic tracking now provides detailed data on the technical and physical performance of every player on a given team in any given match. These outputs are affected by tactical behaviour (coach instructions), pacing strategy, personal playing style of individual players, playing position and match dynamics (match score). As a consequence of the complex interaction between these variables, the observed physical and technical outputs are highly variable. High-speed running efforts during competition are subject to large variation (coefficients of variation ranging from approximately 16 to 30%) among successive matches and across the seasons (Carling, 2013). This variability makes the accurate determination of meaningful changes in performance outputs very difficult to achieve, as the 'noise' within the data is frequently greater than the 'signal' associated with the adaptation. Match performance within football is therefore not a good model for the determination of the physiological changes associated with the training interventions. This necessitates the application of other approaches in order to give more accurate and objective answers.

PRACTICAL CONSIDERATIONS IN THE DELIVERY OF FITNESS-TESTING PROTOCOLS

This section highlights some issues and precautions related to the practical delivery of physiological assessment protocols. The demands of professional teams' schedules make the development and implementation of testing protocols difficult. The high physical requirements of regular games within the competition schedule (often with short recovery periods between them), the complex training requirements and the inclusion of a large amount of travel (both nationally and internationally) all limit the time available to assess the players' performance capabilities. These challenges are particularly relevant to the completion of laboratory-based assessments. While it is clear that this type of approach allows accurate and repeatable evaluations in stable conditions, it does bring with it significant practical challenges.

Laboratory assessments use expensive and sophisticated devices in their evaluations and utilise facilities that are not widely available outside specialist institutions. These types of evaluations may be better associated with periods of the season that have more flexibility with respect to time. For example, pre-season represents a preparatory period during which fitness coaches and sports scientists have the main goal (it is one of the most important aims) of improving the physical condition of players. At such times the need for accurate testing data may be of great importance, thereby justifying the inclusion of these approaches into the team's schedule. The data available in the literature would also provide a scientific rationale for this approach. Changes in fitness level at this time of the year tend to be larger than observed during the competitive season. As such, they are more likely to be detected by more general tests of an individual's broad underlying physiological capabilities. When these changes are not so large, it may become important to complete more sport-specific tests that have the potential to detect subtle changes in performance capability associated with the specific underpinning performance criteria more directly associated with the sport.

Field-based evaluations are frequently the most specific and most commonly performed football tests. The main advantages of these approaches are low cost, easy management and higher levels of both specificity and ecological validity (at times). There are obviously limitations associated with this type of testing in addition to the lower quality of physiological data that are collected compared with laboratory evaluations. These limitations include an inability to always correctly gauge the attainment of maximal effort and a lack of control over factors that can impact test outcome (e.g. environmental conditions). However, field evaluations provide useful information on training and are still the most popular type of assessment.

Sports scientists may be undecided as to whether to use maximal or submaximal tests to evaluate players' fitness status. Maximal tests better represent the football model and (as in the case of yo-yo recovery 1 and submaximal yo-yo recovery) are more sensitive to fitness variations after training periods (e.g. especially yo-yo recovery 1, while submaximal yo-yo recovery did not ever show this capacity). However, the use of exhaustive tests presents some limitations in daily practice. Football players frequently do not reach exhaustion in maximal tests (peripheral fatigue in lower limbs often does not let players get to the stage of being exhausted), and as such, the findings may be difficult to clearly interpret if changes in performance are observable. More importantly, it is difficult to complete maximal evaluations during the season because the time available is limited (due to congestive fixtures). Sometimes, players also do not want to perform maximal tests because they are afraid of getting injured or of accumulating fatigue. Therefore, in some situations submaximal tests could be preferred to maximal evaluations. Moreover, a controlled period of exercise as an indicator of fitness may be a viable alternative to maximal tests. Controlled periods of exercise (such as a part of a test – e.g. a submaximal standardised aerobic circuit) during which sports scientists evaluate HR response to the exercise (as an indicator of fitness) as well as HR in recovery (potentially an indicator of readiness) can offer interesting information on the training process. In daily field-practice it is necessary to perform fitness evaluations and make decisions; thus, quick and non-invasive evaluation methods are essential. A summary of monitoring fatigue strategies in elite team sports athletes was published by Thorpe *et al.*, (2017). We encourage our readers to study this recent publication.

It is recommended that tests should be performed under standardised conditions to ensure repeatability of the data. Standardisation of the surfaces and, where possible, similar environmental conditions are necessary factors (e.g. use of the same shoes is recommended). Technologically advanced devices (e.g. stopwatches compared with electronic timing gates) should, where possible, be preferred to manual instruments as they may help in the elimination of human error. It is also recommended to not use tests that have been individually developed and lack scientific validation (reliability and validity are key pillars in players' evaluations). Taper strategies should be utilised before post-training evaluations, in order to avoid any residual fatigue associated with the training programme. Physical and mental fatigue can mask the real physical state of the players. Staff should take into consideration the player's status at the time of evaluation (e.g. any injuries they may currently have) that can affect the true physical value of the player.

Many football evaluations were not subjected to an accurate validation process, consisting of a number of steps that have to be performed before a test can be considered credible as a conceptual model (construct validity), and in terms of reliability, validity and responsiveness. Validity and reliability are critical parameters in sports science because they can discern the usefulness of a test.

Logical validity is still the most common criterion of test validity (Rampinini *et al.*, 2007). For an in-depth description of these parameters, see the paper by Impellizzeri and Marcora (2009).

THE USE OF FITNESS TESTS TO EVALUATE THE ADAPTATIONS ASSOCIATED WITH CHRONIC TRAINING PROGRAMMES

The previous section highlighted the limitations associated with the use of match performance for providing information on changes in an individual players' fitness status. In this section, we focus exclusively on the potential application of physiological and sport-specific tests as an objective approach to evaluating player performance capabilities. There is convincing scientific evidence of a close relationship between the training process and its outcomes as represented by a test result. Thus, it is logical to assume that any chronic monitoring of players' fitness levels may be achievable by the completion of a relevant test or battery of tests. As such chronic improvements are a product of a long training process (lasting weeks or months), test batteries need to be replicated throughout the annual cycle in order to give a continuous update on the physical status of the players. The inclusion of timely evaluations provides both useful information on the general physical capabilities of the players as well as potential key inputs into approaches used for day-to-day adjustments to the training prescription.

Over the years, coaches and sports scientists have developed several test batteries to identify fitness capacities. These test batteries have been linked to match performance in some circumstances, though such relationships are not easy to accurately identify due to the inherent variability in match performance discussed earlier. These difficulties probably explain why the outcomes of testing evaluations per se fail to be associated with factors such as championship ranking. This does not, however, invalidate the application of this approach to football, as coaches and sports scientists can gain a lot of important objective information by completing these assessments. For example, tests can establish baselines for each player in the squad, identify individual strengths and weaknesses, evaluate the effect of specific training interventions during the season and give practical indications for individualised training for specific playing positions (centre-back, full back, central midfielders, wings and strikers). Moreover, tests can provide a snapshot of the players' performance status after an injury and give useful indications about the success of rehabilitation protocols and return to play. In scientific literature, tests and testing protocols are typically categorised into generic and specific approaches. It is widely accepted that specific assessments are more appropriate for accurately describing the players' physical qualities than general approaches in which the assessments do not accurately reflect the requirements of the sport (Iaia *et al.*, 2009).

Aerobic Evaluations

Aerobic power (VO_2max) is traditionally thought to be a key approach in assessing the aerobic energy system both in sport generally and within football. VO_2max is assessed in the laboratory by a well-controlled protocol (VO_2max in professional football players is around or slightly over 60 ml/Kg min^{-1}), and this approach supports optimal accuracy in the data. VO_2max is one of the most commonly used indicators of aerobic metabolism and power, as it provides an indication of the functional limit of the oxygen transport system in players. VO_2max is considered accurate when a plateau in VO_2 consumption (observed as players near voluntary exhaustion) at the end of an incremental protocol is achieved. It is also indicated by an elevation in HR to its age-predicted maximum and/or by a rise in blood lactate concentration, reflecting anaerobic metabolism (Reilly, 2007). During such an incremental protocol, it is possible to evaluate other parameters thought to be important for aerobic performance, such as the lactate threshold. This represents the point at which lactate begins to accumulate as its production exceeds its removal. Lactate threshold or lactate inflection point (OBLA) is generally around 85% VO_2max. These aerobic fitness parameters provide useful indicators for the fitness coach and sports scientist when they are developing training programmes. During VO_2max or lactate threshold tests it is possible to match HR values to VO_2 and lactate evaluations if HR is recorded. These HR values can then be used during training protocols on the pitch, to guide intensity to the aims of the session (Svensson and Drust, 2005). VO_2max and speed on the treadmill can be matched and used to identify the maximal aerobic speed (MAS). MAS is a useful parameter used to train players on the basis of their aerobic capacity (individualised training). The use of such cardiopulmonary fitness measurements does also have some practical limitations as evidence would suggest that they cannot identify players of differing levels, that they are not associated with HIR distance covered during the match-game, and that they are not sufficiently sensitive to identify small changes in the training state of elite football players (Svensson and Drust, 2005; Wells *et al.*, 2012). These measurements are descriptors of general fitness rather than specific indicators of physiological factors associated with match performance.

The complexity and cost of making accurate assessments in the laboratory means that in general terms teams prefer to perform test batteries that can be completed on the training field. Practical alternatives to laboratory-based protocols for the assessment of aerobic fitness, such as the yo-yo recovery 1 and 2 tests (Bangsbo *et al.*, 2008), have been developed. These tests are highly correlated with traditional approaches to the assessment of aerobic power, and better represent the intermittent model of football as well as better distinguish between professional and amateur football players than cardiorespiratory fitness indices recorded in laboratory tests (Wells *et al.*, 2012). The yo-yo recovery 1 test is the most extensively studied field-fitness test used in football science. Its protocol consists of 20 + 20 m shuttle runs performed at increasing speeds (change of direction 180°), interspersed with 10 seconds of active recovery (walking). Of the two types of test available, Level 1 is longer in duration and slower in speed than Level 2. The general recommendations associated with the tests are that the yo-yo 1 is suitable for testing moderate-fitness players, while the Level 2 test is suitable for professional or well-trained players. The yo-yo 1 test is associated with general intermittent exercise capacity and VO_2max ($r = 0.70$), while performance in the Level 2 test is thought to reflect the ability to perform repeated intense exercise bouts that have a high aerobic-anaerobic energy contribution (Bangsbo *et al.*, 2008). These tests can discriminate between the performances of elite (2,420m), moderate elite (2,190m) and non-elite (1,810m) players, partly confirming their ecological validity in comparison with laboratory evaluations. More information on these tests can be found in the detailed review by Bangsbo *et al.* (2008). An easy and cheap field test that can evaluate MAS is the '45–15' test. This test showed validity and reliability for the assessment of running speed with results that closely resemble individual MAS obtained during laboratory evaluation (on a treadmill). Submaximal evaluations are commonly used with athletes during retraining after an injury when functional capacities are limited, or when there are heavy fixture schedules; thus, aerobic fitness can be evaluated by the submaximal test in the form of a 'submaximal yo-yo recovery test'. This non-exhaustive evaluation involves HR evaluation after six minutes of the test. The submaximal HR showed sensitivity to detecting training adaptations after a training period.

Strength Evaluations

Strength in football is broad and is associated with various types of muscular contractions, such as concentric, eccentric and isometric. As the evaluation of these different types of activity is related to the specific contraction there are many potential modalities that can be used to evaluate strength in football. For example, standardised whole body or specific joint movements can be assessed using free weights or machines, while maximum isometric contractions (load cells) and isokinetic devices can be used for detailed assessments of specific muscle groups. One of the most common practical evaluations used within football is the maximum load that can be lifted in a single repetition (1RM). This evaluation is frequently completed for a given specific exercise (e.g. half squat, bench press) or range of exercises. As the completion of such maximal efforts can be problematic practically, it is possible to perform submaximal tests in this way (e.g. 6RM, 10RM) and to use these data to subsequently estimate the 1RM using specific equations (e.g. Brzycki, 1993). Isokinetic tests can be used for performance and injury prevention evaluations. Isokinetic devices offer facilities for determining torque-velocity curves in isokinetic movements and joint-angle curves from a series of isometric contractions (Reilly, 2007). Static strength may not correctly reflect the ability to develop force and power during dynamic situations and so is probably a poor predictor of muscle performance in sport-specific conditions. Isokinetic assessments can give useful indications of muscular imbalances (injury prevention) that occur naturally or that are a by-product of the rehabilitation process. In this context, isokinetic dynamometry can assess the balance of strength between the hamstrings (H) and quadriceps (Q) muscle groups. These data can then be used to calculate either conventional or functional H/Q ratios that have a practical implication for injury prevention and for evaluation of strength and power improvement. The functional H/Q ratio should be balanced, with a score higher than 0.7 (further publications are still necessary about this topic) (Rahnama *et al.*, 2003), which indicates that the hamstrings' strength can support the force of the quadriceps. These evaluations are typically implemented during the first part of the season (usually during the pre-season and preparation period) in order to have more accurate knowledge of the players' fitness and strength level. This information may help coaches to better plan squad and individual training sessions. Isokinetic assessments are generally implemented during the season or replaced by sport-specific evaluations such as jumps and power tests. More information is reported in the paper from Svensson *et al.* (2005).

Jump height is another common parameter frequently included within test batteries. This is partly due to its ease of evaluation in a practical context. Muscular power is the main performance parameter that can be evaluated by vertical jumping. Power can be calculated if the player's body mass, the vertical distance through which body mass is moved and the flight time are known. Even if the vertical jump is a good measure of muscular performance, the importance of this parameter per se is quite limited, because football players do not perform many maximal jumps during the game. Jump evaluations completed on a force platform might also be useful to evaluate imbalances. A force difference higher than 15% between the lower limbs in a jump test can indicate a possible imbalance and thus may represent an individual with a higher injury risk. Good data from jump protocols requires careful attention to be paid to jump technique and the overall reliability of the protocol.

Speed Evaluations

Sprinting and the ability to accelerate can separate out football players from different levels. Data from performance analysis have shown that more than 90% of all sprints are shorter than 20 metres. Tests that assess the ability to accelerate should therefore be evaluated by including testing protocols in addition to more traditional straight-line sprinting protocols. These capacities can be evaluated by the use of a single sprint test that covers 10, 20 and 30 metres. Data on the performance of such tests (i.e. time) should be recorded by timing gates or accurate timers. Agility and the ability to change direction are also very important in football. These two abilities are the result of a combination of strength, speed, balance and coordination. It is difficult to decide on the most effective test to use, as various protocols exist in the literature with none being recognised as the gold standard. The majority of the available agility tests do not incorporate a decision-making component and as such do not reflect the real circumstances under which such actions take place within the game. Dividing agility testing protocols into those that attempt to purely evaluate the physiological capabilities of the individual (i.e. those without cognitive involvement) and those that include a cognitive component may be useful in comprehensively evaluating this parameter and in the formation of relevant interventions.

Repeated sprinting is another important ability in football. Players have to perform many high-intensity actions with short rest periods (during fatigue status) (Spencer et al., 2005). Under such conditions an individual's energetic homeostasis and buffer capacity are heavily stressed. This makes this fitness attribute distinct from that associated with the completion of a single sprint and therefore worthy of its own assessment protocols within testing batteries. Repeated-sprint ability can be evaluated using a range of different exercise protocols and different exercise modalities. One of the most common protocols uses the following design: six per 40 m (20 + 20 m) shuttle sprints separated by 20 seconds of passive recovery (Rampinini et al., 2007). No gold standard approach is recognised within the literature, though non-specific test protocols with respect to exercise mode or activity protocol (e.g. sprint duration, distance and recovery) should be avoided.

Flexibility and Functional Evaluations

As already discussed, flexibility is identified as a factor associated with both performance and injury prevention; nevertheless, we can find different opinions between the scholars about this topic (Beato, 2017). Some screening tests for flexibility use protocols where strength and flexibility are evaluated at the same time (e.g. functional movement screen, star excursion balance test), while others are limited to an evaluation of flexibility only (e.g. sit and reach). The star excursion balance test is a dynamic balance test requiring multiple reaches with a single foot in a star-like pattern while maintaining balance on the stance leg. This test evaluates eight excursions, while a simplified version (the Y balance test) involves excursions in merely anterior, postero-lateral and postero-medial directions. Both of these evaluations are inexpensive and easy to administer. The functional movement screen is another screening test that is comprised of seven tasks, and it gives a general indication of the flexibility/strength status of the player. A score between 0 and 3 is used to quantify the quality of the movement for each task, and a summative score of all seven tasks is calculated for the overall test result. Up to now, the star excursion balance test has received considerable scientific support, while the functional movement screen needs additional investigations before it can be fully recommended for use with elite players (Li *et al.*, 2015; Overmoyer *et al.*, 2015). It is necessary to remember that flexibility per se is not associated with injury prevention. Prevention programmes and evaluations have to take into account the multifactorial nature of football injuries.

DATA INTERPRETATION

After the conclusion of the data collection for the physical evaluations, it is necessary to analyse, understand and present them. The interpretation of test results is a vital step in the translation of the data into the training process. If interpreted correctly, the data can provide information on players' strengths and weaknesses and hence form a basis for future interventions in the training schedule. The evaluation of the results and the analysis should consider a player's position, as well as his or her anthropometric details, age and other demographic details for the most accurate data interpretation. The completion of some form of statistical analysis is an important and necessary component of data interpretation. Thus, a minimal amount of statistical knowledge may be required if test results are to be used most effectively.

Sports scientists and coaches can compare their own players with athletes of different levels and sporting populations, as well as with data recorded previously using an existing database (i.e. differences among players). Players can be analysed on the basis of an average squad score, according to a specific playing position or according to previous populations that have demonstrated success within the club/sport. The inclusion of such data in a meaningful database is important as it facilitates both cross-sectional and longitudinal comparisons. As a consequence, the development and upkeep of such a database should be a priority of every club. Another key aspect of data analysis is the interpretation of any change in a test score as being meaningful. This can include the interpretation of changes that are improvements as well as those that are reductions in outcome. Statistical approaches that discern the minimum detectable change associated with a testing protocol are important in this regard. The minimum detectable change is the minimum variation that can be interpreted as significant with an acceptable probability level (Pyne *et al.*, 2014). For a large number of tests that are used in football, data on the minimum detectable change are published in the scientific literature. Another easy approach to investigating the minimum improvement was proposed by Hopkins (i.e. 'minimum worthwhile change'). Hopkins suggested considering a variation higher than 0.2 of the sample standard deviation as an important improvement. However, sports scientists may base the evaluation and interpretation of improvements on their sport-specific knowledge; this is very true for industry professionals who have deep background knowledge.

SUMMARY

The multifactorial nature of football requires a complex adaptation of the players (blending physical fitness and technical and tactical skills) for performance. Training for football is therefore a long and complicated process, and it necessitates several acute and chronic evaluations of the training outcome. Acute monitoring represents a daily evaluation strategy that takes into account the players' completed activities and the subsequently individual physiological responses to these activities. Internal and external load parameters may be used to monitor these short-term fitness responses. In contrast, chronic improvements are a product of a long training process. As match performance within football is not a good model for the determination of the chronic changes associated with training interventions, batteries of tests should be applied as they offer more accurate and objective answers. Evaluations should be replicated during the season to give a continuous update on the physical status of the players. Several evaluations can be performed, as laboratory and field tests, in order to know players' status. Laboratory analyses are more sophisticated and accurate, and provide greater comprehension of important physiological parameters than field tests. Field tests do not use expensive instruments, give sport-specific indications associated with performance, but are less accurate than laboratory evaluations. In order to improve the validity and reliability of batteries of tests, it is necessary to use standardised conditions (e.g. taper strategy, similar surface and environmental conditions). This is necessary to limit the effect of external factors (confounders).

CHALLENGES IN THE WORKING ENVIRONMENT

Despite fitness assessment in football being widespread at every level (from amateurs to top clubs), frequently there are some challenges to overcome in the working environment. The degree to which fitness evaluation is applicable is closely associated with the organisational level of the club. It is easy to imagine that top-level clubs have a systematic and well-organised approach to fitness evaluations, while amateur and lower-level clubs do not make use of such technological systems as laboratory assessments. Thus, depending on the characteristics and available resources of the club, it may be possible to plan suitable testing of players. While professional clubs will make use of the most current scientific evidence, as well as qualified sport scientists and technologies, amateur teams will base their strategy on easier and less expensive evaluations (e.g. field tests).

Professional clubs have a busy schedule and involve large amounts of travel, making it hard to carry out testing protocols throughout the competitive season.

These factors limit the club's capability to constantly monitor players' fitness status. Laboratory and maximal evaluations may be more strongly associated with some specific periods of the season (i.e. pre-season and end of pre-season). However, the complexity and cost of making accurate assessments in the laboratory induces teams to opt to perform batteries of tests that can be completed on the training field. Lower-ranking clubs have a different schedule, with a limited number of games and travel, and therefore it is easier for them to organise and plan fitness evaluations. These batteries of tests may be less sophisticated and do not consider physiological evaluations. As reported above, many sport-specific field tests have the potential to detect changes in performance capability associated with sport-specific performance. Planning fitness evaluations during the season (using traditional tests) is sometimes complicated for many reasons (listed in this chapter), such that the utilisation of a standardised controlled period of exercise (as an indicator of fitness) may be a quick and non-invasive evaluation alternative. In conclusion, field and laboratory tests as well as maximal and submaximal evaluations have their own advantages and limitations, and sports scientists should consider these factors when planning their fitness evaluation programme. It is also recommended not to use homemade tests that have been developed without scientific validation.

REFERENCES

Akubat, I., Barrett, S. and Abt, G. 'Integrating the Internal and External Training Loads in Soccer', *International Journal of Sports Physiology and Performance*, 9, no. 3 (May 2014), pp. 457–462.

Bangsbo, J., Iaia, F.M. and Krustrup, P. 'The Yo-Yo Intermittent Recovery Test: A Useful Tool for Evaluation of Physical Performance in Intermittent Sports', *Sports Medicine*, 38, no. 1 (2008), pp. 37–51.

Beato, M., In Response to: 'Hamstring-and-Lower-Back Flexibility in Male Amateur Soccer Players', *Clinical Journal of Sport Medicine*. 2017 Jun 28. [Epub ahead of print]

Brzycki, M., 'Strength testing: predicting a one-rep max from repetitions to fatigue', *JOPERD*. 1993;64:88–90.

Carling, C., 'Interpreting Physical Performance in Professional Soccer Match-Play: Should We Be More Pragmatic in Our Approach?' *Sports Medicine*, 43, no. 8 (August 2013), pp. 655–663.

Di Salvo, V., Gregson, W., Atkinson, G., Tordoff, P. and Drust, B. 'Analysis of High Intensity Activity in Premier League Soccer', *International Journal of Sports Medicine*, 30, no. 3 (March 2009), pp. 205–212.

Hoff, J., Wisløff, U., Engen, L.C., Kemi, O.J. and Helgerud, J. 'Soccer Specific Aerobic Endurance Training', *British Journal of Sports Medicine*, 36 (2002), pp. 218–221.

Iaia, F.M., Rampinini, E. and Bangsbo, J. 'High-intensity Training in Football' (review), *International Journal of Sports Physiology and Performance*, 4, no. 3 (September 2009), pp. 291–306.

Impellizzeri, F.M. and Marcora, S.M. 'Test Validation in Sport Physiology: Lessons Learned from Clinimetrics' (review), *International Journal of Sports Physiology and Performance*, 4, no. 2 (June 2009), pp. 269–277.

Issurin, V.B., 'New Horizons for the Methodology and Physiology of Training Periodization', *Sports Medicine*, 40, no. 3 (1 March 2010), pp. 189–206.

Krustrup, P., Mohr, M., Steensberg, A., Bencke, J., Kjaer, M. and Bangsbo, J. 'Muscle and Blood Metabolites during a Soccer Game: Implications for Sprint Performance', *Medicine and Science in Sports and Exercise*, 38, no. 6 (June 2006), pp. 1165–1174.

Li Y., Wang, X., Chen, X. and Dai, B. 'Exploratory Factor Analysis of the Functional Movement Screen in Elite Athletes', *Journal of Sports Sciences*, 33, no. 11 (2015), pp. 1166–1172.

Mohr, M., Krustrup, P. and Bangsbo, J. 'Fatigue in Soccer: A Brief Review' (review), *Journal of Sports Sciences*, 23, no. 6 (June 2005), 593–599.

Overmoyer, G.V. and Reiser, R.F. 2nd. 'Relationships between Lower-Extremity Flexibility, Asymmetries, and the Y Balance Test', *Journal of Strength and Conditioning Research*, 29, no. 5 (May 2015), pp. 1240–1247.

Pyne, D.B., Spencer M. and Mujika, I. 'Improving the Value of Fitness Testing for Football', *International Journal of Sports Physiology and Performance*, 9, no. 3 (May 2014), pp. 511–514.

Rahnama, N., Reilly, T., Lees, A., and Graham-Smith, P. (2003). 'Muscle fatigue induced by exercise simulating the work rate of competitive soccer', *Journal of Sports Sciences*, 21(11), 933–942.

Rampinini, E., Bishop, D., Marcora, S.M., Ferrari Bravo D., Sassi, R. and Impellizzeri, F.M. 'Validity of Simple Field Tests as Indicators of Match-related Physical Performance in Top-Level Professional Soccer Players', *International Journal of Sports Medicine*, 28, no. 3 (March 2007), 228–235.

Reilly, T. *The Science of Training – Soccer: A Scientific Approach to Developing Strength, Speed and Endurance*, new edn (Routledge, 2007).

Reilly, T., Drust, B. and Clarke, N. 'Muscle Fatigue during Football Match-Play' (review), *Sports Medicine*, 38, no. 5 (2008), 357–367.

Reilly, T. and Williams, A.M. 'Introduction to Science and Soccer', in Reilly, T. and Williams, A.M. (eds.), *Science and Soccer*, pp. 1–6 (Routledge, 2003).

Spencer, M., Bishop, D., Dawson, B. and Goodman, C. 'Physiological and Metabolic Responses of Repeated-Sprint Activities: Specific to Field-Based Team Sports', *Sports Medicine*, 35, no. 12 (2005), 1025–1044.

Svensson, M. and Drust, B. 'Testing Soccer Players', *Journal of Sports Sciences*, 23, no. 6 (June 2005), 601–618.

Thorpe, R.T., Atkinson, G., Drust, B., Gregson, W. 'Monitoring Fatigue Status in Elite Team-Sport Athletes: Implications for Practice', *International Journal of Sports Physiology and Performance*. 2017 Apr;12(Suppl 2):S227-S234.

Vanrenterghem, J., Nedergaard, N.J., Robinson, M.A., Drust, B., 'Training Load Monitoring in Team Sports: A Novel Framework Separating Physiological and Biomechanical Load-Adaptation Pathways', *Sports Medicine*. 2017.

Wells, C.M., Edwards, A.M., Winter, E.M., Fysh, M.L. and Drust, B. 'Sport-Specific Fitness Testing Differentiates Professional from Amateur Soccer Players Where VO$_2$max and VO$_2$ Kinetics Do Not', *Journal of Sports Medicine and Physical Fitness*, 52, no. 3 (June 2012), 245–254.

Zamparo, P1., Bolomini, F., Nardello, F., Beato, M., 'Energetics (and kinematics) of short shuttle runs', *Eur J Appl Physiol*. 2015 Sep;115(9):1985–94.

CHAPTER 7

MONITORING PLAYER LOAD AND FATIGUE STATUS

Prof. Warren Gregson[1], Dr Richard Hawkins[2] and Dr Robin T Thorpe[3]

*Football Exchange, Research Institute for Sport &
Exercise Sciences, Liverpool John Moores University,
UK; Football Performance and Science Department,
Aspire Academy and Qatar FA[1]*
Head of Athletic Training Services, Manchester United FC[2]
Senior Sports Scientist, Manchester United FC[3]

INTRODUCTION

Elite players are now routinely exposed to 2–3 games per week across the domestic season, with international fixtures further increasing this load. Leading players may therefore routinely compete 60 matches per season interspersed with an average of 4–5 days of recovery between matches. These match loads are further increased in those players competing in leagues such as the English Premier League (EPL) due to both the failure to adopt a winter break and the increasing physical demands of match-play over the last decade (Bush *et al.*, 2015).

The availability of players for selection substantially increases a team's chance of success. Given the physical and mental demands placed upon the modern player, training programmes that prepare a player for competition while reducing his or her susceptibility to excessive fatigue, injury and illness are fundamental to the work of the athlete's support team. In recent years, this has led to a surge in the development of methods and technology for monitoring player load (both training and match) and measures that may offer insights into whether the player is adapting positively or negatively to the collective stresses of training and competition. In this chapter, we provide an overview of the approaches to monitoring player load and fatigue status in elite players, including some of the fundamental measurement issues and practical considerations which should be considered by those responsible for the development and implementation of player monitoring systems in the field.

TRAINING PROCESS

Understanding the balance between training load and recovery is fundamental to effective planning and implementation of any training programme. The planning process, often referred to as periodisation, is simply the manipulation of these parameters in such a way as to maximise the desired adaptations in individuals while ensuring that they are suitably recovered in order to maximise their qualities in competition. Training is the application of stress to the body and its ability to recover from that stress. Knowledge of what that stress is and how it can be manipulated to bring about optimal adaptations will determine how efficient a training programme will be. Figure 1a is a simple representation of the supercompensation cycle which demonstrates the role of the training load (stress) and subsequent recovery in the training process. It should be apparent that

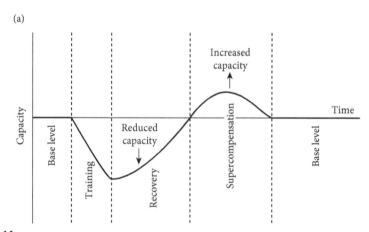

FIGURE 1A The Supercompensation Training Cycle

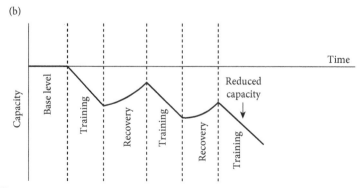

FIGURE 1B The Supercompensation Training Cycle with Insufficient Recovery

training load and recovery are inextricably linked; knowledge of how to manipulate the former while being able to monitor and enhance the effectiveness of the latter will enable a more complete and effective training plan to be implemented. If the training stress is repeatedly too little or too large and the recovery time insufficient or too long then it is highly likely that the training effect will have a negative influence on players' capacities, as represented in Figure 1b. It is the cumulative effect of successive training sessions over time that is the key determinant of whether a training plan succeeds or fails.

TRAINING LOAD

Training load is the product of three components: volume, intensity and frequency. Volume represents the amount of work (quantity); intensity is the quality of the training session; and frequency, sometimes referred to as density, is how often the training is undertaken, determined by how sessions are organised in a given time period. When examining training load, it is important to take into account both the external and the internal load (Figure 2). External load relates to work completed by the athlete independent of his or her internal characteristics and is important for understanding the capabilities and capacities of the player (Halson, 2014). The internal load, or the relative physiological strain resulting from the external training factors, is also crucial to determining both the stress imposed and subsequent adaptation to training (Halson, 2014). In simple terms, the player's individual characteristics will influence the level of stress that a given external load will deliver. Figure 2 shows how these different components fit into the training process and highlight their importance with regard to the planning and monitoring of training programmes.

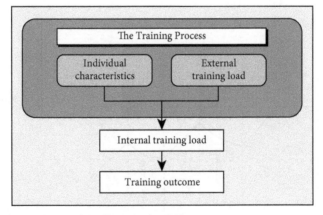

FIGURE 2 The Training Process (Impellizzeri et al., 2005)

TABLE 1 Methods available for assessing internal and external training load

Assessment Method	Measurement	Positives	Negatives
Availability	External load	No expense, easy to analyse	Lacks detail
GPS/local position-ing systems	External load	Lots of information	Expensive, can be time consuming
Heart rate analysis	Internal load	Easy to collect	Moderate expense, requires player compliance
Subjective assess-ments (e.g. RPE)	Internal load	No expense, easy to collect	Requires buy-in and under-standing from players

METHODS OF ASSESSING TRAINING LOAD

As a consequence of advances in technology over the past decade, several monitoring methods are available to coaches and sports scientists to evaluate the various training load components. There are pros and cons to all the methods, and which ones are adopted, together with how much detail is possible, generally depends on the training culture, coaching philosophy and budget. Regardless of which methods are adopted, the validity and reliability of the data remain crucial, and it should also be acknowledged that the power of the information increases over time since a longitudinal profile enables far more detailed analysis to be carried out to support the decision-making processes that ultimately enable players to perform to their potential.

External and internal training load definitions have been provided above, and these will make the means by which these components are calculated easier to understand. Table 1 provides an overview of the typical methods available for assessing external and internal load. External training load can be established using session counts, number of matches, training time and movement analysis, the latter having several levels of detail that can be investigated. In soccer, internal training load is generally assessed using heart rate technology and subjective feedback from players using ratings of perceived exertion (RPE) scales. Calculation of both types of load will now be discussed in more detail, with examples of how the information can be used effectively.

External Training Load

At a basic level, simple training and match availability data can provide an indication of the robustness and readiness of a player over a specific time period. For example, tracking training attendance and minutes played can provide the coach with an

TABLE 2 Player availability summary

Player	Training sessions	Recovery sessions	Days off	Matches available	Minutes played	Training availability (%)	Match availability (%)	Days per game
1	15	5	4	7	570	100	100	4.9
2	17	3	4	7	345	100	100	8.0
3	10	2	1	2	170	48	29	16.4
4	10	4	2	5	450	68	71	6.2
5	20	0	4	7	0	100	100	0.0

indication of the workload individuals have been exposed to (see Table 2). With the ability to compare against previous time periods, this information becomes far more meaningful and can be used to help guide future planning. The example in Table 2 summarises a typical in-season month.

To make accurate inferences from the information contained in Table 2 you would need to be working with the players daily as there are so many factors that can impact decision making; however, the information still provides insight and poses a few questions that coaches and sports scientists should be aware of. For example:

- Player 1 has a low days per game value at the end of the month; is this a level he is regularly exposed to or does his training load need to be adjusted to ensure freshness for future games?
- Player 5 has not been exposed to any games; is his current training exposure sufficient to ensure he can produce the necessary physical output if selected?

These are the types of questions practitioners ask themselves as a result of the data collected. Without it, sometimes key information passes by unnoticed as the focus is generally on day-to-day issues, and consequently important questions that could impact on a player's performance are missed and not acted upon.

Over recent years, semi-automated multi-camera image recognition systems (match load), global positioning satellite (GPS) systems and local positioning measurement systems (match or training load) have become increasing popular in determining the external loads players are exposed to. Although they can provide a considerable amount of information not previously possible, there are cost implications to these systems, whose use can often be beyond the budgets of many professional clubs outside the higher leagues. An example of the detail typically available with GPS systems is given in Table 3. It is important to note that the definitions contained in the table refer to a single session; however, for many aspects of training load assessment, the figures could quite easily be used to represent a specific drill, or a specific time period such as a week, a month or a whole season. Providing individual sessions are analysed, the data can be extended over any time period required.

TABLE 3 Typical GPS parameters captured during training

Parameter	Definition
Total distance (m)	Total distanced covered by a player
Very high-speed running distance (m)	Total distance above a specific speed threshold e.g. >19.8km/h
Sprint distance (m)	Total distance above a specific speed threshold e.g. >25.2km/h
Distance per minute (m/min)	Distance covered per minute over the course of the session
Max speed (km/h)	Maximum speed registered in the training session or drill
Speed exertion (au)	A value calculated from the distance spent in the various speed zones
Body load (au)	A value calculated from the number and severity of impacts over the course of the session
Hi accelerations (no.)	The number of accelerations above a specific threshold e.g. 3.0 m/s/s
Hi decelerations (no.)	The number of decelerations below a specific threshold e.g. -3.0 m/s/s

The extent of GPS use has increased at the elite level over recent years; in continual pursuit of achieving greater understanding of the demands of training, GPS data have been analysed in different ways to calculate further parameters. At an elite level, reference values are useful for evaluating training demands on the squad as a whole and on individuals. However, due to difficulties in obtaining such information from these devices when used in training, practitioners tend to use data from pre-season matches to represent competition demands. Representative elite values are shown in Table 4, the information relating to a premier league team, with the information having been recorded during a five-game pre-season tour in 2014.

There are potential benefits to having this information, as current research trends indicate; recent work in numerous team sports has quantified repeated high-intensity efforts rather than simply reporting high-speed distances, investigating their association with injuries in addition to evaluating occurrences in specific coaching practices and how they reflect certain match demands. Knowing that repeated high-speed efforts include high accelerations as well as high-velocity efforts, it is apparent that these demands provide a better representation of what is taking place in training and therefore can be useful in quantifying training loads, assisting in the planning of specific sessions for teams and individuals, while also adding a further dimension to the quantification of individual workload.

An additional area of development at the elite level involves the analysis of information generated by accelerometers that are commonly incorporated in

TABLE 4 Pre-season match external loads – fully completed halves (n=90, average ± SD)

Parameter	
Duration (min)	46.9 (1.4)
Total distance (m)	5100 (436)
Very high-speed running distance (> 19.8km/h)	268 (111)
Sprint distance (> 25.2km/h)	54 (40)
Distance per minute (m/min)	109 (10.2)
Max speed (km/h)	30 (2.4)
Hi accelerations (no.)	32 (11.8)
Hi decelerations (no.)	39 (11.4)
Body load/dynamic stress load (au)	171 (79.5)

GPS devices. Table 4 shows a body load value that is representative of the number and magnitude of impacts imposed upon players. This value, in conjunction with velocity-based parameters, is increasingly being used to represent a 'mechanical efficiency' for players, which may well be an important development, as it enables sports scientists to identify potential loading issues for players before they result in injury. This is an area that is currently being investigated by many research groups to establish its efficacy in a team sport environment.

Internal Training Load

The internal load, or the relative physiological strain resulting from the external training factors, is crucial in determining both the stress imposed and the subsequent adaptation to training (Halson, 2014). Heart-rate analysis has been utilised for many years in soccer to provide an insight into the internal demands players are exposed to. It is probably the method that coaches and sports scientists are most familiar with even if they have not had experience in using the technology themselves; there is a mass of literature relating to heart-rate analysis in team sports, and more specifically in football, that practitioners are likely to have been subjected to.

Various heart-rate systems are available that have made the collection of data for 20+ players relatively easy, with quick feedback mechanisms available via various reporting options. Once again, there are many ways by which training sessions can be analysed, the most common approach being to provide feedback on amount of time spent in various percentage heart-rate zones (ie integrating an intensity figure and duration to produce a 'dose' response), resulting in an overall training load figure, commonly referred to as 'training impulse' (TRIMP) (Foster *et al.*, 1995). A variety of methods for TRIMP calculation are currently utilised to varying degrees in professional sport. The level of detail and hence accuracy varies between methods, with some simply using arbitrary heart-rate zones and applying a scaling factor to each one, while others use individual zone markers calculated via blood lactate profiling, with each individual player having their own heart-rate intensity curve from which training load is calculated (iTRIMP).

The decision as to which approach to adopt in the measurement and tracking of internal training load is dependent on many factors, none more so than the practitioner's underlying philosophy. Other considerations such as cost and staffing are still important, as are the value of other measures being taken and the level of detail needed. For example, there is some debate as to whether many of the various TRIMP calculations really are representative of internal load since not all have been shown to be correlated with changes in aerobic fitness parameters. In addition, heart rate (HR) does not account for the considerable anaerobic load which players undertake during high-intensity activities. However, that is not to say that these methods do not have any monitoring value especially during certain types of training. Table 5, which provides an overview of heart-rate data from a player at different stages of the season, demonstrates this.

The correct interpretation of these data in isolation is difficult, but so often that is what some sports scientists are faced with. Without having seen the session to provide some qualitative assessment and without GPS data to evaluate external loads, a practitioner could interpret the February session as being insufficient to induce the desired training response in the player, whereas the reality is that the work output in the February session was greater than that observed in September, with a subjective evaluation of load (discussed in more detail below) also being higher. Various interpretations could be made; however, the key point is that only via longitudinal monitoring would it be possible to make a judgement as to the cardiovascular stress the individual is likely to be exposed to and the load required to induce the desired response. Similar to the 'mechanical efficiency' concept referred to above, a 'cardiovascular efficiency' value is increasingly being utilised by practitioners using ratios of heart-rate load and external load to track changes in efficiency over the course of the season. It is evident that the more information that is available, the greater will be the probability of making the correct interpretation with regard to the needs of players and how they respond to specific training sessions.

TABLE 5 Training heart-rate responses at different stages of the season for a single player

Session	Date	HR Load (au)	Time (min) 80–84%	Time (min) 85–89%	Time (min) >90%
6v6 (4x5 min, 2 min recovery)	Sept	220	4	12	7
6v6 (4x5 min, 2 min recovery)	Feb	150	10	8	1

The final monitoring tool to be discussed is that of subjective assessments in the form of ratings of perceived exertion (RPE), which provides a simple, cost-effective, global indication of the player's internal training load. RPE measures have recently been shown to have a correlation with heart-rate measures in football (Kelly *et al.*, 2016). Indeed, compared with HR, RPE may provide a more valid indication of the internal load in team sports such as soccer where the overall training load frequently comprises anaerobic components. This approach is quick to administer and can be applied across all forms of training both on the field and off (eg including gym-based training). As such, RPE represents a universal approach to monitoring the internal training load. There are several different RPE scales in the literature that have been validated. One commonly used in the professional sport setting is the Foster scale shown in Figure 3 (Foster, 2001).

The players simply indicate how hard they found the session, which provides an 'intensity' score. This can then be multiplied by the duration of the training session to provide a 'training load' score. A typical weekly RPE profile for a player is shown in Table 6.

Rating	Descriptor
0	Rest
1	Very, very easy
2	Easy
3	Moderate
4	Somewhat hard
5	Hard
6	
7	Very hard
8	
9	
10	Maximal

FIGURE 3 Ratings of perceived exertion (RPE) scale (Foster *et al.*, 2001)

TABLE 6 Individual player RPE response

Parameter	Monday	Tuesday	Wednesday	Thursday	Friday	Saturday	Sunday
Activity	Training	Training	Training	Training	Training	Training	Match
RPE	2	5	4	6	1	4	8
Duration	30	55	75	70	25	35	90
Training load (au)	60	275	300	420	25	140	720

As with other methods of assessing training load, the information becomes more meaningful when put into context in terms of both the stage of the season and weekly/monthly trends. For example, the total load for the player in the above example is 1940 Arbitrary Units (AU). This may be excessive for this player and some consideration should then be given to subsequent loads; however, it may well be a typical week and the increase in load planned for the following week might then be seen to be suitable.

Insight can be gleaned from simple RPE data that can guide future decision-making relating to the coaching process. It is not uncommon for this type of data to be manipulated further to provide additional information relating to monotony and strain (Foster, 1998). Monotony is a measure of how similar the training stimulus is over the course of a specified time period, and strain is a product of monotony and training load. Using the figures from the table above, the following monotony and strain values can be calculated:

Monotony = Mean Weekly TL / SD Daily Load, ie 270/240 = 1.1
Strain = Monotony x Weekly Load, ie 1.1 x 1,940 = 2,134

In this instance, monotony is low, indicating that there is a large amount of variation in the training load the player has been exposed to, limiting the strain experienced. It is known that by varying the training stimulus, staleness in players can be avoided, and in some instances signs and symptoms of overtraining can be eradicated (this is referred to again later in this chapter). Consequently, being aware of the training-induced stress that players are exposed to will enable them to be managed more appropriately. Although monotony and strain have traditionally been associated with subjective measures, there is no reason why the same principles cannot be applied to other measures discussed in this chapter. It is possible to generate further figures using heart-rate loads, total distances and specific speed threshold distances. Once set up, many of the required calculations should be automated through readily available software such as Excel or more advanced data management systems. Failure to automate in this way could lead to support staff being swamped by too much data that simply cannot be acted upon.

Appropriate Feedback to Support a Training Strategy

It is apparent that the potential exists to collect a vast amount of information from which to make suitable assessments of training load. It is important, however, that data are not collected merely for the sake of it and that the potential 'data tsunami' is managed appropriately; the information obtained via the chosen methods needs to be used to impact upon the coaching process. A key objective of any practitioner when developing a training strategy is to establish what information is important and can be used to assist in the decision making involved in establishing the training requirements of individual players. Generally, training load information is utilised to support the following processes:

1. Evaluation of training sessions and specific drills to support the daily planning for the squad.
2. Development and tracking of individual player profiles and establishment of specific needs in addition to squad training.
3. Supporting the rehabilitation process by evaluating actual workloads against those expected and assisting the return to training and playing pathway.
4. Providing a means by which aspects of player fitness can be continually evaluated.

Throughout this chapter, training load has been discussed as either being internal or external. With only two categories involved, it can be difficult for practitioners to know which external and internal load components to focus on due to the number of potential variables to analyse. With further categorisation, however, it is possible to identify specific areas that may need evaluating, and this can ease the process of selecting the most appropriate sessions or drills required to address the issues identified via the monitoring process. Figure 4 shows one potential categorisation system of training load components. The different components can then be reported on in various formats, as shown in the graph and table representation of weekly training that follows.

The output produced to represent the various training load components is shown in Figure 5. In this instance, total weekly distance has been selected to be represented graphically, while a number of components that represent the various forms of training load are shown in Table 7. Those parameters considered to be the most important can be colour coded based on thresholds set for teams and individuals, drawing attention to key areas. With the appropriate manipulation of data and efficient data management systems practitioners can be informed quickly of key monitoring variables: new loads, changes in load, chronic loads and acute vs. chronic loads (sometimes referred to as 'training stress balance'). These all have

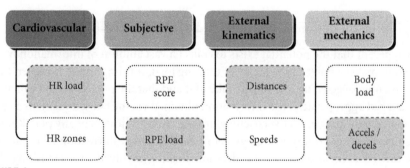

FIGURE 4 Categorisation of Training Load

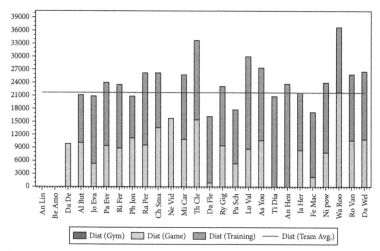

FIGURE 5 Weekly training session summary

TABLE 7 Weekly training load

Player	Mins	RPE	RPE Load (au)	Total Distance (m)	High Intensity Distance (m)	Heartrate Load	High Accelerations
1	256	4.0	1136	21141	883	427	44
2	347	3.0	1138	20869	628	578	79
3	350	4.0	1568	24019	1265	583	63
4	366	3.1	1426	23595	639	611	45
5	313	4.3	1398	20884	985	522	68
6	386	3.7	1581	26277	1184	643	83
7	345	4.8	1769	26141	885	576	82
8	256	3.8	1000	15893	626	427	110
9	391	2.6	1370	25806	803	652	62
10	452	4.6	2165	33801	1693	753	64
11	267	4.2	1023	16286	267	444	75
12	367	3.3	1389	23121	657	611	62
13	276	4.6	1162	17786	311	460	42
14	416	3.1	1454	30074	1608	693	112
15	396	4.4	1813	27418	1395	660	88
16	470	3.9	1793	20740	1063	784	144
17	509	3.9	2067	23724	824	849	138
18	320	4.2	1447	21744	808	534	88
19	423	5.7	2385	17273	581	704	75
20	367	3.8	1513	24070	1138	612	90
Average							

FIGURE 6 Training load reporting

implications for how players are subsequently managed to reduce injury risk and optimise performance.

The way the information gathered is presented and subsequently interpreted is dependent on the requirements of the end user. Consequently, the same information can be presented in a number of ways. Figure 6 depicts a possible structure for reporting to players and coaches.

Data can be easily manipulated to emphasise different points depending on the key processes the data are designed to support. Regardless of how the data are presented, typically the feedback should inform coaches of some or all of the following:

1. Did the session achieve its planned physical load?
2. How did the external load differ from a typical training session for that part of the week for each individual player?
3. Did any player find the session harder than expected?
4. Do any modifications need to be made to subsequent training sessions?
5. What is required from a recovery perspective to prepare for the next training session or game?

Whether insights are being made from session reports or weekly reports, similar questions are being asked, ultimately guiding practice to elicit optimal responses to enhance players' abilities while maximising their readiness for competition. A general premise is that there is a holistic plan to the training week while within the week players are micromanaged accordingly. The monitoring of training load and recovery is integral to the delivery of a suitable training plan. Figure 7 provides the basis for the thought processes that lead to the implementation of strategies.

Summary

Via an appropriate monitoring strategy, training can more effectively be evaluated and subsequent adjustments made to ensure the programme continues

FIGURE 7 Typical in-season weekly training plan

along the desired path. Without such monitoring, all decision-making becomes reliant on subjective opinions predominantly built from experience, lacking the advantages objective information provides. It is the combination of both objective information and subjective experiences that tends to lead to a successful coaching process. There is now available an array of tools to help provide an assessment of training load. The depth of analysis will depend on several factors; however, practitioners and sports scientists alike should continually evaluate the numerous data streams they possess and their usefulness in contributing to the global aims of conditioning in professional football, which are to maintain and/or enhance various player fitness attributes, enhance player readiness for competitive matches and keep players injury free. There are some clear benefits to having an accurate understanding of the loads players have been subjected to and the internal loads achieved as a consequence. Key benefits include the following:

1. They provide the ability to ensure training demands are suitable relative to known match demands.
2. They ensure performance is never compromised by exposing players to too little or too much load, while also avoiding monotony.
3. They enable evaluation of a specific session or drill to see if the desired loads are achieved.
4. They allow players to be monitored during rehabilitation to ensure that a suitable reintegration into normal training takes place.

MONITORING FATIGUE STATUS

As noted earlier in this chapter, the key to developing a successful training programme revolves around effective manipulation of training and match load and recovery in order to attain the desired performance. Routine modifications in training load (frequency, duration, intensity) occur during the annual training cycle, subsequently increasing or decreasing fatigue. Management of this fatigue is essential in mediating adaptation to training and ensuring the athlete is prepared for competition (Pyne and Martin, 2011), and for reducing the athlete's susceptibility to excessive fatigue that may lead to injury and/or illness. Fatigue is a complex and multifaceted phenomenon with a plethora of possible mechanisms originating in the muscle (metabolic fatigue), central nervous system (central fatigue) and mind (psychological fatigue). Indeed, a number of different definitions of fatigue exist depending on the particular circumstances under which it occurs. From a practical perspective, for the purpose of this chapter fatigue will be defined as 'an inability to complete a task that was once achievable within a recent time frame' (Pyne and Martin, 2011).

The Recovery–Overtraining Continuum

The stress associated with a single training session or match leads to acute fatigue lasting minutes or hours and which temporarily impairs a player's physical performance. Alternatively, exercise-induced muscle injury and delayed-onset muscle soreness that often follows a match or training with a high eccentric component may lead to impairment lasting several days. However, with adequate recovery, these symptoms of acute fatigue and functional overreaching (OR) quickly dissipate and are followed by adaptation and performance improvement (see Figure 8). In contrast, in situations where the balance between the stress of training and competition and sufficient recovery is insufficient, an extreme state of OR often referred to as non-functional overreaching (NFOR) is reached. This may lead to a stagnation or decrease in performance that will not return to the desired level for several weeks or months and that will increase the player's susceptibility to injury and illness. With appropriate management of the player's load, the player will recover; however, with a continued mismatch between loading and recovery, the potentially long-term debilitating effects associated with overtraining syndrome (OTS) may arise which may take months to recover from (Meeusen

PROCESS	TRAINING (overload)	INTENSIFIED TRAINING →		
OUTCOME	ACUTE FATIGUE	FUNCTIONAL OR (short-term OR)	NON-FUNCTIONAL OVERREACHING (extreme OR)	OVERTRAINING SYNDROME (OTS)
RECOVERY	Day(s)	Days–weeks	Weeks–months	Months–
PERFORMANCE	INCREASE	Temporary performance decrement (e.g., training camp)	STAGNATION DECREASE	DECREASE

FIGURE 8 Overview of possible stages of training, OR and OTS (Meeusen *et al.*, 2013)

et al., 2013). The ultimate aim of the practitioner, therefore, is to implement monitoring tools which may identify players who are at risk of progressing from a state of OR to one of NFOR.

Problems Posed by Team Sports

As noted earlier, a combination of both external and internal load is important when monitoring training load. This is particularly important when looking to examine the overall recovery status of the player since divergence of external and internal loads may mean the difference between a fresh athlete and a fatigued one (Pyne and Martin, 2011). For example, in 'closed-loop' sports like cycling, where the performance outcome is time, and the power produced by the rider is known to have a relatively precise association with the performance time, the internal load needed to sustain a certain external load (power output) can provide important information regarding the athlete's fatigue status. In contrast to closed-loop sports, in 'open-loop' sports like team sports it is difficult to relate external and internal loads due to the variability in physical performance during sport-specific training and match-play (Gregson *et al.*, 2010). As a consequence, attempts to monitor the fatigue status of team-sport athletes have largely focused on the assessment of internal and external load measures under resting conditions and/or during submaximal exercise assessments on the morning prior to training.

IMPORTANT CONSIDERATIONS UNDERPINNING THE IMPLEMENTATION OF MONITORING TOOLS

Given the multifaceted nature of fatigue, no single measure currently exists to examine the fatigue status of the athlete. Consequently, practitioners working in the field frequently adopt a plethora of monitoring tools in an attempt to generate information pertaining to the overall fatigue status of the athlete (Taylor *et al.*, 2012). However, much of what is currently known in team sports such as soccer has been gleaned from anecdotal accounts since the majority of the relevant data remains protected and unpublished. Furthermore, despite an increasing number of commercially available products, many of these lack the required level of scientific validation. When selecting a tool for this purpose there are several important criteria which it must fulfil. They must be:

1. Valid and reliable
A valid marker of fatigue should be sensitive to changes in training and match loads. Any measurement of fatigue also needs to be interpreted with knowledge about how valid the measurement tool is in terms of the ultimate outcomes

of player performance, illness and/or injury. Another important factor when selecting tests is measurement reliability. The reliability of a test refers to how repeatable a test is within a practically relevant time frame (e.g. between successive days or across a week during the in-season competition phase). An important initial step when adopting any tool is to undertake a well-designed reliability study as opposed to simply deriving estimates from the literature since the practitioner needs to understand the reliability of the tool in their own hands (Atkinson *et al.*, 2007). A test with poor reliability will be unsuitable for tracking changes in the fatigue status of the athlete. Refer to the section on data-analysis consideration later in this chapter for more information on this subject.

2. Non-exhaustive
Prospective tools should limit any additional loading on the athlete. This is particularly important in soccer, where competition occurs on a weekly basis and in some instances on 2–3 occasions a week, meaning that players are required to peak with limited recovery between matches.

3. Time efficient
With squads often comprising 25–30 players, any tool adopted will need to be quick and easy to administer. Morning-measured fatigue-type assessments are often administered as soon as the player arrives at the training facility. As only a short window is available before training occurs, assessments and data processing needs to be quickly undertaken for the information to be readily available to those staff involved in making decisions on what the player's training activity will comprise that day.

4. Non-invasive and cost effective
Invasive tests such as blood sampling are not well accepted and are unlikely to be feasible since assessments are often required on a frequent basis (daily) or on a number of key days across the week (e.g. 2 days pre and post match). Such assessments are also likely to be time consuming, particularly if analysis of the sample is not permitted immediately. The reliance on blood sampling has been reduced to some extent through commercially available saliva-based kits (see immune markers below); however, these may not be well tolerated by the players if undertaken on a daily basis. Furthermore, it can often be difficult to derive a reliable assessment of these parameters under the conditions faced in the training environment. Given the need to obtain fatigue data on a daily basis, it is also important to ensure that tools are financially viable. Even leading clubs with significant financial resources may be limited in their ability to employ methods such as immune assays on a daily basis for large squads of players. Alongside the important factors noted in this section, a cost/benefit analysis is clearly relevant here when deciding on which tools to adopt.

METHODS FOR MONITORING FATIGUE

Athlete Self-Report Measures

Athlete self-report measures (ASRM) are used extensively for assessing the overall well-being of team sport athletes (Taylor *et al.*, 2012). A plethora of ASRM currently exist, including the POMS (Raglin and Morgan, 1994), the DALDA (Coutts *et al.*, 2007), the TQR (Kenttä and Hassmén, 1998) and the REST-Q (Kellmann, 2010), which have been extensively documented in the literature. However, many of these are often extensive and time-consuming to complete, preventing their use on a daily basis with large numbers of team sport athletes. Many team sports therefore often adopt shorter, simplified questionnaires which can be administered on a daily basis (Taylor *et al.*, 2012). A typical example of such questionnaires is shown in Figure 9. Here the players are simply asked to provide a rating from 1 to 7 on each of the three scales.

Scales such as those displayed generally show greater sensitivity to changes in training load compared with the commonly used objective measures detailed below (Saw *et al.*, 2015). For example, among English Premier League (EPL) players, the scales in Figure 9 have been shown to be sensitive to the changes in match and training loads which these players experience during typical weeks during the in-season competition period (Thorpe *et al.*, 2015; Thorpe *et al.*, 2016). For example, Table 8 shows how the morning-measured ratings on each of the three scales progressively improved following the day after a game (post-match day) through to the day before the next game (pre-match day). This type of change

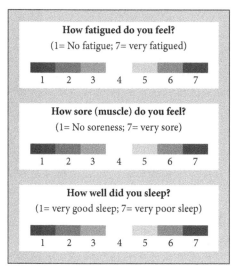

FIGURE 9 Simple ASRM (adapted from Hooper *et al.*, 1995)

TABLE 8 Perceived ratings of fatigue, sleep quality and delayed-onset muscle soreness (DOMS) (AU) across in-season training weeks (mean ± SD).*

| | Day | | | |
Fatigue measure	Post-match day	2 days post-match	4 days post-match	Pre-match day
Fatigue (AU)	3.4 ± 0.6†	4.4 ± 0.7† +	4.5 ± 0.7† +	5.0 ± 0.6
Sleep quality (AU)	3.9 ± 1.2†	4.8 ± 0.9† +	4.7 ± 1.0†	5.2 ± 0.8
DOMS (AU)	3.6 ± 0.6†	4.3 ± 0.7† +	4.4 ± 0.7† +	5.1 ± 0.8

*Note: the higher the rating on each scale, the more enhanced the recovery. † denotes sig. difference vs pre-match day. + denotes sig difference vs post-match day. Scores of 1-7 with 1 and 7 representing very, very poor (negative state of wellness) and very, very good (positive state of wellness respectively)
Data from Thorpe *et al.*, (2016).

would be expected in any sensitive measure in response to the planned training load for that week (Figure 10). The highest load is associated with the match, and following initial recovery (post-match day), we see a gradual rise in load through days 2–5 post match before the load is reduced once again on the day prior to the next game (pre-match day). It should be noted that the efficacy of these ASRM tools is dependent upon a number of theoretical factors (inter-relations between the measure, the social environment and outcomes) and practical factors that need to be addressed within the applied sports setting (Saw *et al.*, 2015). For example, buy-in from both the players and the coaching staff is essential if both valid and reliable information is to be collected.

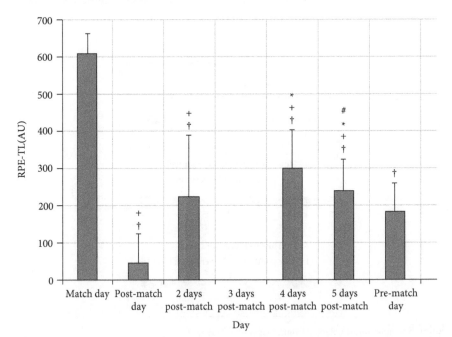

FIGURE 10 Training load (RPE-TL; AU) across in-season training weeks (mean ± SD) (Thorpe *et al.*, 2016)

Autonomic Nervous System (ANS)

The ANS is interlinked with many other physiological systems and therefore significant attention in the literature has centred upon the use of indicators of ANS functioning for determining an athlete's overall adaptation/fatigue status. This is often undertaken by examining indices derived from the sensitivity of the heart rate (HR) to fluctuations in training and competition load, including resting heart rate (RHR), exercising heart rate (HRex), heart-rate variability (HRV) and heart-rate recovery (HRR) (Buchheit, 2014).

Interestingly, much of the available technology targeted at fatigue monitoring has often focused upon a number of the measurements included in this section. Many of these technologies can be very expensive; however, these measures can also be derived manually using basic HR telemetry with the required data processing automated in software packages such as Excel.

Submaximal heart rate (HRex)

Decreases in HR during standardised exercise bouts (e.g. submaximal cycling on a cycle ergometer) have traditionally been associated with increases in aerobic fitness. However, when focused specifically around detecting changes in fatigue status, the majority of available data has reported inconsistent results in non-team-sport athletes, with limited information on team sports such as soccer. For example, in EPL players, HRex failed to fluctuate in response to within-week changes in training and match load (see Table 9) (Thorpe et al., 2016). The use of HRex to detect acute alterations in fatigue status should therefore be done with caution and the results interpreted together with other potential measures of fatigue, such as ASRM.

Heart-rate variability (HRV)

HRV refers to the time interval between heartbeats. It is measured by the variation in the beat-to-beat interval, with increases and decreases in variability thought to be associated with positive and negative adaptation to training.

TABLE 9 HRex (bpm), HRR (%) and Ln rMSSD (ms) across in-season training weeks (mean ± SD). Data from Thorpe et al., 2016

Fatigue measure	Day			
	Post-match day	2 days post-match	4 days post-match	Pre-match day
HRex (bpm)	119 ± 13	117 ± 14	119 ± 15	118 ± 13
HRR (%)	72.1 ± 7.7	71.5 ± 7.5	70.2 ± 7.7	70.9 ± 7.1
Ln rMSSD (ms)	3.31 ± 0.71	3.44 ± 0.69	3.28 ± 0.76	3.33 ± 0.64

† denotes sig. difference vs pre-match day. + denotes sig difference vs post-match day. Scores of 1-7 with 1 and 7 representing very, very poor (negative state of wellness) and very, very good (positive state of wellness respectively)

Sensitivity to changes in training load and performance has mainly been observed in non-team sports. Little evidence, however, currently exists with regard to its sensitivity to fluctuations in training and competition loads observed in football (Thorpe *et al.*, 2015; Thorpe *et al.*, 2016). For example, in EPL players, HRV (Ln rMSSD) did not change across a standard in-season training week (see Table 9) (Thorpe *et al.*, 2016). The sensitivity of HRV to training and competition may be improved when data are averaged over a week or by using seven-day rolling averages rather than single data points due to the high day-to-day variation in these indices (Plews *et al.*, 2013). This suggests that it may provide some valid information over potentially longer periods of time; however, further research is needed to determine whether such approaches enhance the suitability of these measures for use in team-sport populations. Like HRex, the use of HRV to detect alterations in acute fatigue status should be done with caution and the results interpreted together with other potential measures of fatigue, such as ASRM.

Heart-rate recovery (HRR)

Recent findings in endurance sports have shown that post-exercise HRR may serve as a sensitive marker of acute training load alteration, although this association has yet to be seen in team sports. For example, HRR did not fluctuate in response to the within-week training load variability in EPL players (Table 9) (Thorpe *et al.*, 2016). It appears that HRR is responsive to both acute and chronic changes in training load; however, the exact direction of this change and whether HRR can detect fatigue status remain unclear, and the results should be interpreted alongside training status and with caution.

Physical performance

Theoretically, a variety of maximal performance assessments (sprints, repeated sprints, strength/power assessments) can be used to quantify the rate of recovery of performance in the hours and days following training and competition in team sports. However, these types of assessments are exhaustive in nature and time consuming to deliver, meaning that they are often unsuitable for use in team-sport environments to assess ongoing fatigue status. Maximal performance assessments that are quick, efficient and without additional load are the only feasible ones applicable to team-sport players.

Neuromuscular function

Various types of jumps, including squat jump and countermovement jump (CMJ), have been adopted to examine the recovery of neuromuscular function following competition. However, less attention has focused on examining their sensitivity to changes in training load and thus their validity for detecting changes in fatigue status. CMJ has previously not been shown to be sensitive to daily fluctuations in training load in EPL players (Malone *et al.*, 2014; Thorpe *et al.*, 2016). Indeed, CMJ height alone may mask alternative neuromuscular measures and their sensitivity to alterations in load, and in fact emerging evidence suggests that specific neuromuscular variables derived from simple CMJ using specially designed force platforms may be suitable for neuromuscular fatigue detection (Gathercole *et al.*, 2015). The emergence of portable force platform technology will assist with this through enabling practitioners to use these systems whether in their own training facility or when away on training camps.

Functional strength assessments

Both 'fatigue' and 'muscle imbalance' represent two important modifiable risk factors for non-contact injury in professional footballers (McCall *et al.*, 2015). Recent attention has therefore focused upon the use of simple functional strength assessments for examining the fatigue status of players. Indeed, both isometric posterior lower limb muscle strength assessed using a portable force platform (McCall *et al.*, 2015) and hip strength using a hand-held dynamometer (Paul *et al.*, 2014) have been shown to be sensitive to the fatigue induced during match-play. While further research is needed to examine their sensitivity to daily fluctuations in training load, such tests offer real promise for monitoring fatigue status in the field.

Biochemical/hormonal/immunological

A large amount of research has examined a range of biochemical (creatine kinase, C-reactive protein, uric acid), hormonal (testosterone, cortisol) and immunological (salivary immunoglobulin A, IL-6) responses to team sport competition. It is beyond the scope of this chapter to review the collective literature surrounding the responses of such measures in team sports; however, no definitive marker has been derived for examining the potential fatigue status of players. Furthermore, there is currently little longitudinal data, particularly around competition and training phases, relating to team sports. The associated costs, and in some instances the time-consuming nature of their analyses, often mean that many of these measures are impractical for use in the team-sport environment.

Practical Application

In light of the abundance of available measurement tools and the fact that no single tool is likely to provide an overall estimate of fatigue status, the practitioner is faced with the decision of which tool/s to adopt. Such a decision should be informed by the key issues discussed earlier – namely, validity, reliability, time restraints and cost, as well as any additional factors relevant to the specific environment within which they operate. Figure 11 provides an overview of a simple framework which may aid in the selection of appropriate measurement tools based on the available evidence to date. The initial step or foundation should involve some form of simple

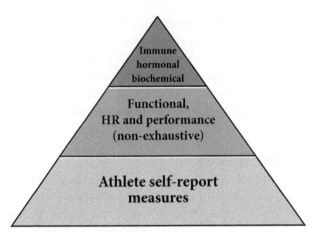

FIGURE 11 Overview of potential approach to the selection of monitoring tools

ASRM that can be easily delivered within the environment in question. Such assessments can be undertaken on a daily basis or on key days within the weekly training cycle – for example, on post-match recovery days (e.g. 1–2 days) in order to ensure the players are sufficiently recovered before entering the training planned for the week ahead. Similarly, assessments could be undertaken two days prior to the next game in order to afford the opportunity to alter the players' loading during the final two training sessions of the week.

Depending on time and resources, subjective ASRM assessments could be supplemented by simple functional strength assessments using a hand-held dynamometer and/or a force platform (e.g. two days after a game and two days prior to the next game). The availability of a force platform will also permit examination of jump parameters that may be more sensitive to fatigue than merely jump height alone. Submaximal exercise/post-exercise assessments of ANS functioning may also accompany these assessments; however, further research is needed to fully elucidate the potential role of ANS measures for routine assessment of fatigue status in team sports such as soccer. Due to cost and/or time restrictions, the assessments listed in the top zone in Figure 11 are likely to be restricted to one assessment per week or even monthly. However, more importantly, issues around both reliability and validity need to be considered by the support team before implementing such assessments.

Data Analysis Considerations

Even in the most controlled circumstances, any human measurement varies on a day-to-day or week-to-week basis. This renders the quantification and interpretation of this variation crucial for practitioners to be able to make robust decisions about the athletes. In order to determine whether a 'true' change in a given measurement of fatigue status has occurred, the practitioner needs to interpret the 'within-subject' variability of measurements (i.e. their reliability or repeatability – see earlier definition in this chapter) against the minimum change of difference that has been deemed to be practically/clinically important (Atkinson, 2003). The selection of this 'minimal clinically/practically important difference' (MCID) in the context of fatigue measurement is challenging, but can be approached using a variety of suggested methods, including the use of expert opinion, evidence syntheses and/or the undertaking of a pilot study. A triangulation of all three of these approaches is desirable (Thorpe et al., 2016). To date, little is known about how valid or prognostic the available measurement tools are for indicating the ultimate outcomes of player performance, illness and/ or injury. Consequently, many practitioners tend to focus on the question of how reliable a measurement tool is using information mainly derived from expertise available within the club.

A relatively simple statistical approach to interpreting change in player status involves comparing a player's score on any given day (e.g. two days post-match) with a typical personalised rating for that particular day derived from previous ongoing data collection. For example, the time-averaged mean and standard deviation (SD) fatigue rating for an individual player two days post-match is found to be 4 ± 1 au. The next step is to select the threshold for suggesting that a particular measurement is high or low enough for the player to be followed up or monitored more closely. This threshold could be a certain number of standard deviations from the mean. For example, 2 SDs could be selected as the threshold, which means that only 5% of any measurements will be outside this range. Consequently, if a player provides a rating of 6 on this particular day, this might be considered an unusual enough measurement for closer scrutiny of the player in conjunction with other members of the medical, performance and/or coaching team. Such analysis can be repeated for any measurement tool or day of interest across the training week. In many clubs, such simple analyses are automated within their data-management systems such as Excel, and appear as alerts (e.g. cell turns red) when any player exceeds a predetermined threshold.

Summary

Given the increase in competition demands in elite team sports over recent years, the quantification of fatigue status has gained increasing importance among practitioners. Maximal physical performance assessments (sprints, repeated sprints and maximal voluntary contractions) that are traditionally used to quantify recovery and fatigue in athletes are unsuitable in team-sport environments due to their exhaustive and time-consuming nature. Consequently, quick, simple and non-invasive tools such as ASRM, ANS HR indices and jump characteristics have received increasing interest among practitioners. Practitioners utilising such measures must consider the 'within-subject' variability of measurements against the MCID to determine whether a 'true' change in a given measurement of fatigue status has occurred.

CHALLENGES IN THE WORKING ENVIRONMENT

The areas discussed in this chapter have evolved considerably in recent years, reflecting advances both in technology and in the expertise available to clubs. The fundamental reason for monitoring training load and fatigue status is to inform relevant decisions within the coaching process. In order to maximise the impact of this, it is essential that the correct systems and processes are implemented. For example, some form of data-management system is essential to assist with the storage and processing of the vast quantities of data produced in today's modern clubs. By making use of such a system, more time is made available for the production of meaningful insights and for focused discussion with the players and relevant coaching staff as part of the feedback process. Making such processes as efficient and effective as possible also has the benefit of creating the opportunity for additional and/or more detailed assessments without impacting on other areas of the support process. With all the data collected by practitioners and sports scientists discussed in this chapter, the adoption of appropriate feedback mechanisms to provide both relevant and timely information to coaches is one of the most crucial elements of the training process in ensuring that the gathered information is used appropriately. There are excellent practitioners all over the world who use feedback systems of varying degrees of complexity that fit within the culture they operate. There is no one-size-fits-all system; however, there is a requirement to understand the needs of the coaches with whom practitioners work and to provide feedback in such a way that the recipients of the information can use it appropriately to support the coaching process.

Technology in many areas has continued to enhance our ability to derive more detailed insights regarding athlete load and fatigue status. Despite this, many examples remain of technologies that have not been subjected to the required level of scientific rigour. This is often due to commercial reasons, with companies eager to take their product to market as soon as possible, alongside practitioners eager to apply new approaches in the hope of achieving some competitive edge. This 'working fast' approach is common in elite sport (McCall et al., 2016), and indeed at the highest level in many professions. However, it is essential that clubs strike a balance between embracing new technology and challenging the providers to demonstrate the required level of scientific rigour. Indeed, many elite clubs are now routinely engaged in research and development programmes either internally or in collaboration with external partners. Ultimately, practitioners have a duty of care to the player to fully understand the tools being utilised in their programme.

REFERENCES

Atkinson, G. 'Does Size Matter for Sports Performance Researchers?' *Journal of Sports Sciences*, 21, no. 2 (2003), pp. 73–74.

Atkinson, G. and Nevill, A.M. 'Method Agreement and Measurment in the Physiology of Exercise', in Winter, E.M., Jones, A.M., Davison, R.C., Bromley, P.D. and Mercer, T.H. (eds.), *Sport and Exercise Physiology Testing Guidelines: The British Association of Sport and Exercise Science Guide. Volume II: Exercise and Clinical Testing*, pp. 41–48 (Routledge, 2007).

Buchheit, M. 'Monitoring Training Status with HR Measures: Do All Roads Lead to Rome?' *Frontiers in Physiology*, 5 February 2014. doi:10.3389/fphys.2014.00073.

Bush, M., Barnes, C., Archer, D.T., Hogg, B. and Bradley, P.S. 'Evolution of Match Performance Parameters for Various Playing Positions in the English Premier League', *Human Movement Science*, 39 (2015), pp. 1–11.

Coutts, A.J., Slattery, K.M. and Wallace, L.K. 'Practical Tests for Monitoring Performance, Fatigue and Recovery in Triathletes', *Journal of Science and Medicine in Sport*, 10, no. 6 (2007), pp. 372–381. doi:10.1016/j.jsams.2007.02.007.

Foster, C. 'Monitoring Training in Athletes with Reference to Overtraining Syndrome', *Medicine & Science in Sports & Exercise*, 30, no. 7 (1998), pp. 1164–1168.

Foster, C., Florhaug, J.A., Franklin, J., Gottschall, L., Hrovatin, L.A., Parker, S., Doleshal, P. and Dodge, C. 'A New Approach to Monitoring Exercise Training'. *J Strength Cond Research* 15(1) (2001), pp. 109–115.

Gathercole, R., Sporer, B., Stellingwerff, T. and Sleivert, G. 'Alternative Countermovement-Jump Analysis to Quantify Acute Neuromuscular Fatigue', *International Journal of Sports Physiology and Performance*, 10, no. 1 (2015), pp. 84–92.

Gregson, W., Drust, B., Atkinson, G. and Salvo, V.D. 'Match-to-Match Variability of High-Speed Activities in Premier League Soccer', *International Journal of Sports Medicine*, 31, no. 4 (2010), pp. 237–242.

Halson, S.L. 'Monitoring Training Load to Understand Fatigue in Athletes', *Sports Medicine*, 44, Suppl. 2 (2014), S139–S147.

Hooper, S.L., Mackinnon, L.T., Howard, A., Gordon, R.D. and Bachmann, A.W. 'Markers for Monitoring Overtraining and Recovery', *Medicine and Science in Sports and Exercise*, 27, no. 1 (1995), pp. 106–112.

Impellizzeri, F.M., Rampinini, R. and Marcora, S.M. 'Physiological Assessment of Aerobic Training in Soccer', *Journal of Sports Sciences* 23, no. 6 (2005), pp. 583–592.

Kellmann, M. 'Preventing Overtraining in Athletes in High-Intensity Sports and Stress/Recovery Monitoring', *Scandinavian Journal of Medicine & Science in Sports*, 20, Suppl. 2 (2010), pp. 95–102.

Kelly, D.M., Strudwick, A.J., Atkinson, G., Drust, B. and Gregson, W. 'The Within-Participant Correlation Between Perception of Effort and Heart Rate-Based Estimation of Training Load in Elite Soccer Players', *Journal of Sports Sciences*, 34, no. 14 (2016), pp 1328–1332.

Kenttä, G. and Hassmén, P. 'Overtraining and Recovery. A Conceptual Model', *Sports Medicine*, 26, no. 1 (1998), pp. 1–16.

Malone, J.J., Murtagh, C., Morgans, R., Burgess, D., Morton, J.P. and Drust, B. 'Countermovement Jump Performance is Not Affected during an In-Season Training Microcycle in Elite Youth Soccer Players', *Journal of Strength and Conditioning Research*, 29, no. 3 (2014), pp. 752–757.

McCall, A., Davison, M., Carling, C., Buckthorpe, M., Coutts, A.J. and Dupont, G. 'Can Off-Field "Brains" Provide a Competitive Advantage in Professional Football?' *British Journal of Sports Medicine*, 50, no. 12 (2016), pp. 710–712.

McCall, A., Nedelec, M., Carling, C., Le Gall, F., Berthoin, S. and Dupont, G. 'Reliability and Sensitivity of a Simple Isometric Posterior Lower Limb Muscle Test in Professional Football Players', *Journal of Sports Sciences*, 12 (2015), pp. 1298–1304.

Meeusen, R., Duclos, M., Foster, C., Fry, A., Gleeson, M., Nieman, D., Raglin, J., Rietjens, G., Steinacker, J. and Urhausen, A. 'Prevention, Diagnosis, and Treatment of the Overtraining Syndrome: Joint Consensus Statement of the European College of Sport Science and the American College of Sports Medicine', *Medicine & Science in Sports & Exercise*, 45, no. 1 (2013), pp. 186–205.

Paul, D.J., Nassis, G.P., Whitely, R., Marques, J.B., Kenneally, D. and Chalabi, H. 'Acute Responses of Soccer Match Play on Hip Strength and Flexibility Measures: Potential Measure of Injury Risk', *Journal of Sports Sciences*, 32, no. 13 (2014), pp. 1318–1324.

Plews, D.J., Laursen, P.B., Stanley, J., Kilding, A.E. and Buchheit, M. 'Training Adaptation and Heart Rate Variability in Elite Endurance Athletes: Opening the Door to Effective Monitoring', *Sports Medicine*, 43, no. 9 (2013), pp. 773–781.

Pyne, D.B. and Martin, D.T. 'Fatigue Insights from Individual and Team Sports', in Marino, F.E. (ed.) *Regulation of Fatigue in Exercise*, pp. 177–185 (Nova Science, 2011).

Raglin, J.S. and Morgan, W.P. 'Development of a Scale for Use in Monitoring Training-Induced Distress in Athletes', *International Journal of Sports Medicine*, 15, no. 2 (1994), pp. 84–88.

Saw, A.E., Main, L.C. and Gastin, P.B. 'Monitoring the Athlete Training Response: Subjective Self-Reported Measures Trump Commonly Used Objective Measures: A Systematic Review', *British Journal of Sports Medicine*, 50, no. 5 (2015), pp. 281–291.

Taylor, K., Chapman, D.W., Cronin, J.B., Newton, M.J. And Gill, N. 'Fatigue Monitoring in High Performance Sport: A Survey of Current Trends', *Journal of Australian Strength and Conditioning*, 20 (2012), pp. 12–23.

Thorpe, R.T., Atkinson, G., Drust, B. and Gregson, W. 'Monitoring Fatigue Status in Elite Team Sport Athletes: Implications for Practice', *International Journal of Sports Physiology and Performance*, 12, Suppl 2 (2017), pp. 227–234.

Thorpe, R.T., Strudwick, A.J., Buchheit, M., Atkinson, G., Drust, B. and Gregson, W. 'The Monitoring Fatigue Status During the In-Season Competitive Phase in Elite Soccer Players', *International Journal of Sports Physiology and Performance*, 10, no. 8 (2015), pp. 958–964.

Thorpe, R.T., Strudwick, A.J., Buchheit, M., Atkinson, G., Drust, B. and Gregson, W. 'The Tracking of Morning Fatigue Status Across In-Season Training Weeks in Elite Soccer Players', *International Journal of Sports Physiology and Performance*, 11, no. 7 (2016), pp. 947–952.

CHAPTER 8

NUTRITION FOR SOCCER

Prof. James P. Morton and Prof. Graeme L. Close

Football Exchange, Research Institute for Sport & Exercise Sciences, Liverpool John Moores University, UK

INTRODUCTION TO THE ROLE OF THE SPORTS NUTRITIONIST

Sports nutrition is one of the most rapidly growing sub-disciplines of sports science and its importance is becoming increasingly recognised in professional soccer. At present, many professional clubs (at least in the United Kingdom) employ individuals on a consultancy or part-time basis where they usually provide a nutrition service primarily focusing on first-team players, but also providing support to academy-level players. In the UK, there is currently no formal sports nutrition career path and practitioners in professional soccer tend to originate from dietetics or sports science backgrounds. The Sport and Exercise Nutrition Register (SENr) is now the governing body for accredited sports nutritionists within the UK and it is recommended that clubs source an accredited practitioner when providing a nutrition service to their players. Regardless of career entry, it is the authors' opinion that all sports nutritionists and dieticians (or performance nutritionists, as they are often called) should work towards a common objective – namely: 'To provide scientifically sound and individualised nutritional interventions which aim to maximise performance, training adaptations and recovery as well as ensuring athlete well-being and education at all times.'

To this end, the nutritionist should perform a variety of roles and have numerous responsibilities (see Table 1) and work closely with various members of the club's support staff, including fitness (and strength and conditioning) coaches, sports scientists, physiotherapists (and masseurs), club doctors, club chefs and, of course, the players and coaching staff themselves. Effective and clear communication between all of the aforementioned staff is essential to ensure a high-quality and, above all, consistent service provision.

TABLE 1 Typical responsibilities of the sports nutritionist working in professional football

General Responsibilities

- Devise a scientifically sound nutritional philosophy emphasising a 'food first' approach and communicate it to all key stakeholders.
- Devise, implement and monitor a scientifically sound, safe and legal sports supplement policy.
- Devise, implement and monitor training-day nutritional and hydration strategies relevant to both foods and supplements.
- Devise, implement and monitor match-day nutritional and hydration strategies (both home and away) relevant to both foods and supplements.
- Devise, implement and monitor nutritional and hydration strategies for travelling.
- Monitor body composition and develop and implement strategies to ensure ideal player values.

Individual Player Responsibilities

- Undertake one-to-one player consultations and devise and implement individualised nutrition, hydration and supplement strategies to maximise performance, training adaptations and recovery.
- Devise and implement individualised nutrition, hydration and supplement strategies to achieve ideal body composition.
- Devise and implement individualised nutrition, hydration and supplement strategies for injured players.
- Liaise with players' parents/guardians/housekeepers or partners (where appropriate) to ensure effective nutritional support.
- Enhance general health of the player.

Educational Responsibilities

- Develop group and individual strategies to ensure continual player and staff education on sports nutrition–related issues (using group presentations/booklets/webinars, etc).
- Develop and implement a shopping and cooking education programme for players, partners, houseparents, staff, etc where appropriate.
- Educate staff within the club and run internal continuing professional development (CPD) programmes.

Personal Responsibilities

- Gain appropriate academic and professional qualifications.
- Ensure continual critical evaluation of classic and contemporary sports nutrition topics and, if possible, engage in academic research.
- Understand the culture of the sport.
- Implement and adhere to own ethical code of conduct.
- Develop professional, practical and technical skills through ongoing CPD and reflective practice.
- Keep accurate and professional notes.

In this chapter, we provide an overview of the theoretical basis of sports nutrition in terms of the macronutrient (i.e. carbohydrates, protein and fats), micronutrient (i.e. vitamins and minerals) and fluid requirements for professional soccer players, as well as briefly outlining some evidence-based supplements that can enhance physical performance and training adaptations. This overview provides a basis for subsequent sections where we outline practical nutrition strategies to implement on both match days and training days. Finally, we close by offering some reflections on challenges within the working environment, and place particular emphasis on the cultural, political and financial constraints associated with working as a sports nutritionist in professional soccer.

ESSENTIALS OF SPORTS NUTRITION

Overview of Energy Metabolism and Storage

Prior to intervening with a nutritional strategy, we consider it vital that practitioners possess a sound understanding of exercise metabolism so that appropriate consideration has been given to both energy storage and substrate utilisation during subsequent exercise. Although a detailed understanding of such processes is beyond the scope of the present text (readers should consult MacLaren and Morton, 2011), it is pertinent to at least provide a brief overview here (see Table 2). It is noteworthy that although carbohydrates (CHO) supply the major energy source for moderate-to-high-intensity exercise such as > 70% VO_2max (van Loon

TABLE 2 Overview of energy storage within key tissues of the human body. Values are considered representative of a 75kg male.

Substrate	Amount (kg)	Energy (kcal)
Carbohydrate:		
Plasma Glucose	0.02	78
Liver Glycogen	0.1	388
Muscle Glycogen	0.4	1,550
Total	0.52	2,000
Fat:		
Plasma Free Fatty Acids	0.0004	4
Plasma Triglycerides	0.004	39
Adipose Tissue	10	83,333
Intramuscular Triglycerides	0.3	2,616
Total	10.3	86, 000

et al., 2001), the absolute amount of CHO that can be stored is typically limited to around 500 g and is effectively depleted by the end of two hours of exercise. In contrast, the supply of fat (often referred to as lipids) sources within the body is much more plentiful but lipids can only supply energy for low-to-moderate-intensity exercise (i.e. <60% VO_2max). For soccer match play, it is therefore crucial that players begin the game with maximal CHO stores so as to maintain high-intensity performance throughout the course of a 90-minute game. However, for training days (when typical training intensity is moderate and distance covered is <5km), consuming a daily diet that is high in CHO may lead to elevated body fat and as such, practitioners should pay particular attention to CHO intake when faced with the requirement to lose body fat.

Carbohydrates (CHO)

CHO and Soccer Performance

The importance of muscle glycogen for soccer match-play was recognised as early as the 1970s (Saltin, 1973), though is perhaps best illustrated by the data of Krustrup *et al.* (2006). Indeed, the latter authors observed that pre-game muscle glycogen was 449 ± 23 mmol.kg^{-1} dw and decreased to 225 ± 23 mmol.kg^{-1} dw immediately after the match. These observations highlight that certain players started the game with what would be considered sub-optimal muscle glycogen availability (likely due to inappropriate dietary practices in the days leading up to competition). Although post-game glycogen values in whole muscle suggested sufficient glycogen available to continue exercising, analysis of individual muscle fibre types revealed that 50% of fibres could be classified as *empty* or *almost empty*. This pattern of depletion or near depletion was evident in type 2 muscle fibres, those fibres responsible for sprinting and high-intensity activity. The glycogen depletion that was found in these muscle fibres is likely a contributing factor underpinning the progressive decline in the amount of high-intensity running and sprinting that occurs throughout the course of a game (Mohr *et al.*, 2003). These findings highlight the potential role of muscle glycogen depletion as a key factor contributing to nutritional-related soccer-specific fatigue.

Given the body's limited capacity to store muscle and liver glycogen, it is crucial that the daily diet contains adequate CHO to enable it to effectively prepare for and recover from repeated training sessions and games. Indeed, in terms of match-specific performance, commencing match-play with elevated muscle glycogen stores increases total distance covered (Saltin, 1973) as well as high-intensity activity (Balsom *et al.*, 1999). Furthermore, consuming additional CHO during exercise (in the form of sports drinks) improves intermittent exercise capacity (Foskett *et al.*, 2008;) and the ability to perform technical skills such as passing and shooting. The enhanced performance seen with feeding CHO during exercise may be due to such factors as the prevention of hypoglycemia, since blood glucose values <3.5 mmol.L^{-1} have been observed during soccer match-play (Krustrup *et al.*, 2006), as well as the maintenance of high CHO oxidation rates, muscle glycogen sparing, and direct effects on the central nervous system.

CHO and the Glycaemic Index

Although carbohydrates have been traditionally considered as simple or complex (on the basis of their chemical structure), it is more appropriate to categorise CHO-containing foods on the basis of their glycaemic index (GI). The GI is a numerical scale which ranks CHO foods on their ability to raise circulating glucose concentrations. Glucose or white bread is the reference food and is given a numerical value of 100. Foods categorised as high GI (HGI), moderate GI (MGI) and low GI (LGI) are typically considered as those with scores of >70, 55–70 and <55, respectively. The most recent published database on GI values was published in 2008 and readers should consult this database when formulating nutritional plans (Atkinson *et al.*, 2008). By way of example, porridge is considered a moderate GI food (58) whereas breakfast cereals such as cornflakes are considered a high GI food (72).

Considering the differential effects of HGI and LGI foods on influencing the pattern of fuel use during exercise, it is important to appreciate how the GI concept can be usefully applied to the soccer player. For example, consuming LGI foods in the hours before exercise may confer a metabolic advantage as they increase the use of fat as a fuel, help maintain more stable plasma glucose concentrations and spare the use of muscle glycogen during exercise. As such, these food sources are useful choices to include in the pre-match or pre-training meal. Conversely, because of their capacity to rapidly elevate blood glucose, HGI carbohydrates are superior to LGI in the post-exercise recovery period as they promote muscle glycogen re-synthesis (Burke *et al.*, 1993). Clearly, the type of CHO consumed can have a more influential role than the quantity of CHO per se. In the practical setting, it is therefore prudent to vary the GI of the available CHO foods according to the immediate goal.

CHO Requirements for Soccer Players

Given the importance of CHO for exercise performance, guidelines for CHO intake for athletes were traditionally representative of a *one-size-fits-all* approach where high daily CHO intakes (eg 8 g.kg^{-1}) were advised. However, it is now recognised that CHO intake (in terms of timing, quantity and type) should vary according to daily training demands and the fixture schedule of the particular week. Furthermore, there is growing evidence that completing and recovering from repeated training sessions with consistently high levels of CHO can actually reduce the magnitude of aerobic enzyme increases of skeletal muscle (see Bartlett *et al.*, 2014). Clearly, the role of CHO has moved beyond that of a simple energy store and sports scientists now recognise the importance of glycogen as a signalling molecule that regulates training adaptations rather than just providing energy. Using a periodised approach to CHO intakes, we present an overview of suggested CHO intake by a professional soccer player during a typical week in which consecutive games are interspersed by seven days (see Table 3).

TABLE 3 Suggested strategy to periodise CHO intake during the weekly schedule of a professional soccer player. HGI = high glycaemic index. L/MGI = low/moderate glycaemic index.

Specific Situation	Suggested CHO Intake	Additional Comments
Day before game	6–10g.kg^{-1}	HGI CHO foods and drinks to augment glycogen stores for competition on the following day.
Breakfast on match day	1–3g.kg^{-1}	L/MGI CHO foods and drinks consumed. For a 3 pm kick-off, this meal should be consumed between 8 and 9 am.
Pre-match meal	1–3g.kg^{-1}	L/MGI CHO foods and drinks consumed. This meal should be consumed 3–4h prior to kick-off. For midday kick-offs, this meal would effectively be breakfast.
During match	30–60g.h^{-1}	HGI CHO in the form of 6% CHO drinks or sports gels. Players could take advantages of breaks in play to consume small but regular CHO intake to avoid gut discomfort. Additionally, the half-time break should be used for re-fuelling according to the player's preferred approach. Players should practise fuelling strategies during training in order to develop individually suited strategies.
Post-match	1.2g.kg^{-1} h^{-1}	HGI CHO foods and drinks consumed for several hours post match so as to promote glycogen re-synthesis.
Day after game	6–10g.kg^{-1}	HGI CHO foods and drinks consumed so as to promote glycogen re-synthesis.
General training day	3–6 g.kg^{-1}	Combination of L/MGI and HGI CHO foods and drinks consumed to ensure adequate CHO availability for training and recovery purposes depending on the specific energy demands of the particular training day as well as individual training goals. For players wishing to lose body fat, 4g.kg^{-1} would prove beneficial (in conjunction with increased protein intake – eg 2g.kg^{-1}), and L/MGI choices should be emphasised.

Protein

Protein Turnover – Synthesis vs. Degradation

Protein is often considered essential for athletes involved in weight training to promote muscle growth. In reality, however, proteins have a variety of functions that extend far beyond the mere requirement to build muscle. Indeed, proteins not only give our muscles the basic structure they need to perform, they also provide the building blocks to make the many thousands of enzymes that are needed to provide energy from the breakdown of carbohydrates and fat. In the fasted state, the stress of intense exercise causes our muscle protein stores to actually break down (referred to as *protein degradation*), but that, of course, can be detrimental to training adaptation as it leads to negative protein balance. However, in the presence of adequate protein feeding, the *combined* effects of exercise and protein ingestion result in the formation of new proteins (referred to as *protein synthesis*), such that a positive protein balance occurs (Levenhagen *et al.*, 2002; Tipton *et al.*, 1999). It is these repeated changes in protein turnover (in favour of protein synthesis to yield a positive protein balance) in response to every exercise session which ultimately form the molecular basis of how our muscles adapt and recondition to the demands of heavy training (Coffey & Hawley, 2007). These transient changes in protein synthesis eventually lead to the up-regulation of specific proteins (e.g. myofibrillar and/or mitochondrial) such that we can better withstand the physical demands associated with the next exercise bout.

Essential and Non-Essential Amino Acids

In order for optimal training adaptation to occur (i.e. to facilitate protein synthesis), it is essential that protein be ingested as soon as possible before the exercise stimulus. Protein-rich foods and supplements contain the key *amino acids* that are used as the building blocks to make new proteins in our muscles. There are 20 amino acids that are required to form new proteins (see Table 4), 8 of which are described as essential (i.e. they can only be obtained from the diet) and 12 of which are known as non-essential (i.e. the body can make them). The amino acids of leucine, valine and isoleucine are collectively known as the branched amino acids (BCAAs) and are especially required to facilitate muscle protein synthesis. Of all the BCAAs, leucine has been identified as particularly important for muscle protein synthesis as it can also act in a signalling role, instructing the molecular machinery to initiate protein synthesis pathways (Drummond and Rasmussen, 2008).

Protein Requirements for Soccer Players

A scientific consensus on the optimal daily protein requirements for soccer players has not yet been reached. Nevertheless, based on the current daily recommendations for endurance- (1.2-1.4g.kg^{-1}) and strength- (1.7-2.0g.kg^{-1}) based athletes, it is

TABLE 4 Overview of essential and non-essential amino acids.

Essential	Non-Essential
Isoleucine	Alanine
Leucine	Arginine
Lysine	Asparagine
Methionine	Aspartate
Phenylalanine	Cysteine
Threonine	Glutamate
Tryptophan	Glutamine
Valine	Glycine
	Histidine
	Proline
	Serine
	Tyrosine

probably sufficient to advise as for the latter given that soccer players perform both aerobic and resistance training during a typical week. As such, a 75kg player would need between 135 and 150g per day. Additionally, players may need to exceed this intake during heavy training periods that are designed to reduce body fat but preserve muscle mass (Mettler *et al.*, 2010).

Perhaps more important than total daily protein intake, however, is the pattern of ingestion of protein intake throughout the day. In this regard, recent research suggests that an intake consisting of 20–30g portions consumed every three hours is superior to larger portions consumed less frequently (Moore *et al.*, 2012). In the context of exercise, it is also advised that protein is consumed within 60 minutes prior to exercise (Tipton *et al.*, 2001) and immediately post exercise (Moore *et al.*, 2005; Howarth *et al.*, 2009), where 20g is likely sufficient in both instances (Moore *et al.*, 2009). Practical examples of 20g of protein sources are shown in Table 5. Furthermore, because of their high leucine content and rapid digestion, whey protein supplements are superior to casein and soy-based supplements for activating muscle protein synthesis (Phillips *et al.*, 2009; Tang *et al.*, 2009). Liquid forms of protein have also been shown to induce a more rapid rise in plasma amino acids than solid foods and as such, may not only be a convenient form of provision but also a superior strategy in the post-exercise period (Burke *et al.*, 2012).

Fat

Fat has historically been viewed in a negative light and as a result, many soccer players believe they should eliminate all fats from their diet. However, although

TABLE 5 Practical strategies to obtain approximately 20g of protein.

Animal Sources
• 1 x chicken/turkey fillet
• 1 x fish fillet (e.g. 100g standard salmon fillet)
• 1 x small tin of tuna in brine
• 3 medium eggs
• 200g cottage cheese (⅔ small tub)
• 200g Greek yogurt
Non-Animal Sources
• 150g Quorn mince (75g is a typical portion)
• 400g red kidney beans (1 large tin)
• 300g chick peas (⅔ large tin)
• 100g almonds
Liquid Sources
• Whey/casein protein shake
• 1 x pint of milk

excessive intake of fat is a problem for general health and weight control (as is over-consumption of any macronutrient), too little dietary fat is also a problem for optimal health. The body needs an adequate intake of essential fatty acids (such as omega-3 and omega-6 fatty acids) as well as the fat-soluble vitamins A, D, E and K. It should also be noted that fats are required during exercise as an energy source, especially when carbohydrate stores become depleted, as happens when the exercise period is longer than 60–90 minutes, which can occur both in training and in the late stages or extra time periods of soccer games.

Types of Dietary Fat

Fats are generally classified as saturated or unsaturated, depending on their chemical structure. Unsaturated can then be further subdivided into mono-unsaturated (MUFA) and poly-unsaturated (PUFA). It is important to acknowledge that, despite some foods being described as saturated or unsaturated fats, all fats contain a mixture of fatty acids and they are simply classified according to whichever fat source they contain the most of. Traditionally, saturated fats have been classed as 'bad fats' and the advice has been to consume them in moderation, whereas unsaturated fats have been classed as 'good fats', although emerging evidence would suggest that this classification might also be an over-simplification.

A major problem with the notion of removing saturated fats from the diet is the issue of what to replace them with. Studies have clearly demonstrated that reducing saturated fat intake will be of no benefit, and can even cause more harm if the saturated fats are replaced with refined carbohydrates such as sugary drinks, mashed potatoes and white bread, for example (Hu, 2010). In contrast, replacing some saturated fats with unsaturated fats, including foods such as salmon, nuts, avocados and seeds, has been shown to improve health. Moreover, individual saturated fatty acids have differing effects on blood lipid levels depending upon their composition. For example, lauric acid (found in high concentrations in coconut oil) despite being a saturated fatty acid, actually decreases the total-to-HDL cholesterol ratio, due to an increase in HDL cholesterol. Therefore, with regard to saturated fats and health, it may be unwise to advise soccer players about good and bad fatty acids and better to simply give advice regarding the best types of food to eat (Astrup *et al.*, 2011). The simple message to the soccer player is to choose 'natural' fats and avoid processed ones, especially 'trans fats' (e.g. margarine, pastry, confectionary products), which should without question be eliminated from the player's diet. Trans fats increase LDL cholesterol and lower HDL and are therefore a major risk factor for cardiovascular disease (Mozaffarian *et al.*, 2006).

A further class of PUFA is that of the essential fatty acids (EFA). Just like essential amino acids, essential fatty acids cannot be made by the body and must be obtained through the diet to achieve optimal health. The EFA are classified as omega-3 (n-3) and omega-6 (n-6) fatty acids. Generally, athletes consume sufficient omega-6, but diets often lack omega-3. The main dietary source of omega-3 is oily fish (mackerel, salmon, tuna, herring, etc) and therefore soccer players should be encouraged to eat wild oily fish on a regular basis, or to consider taking a high-quality fish oil supplement.

Efficacy of High Fat Diets for Athletes

Given that it is well documented that performance in prolonged endurance events is limited by endogenous carbohydrate stores, many exercise scientists have become interested in strategies which could increase lipid oxidation and thereby spare glycogen utilisation. One such strategy is *fat adaptation*, a nutritional approach in which athletes consume a high-fat (and low-CHO) diet for a period of up to two weeks, during which they perform their normal intensity and volume of training, followed by 1–3 days of a high-CHO diet and a taper in training volume (Yeo *et al.*, 2011). Five days of fat adaptation increases the use of fat as a fuel and reduces the use of CHO during exercise undertaken on both day 6 and 7 despite CHO restoration on day 6. While the restoration of muscle glycogen is of obvious benefit, it is remarkable that fat utilisation is still enhanced under these conditions, considering that high glycogen availability usually enhances glycogen utilisation. The increased reliance on fat as a fuel induces a sparing of muscle glycogen utilisation but does not affect plasma glucose utilisation.

In terms of reducing CHO oxidation rates, available data suggest the enzyme pyruvate dehydrogenase (PDH) as a major control point. Indeed, fat adaptation reduces PDH activity at rest as well as during both submaximal and supramaximal exercise. The suitability of high-fat diets for soccer performance is therefore questionable as this lessening of PDH activity is problematic when there will be the need for periods of high-intensity exercise such as sprinting (and thus, for high CHO oxidation rates). For the outfield player, it is therefore likely that sustained periods of high-fat diets are not beneficial, though short periods of high-fat/low-CHO diets may be beneficial for weight loss.

Fluids

Dehydration and Soccer Performance

Given the intense energy demands of soccer match-play, metabolic heat production can increase rectal and muscle temperature to >39°C (Mohr et al., 2004). Sweat losses of 2 litres have been observed during both match-play and training (Maughan et al., 2007), even when the ambient temperature is <10°C. For a 75kg player, this sweat loss equates to >2% dehydration, and if appropriate fluid intake is not consumed, performance could be impaired. Dehydration of this magnitude reduces repeated-sprint capacity (Mohr et al., 2010) as well as soccer dribbling performance (McGregor et al., 1999). Potential mechanisms underpinning dehydration-induced decrements in physical and mental performance include increased core temperature, cardiovascular strain, muscle glycogen utilisation and impaired brain function (Gonzalez-Alonso, 2007).

From observations of players during training and match-play, sweat loss and dehydration appear to be lower in temperate environments (<10°C) than in warm ones (25–35°C) (Kurdak et al., 2010). To compensate for the warmer conditions, however, players voluntarily consume significantly more fluid during training. The development of fatigue during match-play is also more pronounced during high ambient temperatures (Mohr et al., 2010). In addition to fluid loss per se, sweat contains electrolytes such as sodium, chloride, potassium, calcium and magnesium. Loss of sodium is the most significant for athletes (given its role in promoting fluid retention), and soccer players can lose between 2 and 13g during training or match-play (Maughan et al., 2007; Kurdak et al., 2010). The importance of high salt losses is also underscored by observations linking them to exercise-related muscle cramps (Bergeron, 2003), and for this reason, it is important to identify players who are *salty sweaters* so as to develop individually tailored hydration strategies.

Practical Assessment of Hydration Status

In developing individualised hydration strategies, it is important to perform *regular* estimations of pre-exercise hydration status in order to identify those players who may need particular attention. Within the field setting of training grounds or on match days, assessments of pre-exercise urine osmolality and colour provide reasonably inexpensive and informative measures. Osmolality values <700 mOsmol.kg^{-1} are suggestive of euhydration (i.e. a balanced state), as is a urine colour that is pale yellow (note that excessive vitamin B intake can also promote urine colour changes). Urine indices of hydration are sensitive to changes in posture, food intake and body water content and for this reason, a urine sample passed upon waking is often advised as the criterion sample. However, values indicative of dehydration at this time (e.g. 7 am) may not mean the player is dehydrated upon commencing training at 10.30 am, assuming that appropriate fluid intake has been consumed upon waking and with breakfast. The same can be said for match day, in that samples suggestive of dehydration collected prior to the pre-match meal may not mean players are dehydrated at kick-off. Where practical, players should therefore be assessed at both time-points so as to initially identify players who are causes for concern and to verify that any subsequent hydration strategies implemented are effective, ensuring a state of euhydration prior to competition. Soccer players tested prior to an evening kick-off exhibited pre-game osmolality values >900 mOsmol.kg^{-1} in a study by Maughan *et al.* (2007), despite the fact that they would have had the morning and afternoon to hydrate. Such values are indicative of 2% dehydration and effectively mean that those players were commencing the game dehydrated, thereby running the risk of impaired physical and mental performance.

Fluid Requirements for Soccer Players

It is difficult to provide fixed prescriptive fluid recommendations for soccer players due to player differences in workload, heat acclimatisation and training status, and also because of match-to-match variations in ambient temperature. Nevertheless, in order to offset the negative effects of dehydration on performance, the American College of Sports Medicine advises fluid ingestion at a rate that limits body mass loss to <2% of pre-exercise values (Sawka *et al.*, 2007). More recent guidelines suggest that merely drinking to thirst is sufficient to offset negative effects of dehydration (Noakes, 2010). Regardless of the precise amount, players should not aim to drink to gain mass during exercise as this can lead to water intoxification, a condition known as hyponatremia (a serum sodium concentration <135 mmol.L^{-1}), which in extreme cases is fatal (Almond *et al.*, 2005).

It is recommended that 5–7ml.kg^{-1} of fluid is consumed at least 3–4 hours prior to the game (Sawka *et al.*, 2007). Additionally, if the individual does not produce urine or if the urine remains dark coloured, a further 3–5 ml.kg^{-1} could be consumed about 2 hours before kick-off. Drinking within this time schedule should allow for fluid absorption and enable urine output to return to normal levels. Consumption of sports drinks at this time, as opposed to water, is beneficial given that they contain not only electrolytes but also additional CHO. For training days, fluid intake should be consumed upon waking (before travelling to training) and with breakfast, which soccer players usually consume at the training ground.

In order to promote a drinking strategy which prevents weight losses >2%, players should routinely weigh themselves nude before and after exercise to ascertain whether their habitual drinking patterns are effective. Players should have individually labelled drinks bottles so that support staff can monitor habitual fluid intake and, furthermore, any urine passed during exercise should be accounted for when calculating sweat loss. Cold beverages (10°C as opposed to 37 or 50°C) are beneficial for minimising the rise in body temperature during exercise (Lee and Shirreffs, 2007), and sports drinks are considered superior to water due to their provision of electrolytes and CHO. Sports drinks should be in the range of 2–8% CHO (administered as glucose polymers) as both high CHO concentration and osmolality can delay gastric emptying (Vist and Maughan, 1995). It is important that players try out different fluid intake strategies during training in order to develop individually suited approaches which maximise gastric emptying, fluid absorption and CHO delivery, yet are suited to their taste and do not cause gastrointestinal discomfort during match-play. Finally, there is no need for aggressive re-hydration strategies post training (unless there is an afternoon training session and the ambient temperature is high) or after match-play as the normal schedule would allow for appropriate re-hydration within several hours of the period of exercise. Nevertheless, those players identified as salty sweaters may benefit from the addition of sodium to drinks or foods or from the provision of salty snacks so as to promote fluid retention.

Vitamins and Minerals

Micronutrients are compounds that are required in small quantities (<1g) to maintain normal physiological function. Although micronutrients do not directly supply energy for human performance, they play essential roles in many metabolic pathways. Broadly speaking, micronutrients can be divided into vitamins and minerals. While it is accepted that deficiency in most micronutrients could adversely affect health and performance, it is also known that some micronutrients taken in excess could be equally harmful to health.

Vitamins

Vitamins are organic compounds that are essential for normal physiological functioning of the body. Although vitamins are only required in small amounts, they must be consumed in the diet (with the exception of vitamin D, which is mainly obtained from sunlight). Vitamins are generally categorised as fat soluble (A, D, E and K,) and water soluble (e.g. the B vitamins and C). In the UK, dietary reference values (DRVs) have been established with regard to daily micronutrient intakes. The three DRV levels are:

- Recommended nutrient intake (RNI) – the amount of the nutrient needed to be adequate for 97.5% of the population.

- Estimated average requirement (EAR) – the average requirement for the population (i.e. adequate for 50% of the population).
- Lowest reference nutrient intake (LRNI) – the amount required to be adequate for only 2.5% of the population.

For some micronutrients there are insufficient data to set DRVs. Where possible, however, safe upper limits (SUL) are set for all micronutrients, and this represents a level that can be consumed daily over a lifetime without significant risk to human health. For some micronutrients, even an SUL cannot be established due to a lack of data. However, this does not mean that these are safe to take in excessive amounts as the effects are unknown and may still be toxic. It should also be stressed that some RNIs vary from country to country. Finally, all RNIs are designed to be adequate for nearly all healthy individuals and are not set for optimum sporting performance. There are currently no recommended daily intakes specifically designed for athletes, and therefore the best advice at present is to ensure that athletes are not deficient, or even only marginally sufficient, in any micronutrients.

Fat-Soluble Vitamins

The fat-soluble vitamins are predominantly stored in the liver and in adipose tissue for later delivery into other tissues (see Table 6). The major advantage of fat-soluble vitamins over water-soluble vitamins is that they can be stored. This means that if the daily intake is low, the body can turn to its stores for a supply, and when intake is high the stores can be replenished. The storage capacity of vitamins is particularly important when trying to establish whether an athlete's diet lacks any

TABLE 6 Major fat-soluble vitamins, their physiological role, typical food sources, the likelihood of deficiency in athletes and RNI for non-pregnant women

Vitamin	Physiological Role	Food Source	RNI (non-pregnant women)
A	Antioxidant. Eye function, cell growth and division	Oily fish, liver, egg yolk, milk, butter, carrots and apricots.	700mg (males) 600mg (females)
D	Facilitates the utilisation of calcium, cell differentiation, immunity, skin cell development and muscle function	Oily fish, eggs and fortified foods.	No DRVs because of sun-related synthesis 0.01 mg/day advised if confined indoors
E	Major fat-soluble anti-oxidant. Growth and development	Almonds, peanuts, shrimp, sunflower seeds, corn oil.	No DRVs, but 4mg for males and 3mg for females considered adequate.
K	Essential for blood clotting and formation of some proteins	Broccoli, cabbage, liver, cauliflower, spinach.	No DRVs, but 1mg/kg body weight considered adequate.

fat-soluble vitamins. Food diaries completed for 3–5 days are commonly used to assess a player's diet, although this may not be long enough to detect deficiencies in fat-soluble vitamins. A second important consideration regarding the fat-soluble vitamins is that because the body stores them, excessive intake can be a problem to health. Vitamin D is somewhat unique given that it is mainly synthesised from sunlight exposure. During the winter months in the UK, if sunscreen is applied or if players cover their skin, vitamin D cannot be synthesised and this may render them at risk of a deficiency. There is growing evidence that athletes should be tested for vitamin D deficiency, given its unique route of entry.

Water-Soluble Vitamins

Water-soluble vitamins include vitamin C and the B vitamins (see Table 7). Unlike fat-soluble vitamins, the body does not store these vitamins. Excessive intake of water-soluble vitamins results in tissue saturation and those surplus to requirements are excreted in the urine. High doses of water-soluble vitamins are unlikely to be toxic if taken in excess, although there are some exceptions to this, such as vitamin B_6, which can result in peripheral nerve damage (Cohen and Bendich, 1986). The inability to store water-soluble vitamins means that if daily intake is low, tissue levels are low, as there are no stores to draw upon. It is therefore important that the daily requirements of these vitamins are met each day to ensure adequate status. Many athletes have been advised that high doses of B vitamins (energy) and C (immune function) are beneficial to health and performance. While low B vitamins could be a problem, in reality this is rarely the case. Moreover, if a soccer player does indeed have low B vitamin status it would be more beneficial to treat the cause of this (usually inadequate calorie intake or poor food choices) rather than simply supplementing their diet with B vitamins. A typical commercially available supplement of vitamin C can contain 1,000mg, which is 25 times the recommended nutrient intake (RNI) for this vitamin (the RNI in the UK is 40mg). The reasons given for increasing vitamin C intake are to increase immune function and to boost antioxidant levels, although the evidence is questionable (Close et al., 2006; Gleeson, 2007) and probably reflects commercial sales hype rather than scientific fact.

Minerals

Minerals are essential inorganic compounds that are crucial for normal physiological function, as well as being important in many aspects of metabolism. Minerals are stored in the human body in various tissues. There are at least 20 different minerals that must be consumed in adequate amounts to allow normal physiological function. There is evidence that in athletes attempting to lose weight or undertaking vigorous training regimes, some mineral deficiencies can occur (Clarkson, 1991; Manore, 2002). The minerals that are most likely to be deficient during low-calorie diets are calcium, iron and zinc (see Table 8). The bioavailability (i.e. the ability to absorb it from the diet) is also lower for minerals (Turnlund,

TABLE 7 Major water-soluble vitamins, their physiological role, typical food sources, the likelihood of deficiency in athletes and RNI for non-pregnant women

Vitamin	Physiological Role	Good Food Sources	RNI (non-pregnant women)
C	Major water-soluble anti-oxidant. Iron absorption. Important in skin, gum and blood vessel health.	Asparagus, grapefruit, limes, oranges, lemons, broccoli, sprouts.	40mg
B$_1$ (Thiamin)	Important in carbohydrate and amino acid metabolism (energy).	Almonds, liver, peanuts, wholegrain bread and cereals, green peas.	1.4mg (males) 1.0mg (females)
B$_2$ (Riboflavin)	Important in carbohydrate metabolism (energy).	Asparagus, broccoli, spinach, bananas, mushrooms, tuna, dairy products.	No DRVs, but 1.1mg/day for females and 1.3mg/day for males prevents deficiencies.
B$_3$ (Niacin)	Important in carbohydrate, fat and amino acid metabolism (energy).	Liver, meat and fish, milk, eggs, avocados, tomatoes, legumes, carrots.	17mg (males) 13mg (females)
B$_5$ (Pantothenic Acid)	Needed to synthesise co-enzyme A and important in carbohydrate, fat and amino acid metabolism (energy).	Chicken, beef, potatoes, tomatoes, liver, egg yolk, broccoli, whole grains.	No DRVs, but 3mg considered safe.
B$_6$ (Pyridoxine)	Haemoglobin formation and important in carbohydrate metabolism (energy).	Bananas, fish, spinach, tuna, egg yolk, chicken.	1.4mg (males) 1.2mg (females)
B$_{12}$ (Cobalamine)	Haemoglobin formation and prevention of anaemia. Carbohydrate metabolism (energy). Plays role in nervous system.	Beef, dairy products, chicken, egg yolk, tuna.	1.5µg
Folic acid	Cell division and important in the production of some proteins	Meat, liver, green leafy vegetables, legumes, fruit.	200µg
Biotin	Important in carbohydrate, fat and amino acid metabolism (energy).	Egg yolk, liver, kidney, meat.	No DRVs, but 10–200µg considered safe and adequate.

TABLE 8 Common minerals that athletes may be deficient in, their physiological role and typical food sources

Mineral	Physiological Role	Food Source	RNI (non-pregnant women)
Calcium	Important in muscle contraction and transmission of nerve impulses. Involved in developing strong bones.	All dairy products, including milk, cheese and yogurt. Small fish with bones (e.g. sardines), beans and broccoli.	700mg/day
Iron	Important in the transport of oxygen	Red meat, liver, broccoli, spinach, fortified cereals, eggs, dried fruits, nuts and seeds.	8.7mg (males) 6.7mg (females)
Magnesium	Muscle contraction and transmission of nerve impulses.	Meats and dairy, vegetables and potatoes, bread and cereals, nuts (brazil nuts, almonds and cashews), mushrooms.	300mg (males) 270mg (females)
Zinc	Assists immune function and is an antioxidant. Helps protein digestion, and assists in some energy pathways.	Liver, kidney, red meat, seafood, poultry, milk, whole grains, leafy and root vegetables.	5.5–9.5mg (males) 4–7mg (females)

1991) than for vitamins and as such, it can sometimes be harder to ensure adequate mineral status. However, most research has suggested that, providing athletes are not eliminating food groups, are eating a well-balanced diet and are consuming adequate calories in relation to their energy expenditure, there should be no major risk of inadequate mineral intake. Unlike vitamins, the margin of safety between the RNI and toxicity is less for minerals, so particular care should be taken when using mineral supplements.

Assessment of Micronutrient Deficiencies
Factors that could contribute to micronutrient deficiencies include:

- Eliminating food groups from diet either due to food dislikes or allergies or for moral reasons.

- Utilising a low-calorie diet when attempting to reduce body fat.
- Utilising a very low-fat diet, which could affect the fat-soluble vitamins.
- A lack of variety in the diet.

In practice, unless the soccer player fits into one of the scenarios above, it is highly unlikely that he or she will be deficient in any micronutrients. The first course of action if an athlete (or coach) is concerned about the micronutrient intake is to complete a detailed food diary and get this analysed by a suitably qualified individual (a registered dietician or a registered sports nutrition consultant). If there may be cause for concern following dietary analysis, subsequent blood analysis may be required. Caution should be taken if using companies that claim to measure micronutrient deficiencies for athletes and then promote the use of their own mega-dose expensive supplements to correct these 'deficiencies', since the validity and reliability of their tests is highly questionable.

Supplements

General Function and Usage of Supplements in Athletes

The sports supplement industry is a multi-billion-pound business that is one of the most rapidly growing and dynamic components of the sports nutrition profession. At present, there are thousands of commercially available supplements that all purport to improve muscle strength, power, speed and endurance as well as to prevent (and promote recovery from) illness and injury. Given that all of the aforementioned indices of physical fitness are relevant to the professional footballer, it is unsurprising that elite players, coaches and sports science staff are often overwhelmed when faced with the challenge of developing a practical and evidence-based supplement strategy that is ergogenic (i.e. that enhances physical performance) during football match-play and in training. Additionally, many of the sports supplements commonly used by professional players are also commercially driven (as opposed to evidence based) and their use is based on lucrative sponsorship deals to the individual player, club and/or governing body of the professional league in question. Nevertheless, it is clear that supplements should be consumed alongside a daily diet that is already considered sufficient for both macro- and micronutrient content and should be administered with the strategic aim of improving match-day performance, promoting training adaptations and maximising recovery.

Developing a Safe and Legal Supplement Strategy

Once the soccer player's general diet is considered well-balanced in meeting macro- and micronutrient requirements, there may be some instances where a targeted supplement plan *may* be of use, but this should only be prescribed by qualified individuals who are up to date with the current soccer-specific doping regulations. It is crucial that if the soccer player does use supplements, they should only use ones that have been independently drug tested. A commonly used laboratory that performs such testing is the HFL lab, and on its website (www.hfl.co.uk) you can find a list of companies that routinely test their products. Soccer players must also be aware that although a product has been tested, this does not guarantee that the supplement is drug free, and ultimately it has to be the soccer player's own decision if they do decide to take supplements.

In the authors' own practice, the following questions are always asked to help decide if a supplement will be advised:

1. Is there a need for the supplement? (i.e. can't you get the optimum amount in a normal diet?)
2. Is there a clear scientific rationale for the use of the supplement?
3. Are there any health risks associated with the use of the supplement?
4. Does the supplement contain any prohibited substances?
5. Is there an independently tested product available?

If the answer to all five of these questions is yes, then there may be grounds to consider the use of such a supplement.

Developing a Practical Supplement Strategy

Due to space constraints, it is not possible to provide a thorough review of those supplements that it may be practical for players to take in order to improve match-play performance and training adaptations. However, a number of potential practical supplement strategies are presented below, and the reader is directed to Morton (2014) for further reading. It should be noted that these recommendations are not intended to be immediately applicable or relevant to every player. Indeed, supplements should not be administered as a one-size-fits-all approach, as players are training for different goals (e.g. some for body composition issues, others for injury rehabilitation, etc) and have different training loads. Rather, these strategies could be adopted as initial starting points with which to experiment during non-competitive situations so as to fine-tune individual approaches to supplementation for competition and important phases of training.

- Ingestion of caffeine 30–60 minutes prior to match-play can improve cognitive, physical and technical elements of performance. Ergogenic effects are achieved with 2–6mg/kg body mass in either capsule, fluid or gel format (Burke *et al.*, 2013). Pre-training ingestion of caffeine can be readily achieved by drinking coffee with the breakfast meal.
- Creatine can enhance repeated-sprint performance during match-play, promote post-exercise muscle glycogen re-synthesis and also augment training-induced gains in lean mass, strength and power. To achieve ergogenic effects, play-ers can undertake a five-day loading dose (4 x 5g per day) followed by a daily

maintenance dose (eg 3–5g). Alternatively, a more practical strategy may be to consume 3g daily, though it is noteworthy that longer periods are required (e.g. 30 days) to augment muscle creatine stores (Hultman *et al.*, 1996).

- Supplementation with β-alanine (1.6–6.4g per day) augments muscle carnosine stores within several weeks, and these can subsequently buffer the metabolic acidosis associated with high-intensity exercise, thereby improving repeated-sprint performance. To minimise symptoms of paraesthesia (i.e. tingling of the skin) associated with supplementation, players should consume 'slow-release' formulas in even doses spread throughout the day (Stellingwerff *et al.*, 2012).

- Pre-match nitrate supplementation (especially using an intense loading dose of 30mmol in 36 hours) may improve repeated-sprint performance (Wylie *et al.*, 2013). This may be achieved by consuming concentrated beetroot juice the day before match day as well as in the hours before the game.

- Post-match and post-training ingestion of 20–30g of whey protein can induce maximal rates of muscle protein synthesis (MPS), thereby promoting recovery and training adaptation, respectively (Moore *et al.*, 2009). To promote overnight recovery, players may consume 30–40g of casein protein prior to sleeping (Res *et al.*, 2012).

- Daily consumption of 5,000 IU vitamin D during the winter months can restore any seasonal decline in vitamin D to levels deemed to be sufficient (Close *et al.*, 2012), thus promoting immune and bone function and potentially improving training adaptations through modulation of MPS (Owens *et al.*, 2014).

NUTRITION FOR MATCH DAY

Overview of Nutritional-Related Causes of Fatigue

Fatigue in soccer match-play is commonly observed as *progressive* fatigue that manifests itself as a decline in both physical performance (e.g. progressive reduction in sprints) and technical performance (e.g. reduced quality of technical skills) during the course of the game (Mohr *et al.*, 2003). Players may also experience *temporary* fatigue, defined as a marked reduction in physical performance in the minutes following a particularly physically demanding period of the game (Mohr *et al.*, 2003). In addition to their relation to physical fitness, there is strong evidence supporting the theory that both forms of fatigue may have nutritional causes. In the case of progressive fatigue, obvious candidates are reduced availability of carbohydrate (i.e. muscle glycogen and circulating glucose) and dehydration. Temporary fatigue is likely mediated by metabolic disturbances within the muscle caused by the prior period of high-intensity exercise (e.g. acidosis, extra-cellular accumulation of potassium, phosphocreatine (PCr) depletion), and hence a variety of ergogenic aids, such as creatine, β-alanine (both of which require weeks of supplementation to be effective) and caffeine (effective within 60 minutes of consumption) may help maintain physical performance in this instance.

Nutrition on the Day(s) Before Match Day

Given the role of muscle glycogen in fuelling moderate- and high-intensity exercise, the major goal of nutritional interventions on the days prior to the game should be to maximise pre-game muscle and liver glycogen stores (i.e. CHO loading). Trained athletes can achieve high glycogen stores with as little as 24–36 hours of a CHO-rich diet (Bussau et al., 2002), providing that training demands are of low intensity (fortunately, managers and coaches usually schedule light training sessions on the day prior to match day). To fully achieve high glycogen storage within this time-scale, players should ensure increased portion sizes and increased frequency of HGI foods and drinks on the day prior to match day, as HGI carbohydrates are superior to LGI-based sources (Burke et al., 1993). An example of a CHO loading strategy is shown in Table 9.

TABLE 9 Practical example of a CHO loading strategy containing approximately 8g.kg^{-1} CHO for a 75kg player. Note that for illustrative purposes, only CHO contents are shown, though in practice, regular protein feeds with main meals and snacks would also be provided.

Food and Drink Schedule	Time	Description	Approximate CHO Content(g)
Breakfast	8:00	Large bowl of HGI cereal (50g) with 200ml semi-skimmed milk	50
		Two slices of white toast with jam	45
		Large glass of orange juice (400ml)	40
Mid-morning snack	10:30–11:00	One banana	20
		500ml sports drink	35
		Energy bar	40
Lunch	13:00–13:30	Ham salad (lettuce, tomato) on white baguette	100
		Creamed rice pudding	35
		500ml sports drink	35
Mid-afternoon snack	15:00	500ml chocolate milk	50
		Energy bar	40
Dinner	17:30–18:00	Large portion of pasta (200g)	60
		Tomato-based sauce (125g)	15
		500 ml sports drink	35
Evening snack	21:00	Large bowl of HGI cereal (50g) with 200ml semi-skimmed milk	50
		TOTAL	650

Pre-Match Meal

Soccer players commonly make the mistake of believing that the pre-match meal is the most important meal for match-day performance, and this can often lead to poor practices – for example, consuming the wrong quantity and type of foods, and doing so too close to kick-off. Assuming that players have correctly CHO loaded in the 24–36 hours prior to match day, the purpose of the pre-match meal is to simply *top up* CHO availability, and players should therefore be careful not to overeat at this time. The pre-match meal is of course also dependent on the location and timing of the match. For example, for a regular 3 pm Saturday kick-off, nutritional preparation on match day would consist of a light breakfast, with the main pre-match meal consumed at around 11.30 am. For an evening kick-off between 7.45 and 8 pm, match-day nutrition would be extended and the pre-match meal should be consumed at around 4.30 pm. Finally, at the opposite end of the spectrum is the lunchtime kick-off (usually between noon and 1 pm), and in this situation, match-day nutrition would be limited, with breakfast effectively serving as the pre-match meal.

Regardless of the timing of the game, it is always advised that the pre-match meal should be reasonably high in both CHO (approximately 2g.kg^{-1}) and protein (e.g. 20–30 g) content and consumed within 2.5–3 hours prior to kick-off so as to allow sufficient time for digestion and to avoid gastrointestinal problems and feelings of gut fullness. It is important that the stomach be reasonably empty at the time of commencing the match so that digestion and absorption of food do not compete with the exercising muscles for blood supply. Furthermore, consumption of high-fibre (e.g. vegetables) and high-fat foods (even those associated with protein sources, such as red meat and cheese) should be avoided given that they slow down the rate of gastric emptying.

In an attempt to maintain stable blood glucose concentrations during match-play, players may wish to emphasise LGI and MGI carbohydrates as opposed to HGI foods (Wee *et al.*, 2005) though the GI effects during high-intensity intermittent exercise (Little *et al.*, 2009; Little *et al.*, 2010) are less pronounced than they are during continuous exercise. Furthermore, consuming CHO during match-play (as players are advised to do) may negate any potential metabolic advantages of consuming LGI foods prior to exercise (Burke *et al.*, 1998). Nevertheless, players' access to energy intake during games is usually limited to unscheduled breaks (e.g. breaks in play due to injuries) and half-time. For this reason, it is probably more beneficial to emphasise LGI and MGI CHO choices at pre-match meals especially in situations where players may not have CHO loaded appropriately and thus glycogen availability may not be optimal. Many players have customary pre-match meals and are often superstitious about their pre-game preparations. For such individuals, it may be beneficial to let them consume their *preferred* meal (regardless of whether it is LGI or HGI), though the basic principles of ensuring adequate CHO and protein provision and low fat and fibre should

TABLE 10 Practical examples of pre-match meals containing approximately 2g.kg^{-1} CHO for a 75kg player (i.e. 150g)

Option 1

Cereal with semi-skimmed milk + 500ml sports drink + 2 slices of wholemeal toast with jam + 1 banana

Option 2

Basmati rice + salmon fillet + 500ml sports drink + rice pudding

Option 3

Griddled chicken strips with fettuccini and a low-fat tomato-based sauce + mixed fruit and yogurt + 500ml sports drink

Option 4

Homemade chicken burgers on a large wholegrain roll + potato wedges and side salad + 500ml sports drink

always remain. Finally, players should ensure they begin the game in a euhydrated state, and consumption of approximately 500ml of an electrolyte-based drink upon waking and with the pre-match meal is advised. Examples of pre-match meals are shown in Table 10.

Nutrition 60 Minutes Before Kick-Off

In the 30–60 minutes before the game, some players also choose to consume additional carbohydrate in the form of sports drinks, gels or bars. In such situations, some caution is advised for those individuals who may experience rebound hypoglycemia, a condition in which insulin and contraction-induced increases in glucose uptake induce a rapid fall in blood glucose within minutes of the game, causing the player to become light-headed and nauseous (Jeukendrup and Killer, 2010). In individuals who are susceptible to rebound hypoglycemia, the response can be induced with as little as 20g of CHO, equivalent to approximately 350ml of a 6% sports drink. Pre-exercise feeding within this period should therefore be practised initially in training sessions in order to carefully monitor for any associated side effects.

In addition to CHO feeding, this period would also be an appropriate one in which to include any ergogenic aids to increase performance or perhaps to increase recovery. In this regard, 2–4 mg.kg^{-1} of caffeine (in either capsule, liquid or gel format) may benefit players in terms of increased mental and physical performance, and the ingestion of 6–8g essential amino acids has been shown to increase post-exercise muscle protein synthesis (Tipton *et al.*, 2001), thereby having beneficial implications for post-match recovery (Jackman *et al.*, 2010). At this stage, any increases in urine production (as a result of earlier hydration strategies) should normalise and players should ensure they begin the game in a voided state.

In-Game and Half-Time Nutrition

During the game itself, nutritional aims are to maintain appropriate levels of energy availability and to avoid excessive dehydration such that performance decrements do not occur. In terms of the dose of CHO that can be used from feeding CHO during exercise, maximal utilisation rates from glucose polymers are approximately 1g.min^{-1} (Jeukendrup, 2010), and players are therefore advised to consume 30–60g per hour. Such doses are equivalent to 500–1000ml of conventional 6% sports drinks, though ingestion of such volumes of fluid are unlikely given that opportunities for fuelling are limited to natural breaks in play. Players should therefore take advantage of the half-time period and those unscheduled breaks in play to obtain necessary fluid and energy intake.

Assuming players have fuelled appropriately the day before and at the pre-match meal, there is likely to be no need for additional CHO within the first half period. Rather, fuelling strategies should likely predominate in the half-time period and at regular periods in the second half. Rates of CHO oxidation are largely similar regardless of whether CHO is provided in fluid or gel form or as sports bars (Pfeiffer *et al.*, 2010a, 2010b), and thus players should be provided with their preferred source to encourage appropriate energy intake. The provision of gels or sports bars is particularly useful for those players who prefer water for hydration as opposed to sports drinks, as well as for those who prefer not to drink much fluid at all. In relation to fluid intake itself, it is difficult to prescribe definitive guidelines owing to variations in, for example, ambient temperature, fitness levels, acclimation status and intensity of the game. The American College of Sports Medicine currently advises a drinking strategy which limits fluid loss to <2% of body mass, though more recent guidelines advise that drinking to thirst is sufficient (Noakes, 2010).

Post-Match Nutrition

The goal of post-match nutrition is to replenish both muscle and liver glycogen stores as well as to promote protein synthesis so as to facilitate remodelling and repair of muscle tissue. Additionally, there is the obvious requirement of rehydration and the need to offset the effects of exercise-induced suppression of immune function. In relation to muscle glycogen synthesis, the general consensus is that consuming 1.2g.kg^{-1}.h^{-1} of HGI carbohydrates for 3–4 hours is optimal to facilitate short-term glycogen re-synthesis (Beelen *et al.*, 2010). For a 75kg player, this would equate to repeated intakes of 90g of CHO. Importantly, post-match feeding should begin immediately (i.e. in the changing room), as this is when the muscle is most receptive to glucose uptake and the enzymes responsible for

TABLE 11 Practical examples of post-match recovery strategies that could be available in the changing room immediately after games to help facilitate muscle glycogen re-synthesis and protein synthesis

Changing Room Options (i.e. consume between 4.45 and 5.15 pm for a 3 pm game)
Recovery shake (both CHO and protein based)
Potato wedges and chicken skewers
Chicken panini and sports drink
Sushi and sports drink
Chicken and paella/pasta pots
Rice pudding and protein shake
Chicken goujons and sports drink
Fruit-based protein smoothies
Muffins and protein shake

glycogen synthesis are most active (Ivy *et al.*, 1988). Whether the CHO is provided in solid or in liquid form is immaterial and should be left to the player's preference. In practice, therefore, a selection of high-CHO snacks and drinks should be readily available in the changing room post game (see Table 11). Additionally, these meals should contain moderate protein intake so as to support post-exercise protein synthesis.

It is noteworthy that the addition of creatine to CHO feeding in the days after glycogen-depleting exercise has been shown to augment glycogen storage levels (Robinson *et al.*, 1999). This approach to post-game feeding may be particularly applicable during times of intense fixture schedules. Finally, in situations where muscle damage has occurred due to lengthening contractions, muscle glycogen re-synthesis can be impaired even when there is high CHO intake (Costill *et al.*, 1990). For those players who experience regular symptoms of muscle damage post game, consuming additional macronutrients (e.g. protein) and other supplements (e.g. antioxidants and HMB) in an attempt to reduce the severity of muscle damage may prove beneficial. In addition to muscle glycogen re-synthesis, it is important to incorporate strategies which promote the restoration of liver glycogen. For this purpose, fructose is more effective than glucose (Decombaz *et al.*, 2011), and thus the provision of fructose-rich foods (e.g. fresh fruit/juice/smoothies etc) in the changing room or the addition of fructose to recovery drinks is recommended.

Day After Match Nutrition

In addition to nutrition in the hours after the game, it is important that appropriate feeding strategies are adhered to in the days after the game in order to facilitate replenishment of energy stores, promote repair and facilitate recovery from any muscle damage. To facilitate this process, it is advisable to consume a similar CHO-loading diet to the one that was consumed on the day prior to the game, as well as consuming regular protein feeds every three hours. Additional supplemental strategies to reduce muscle damage (e.g. BCAAs, antioxidants, HMB) and maintain immune function (e.g. vitamin C, zinc, glutamine, probiotics, colostrum) may also be useful. Finally, it is worth noting that in the case where successive games have only a matter of days between them (such as a domestic league game at the weekend followed by a mid-week European fixture), three days of a high-CHO diet will likely be required in an attempt to fully replenish muscle glycogen stores (Gunnarsson *et al.*, 2013).

NUTRITION FOR TRAINING

Overview of Training Adaptations, Goals and Structure

While the role of nutrition in modifying performance is well documented, its role in determining the quality and extent of adaptations to training is often less appreciated by players and coaching and backroom staff. Furthermore, certain players may have specific training goals, such as the requirement to reduce body-fat levels or to increase lean muscle mass, and in such cases the nutritional strategy should be aligned accordingly. It is therefore difficult in this present text to provide definitive guidelines in terms of quantity and type of food to be consumed throughout the training day. Rather, in the text to follow, we have chosen to provide some *general* recommendations for training-day nutrition and to offer further key principles for specific situations. Furthermore, the following discussion is based on the typical training structure of a professional football club within the English Premier League, where training typically commences at 10.30 am and consists of a 60–90min field-based session that may or may not be followed by a 30–45min gym-based session.

Breakfast

It is common practice for players to consume breakfast at the club training ground upon arrival (e.g. 9–9.30 am). Given the requirement for adequate digestion prior to training, it is advisable that breakfast is not consumed any later than this. Furthermore, because of the capacity for LGI and MGI carbohydrates to promote lipid oxidation and maintain stable plasma glucose concentrations and spare muscle glycogen levels, it is advisable to emphasise these choices as opposed to HGI-based sources. Contrary to popular belief, the typical training intensity of professional soccer players is not overly high (players cover an average of 5km per day), and therefore there is no need for excessive CHO intake at this time (especially considering the requirement to maintain low body-fat levels). In this

TABLE 12 Summary of good and poor/moderate food choices to consume at breakfast

Good Choices	Poor/moderate choices (note that these HGI foods could be considered suitable on CHO-loading days)
• Porridge, natural muesli, All-Bran, Alpen, Fruit & Fibre (with milk)	• Frosties/Rice Krispies/Cornflakes/CocoPops/ Frosted Wheats/Sugar Puffs/Cheerios
• Poached, scrambled or boiled eggs	• High-sugar cereal bars
• Grilled fish/smoked salmon/mackerel/ ham	• White toast/bread/baguettes
• Wholegrain toast	• Croissants
• Greek yogurt and fresh fruit	• Pancakes
• Water/electrolyte drink, tea, coffee, fruit juice/smoothies	• Crumpets

regard, CHO intakes of <100g are more than sufficient to complete typical training workloads.

Although players are typically good at consuming adequate CHO at breakfast, it is a common mistake to not consume sufficient protein at this time. This is particularly important considering that protein was probably last consumed in the evening meal the day before. If players don't consume adequate protein at breakfast, protein breakdown during training will be accelerated, thus inducing negative protein balance and thereby creating metabolic conditions unfavourable to training adaptation. An intake of approximately 20g of high-quality protein is therefore essential prior to training. A summary of suitable foods to consume at breakfast is given in Table 12.

In-Training Nutrition

As alluded to earlier in relation to the typical training demands and duration of a pitch-based session, there is likely no requirement for consuming conventional CHO-based sports drinks during the session itself. Furthermore, there is growing evidence that CHO intake during exercise (when the intensity of exercise does not warrant it) can actually lessen the magnitude of the skeletal muscle adaptations (Bartlett *et al.*, 2014) that are the actual goal of the training session. Rather, for normal training days when training intensity and duration is not high, it is likely more beneficial to maintain adequate hydration through the provision of electrolyte-containing drinks with a CHO content <2%. In the typical ambient temperatures of the UK, it is likely that drinking to thirst is sufficient in this instance, though simple hydration-monitoring strategies would be useful to monitor any players with particularly high sweat rates. Scheduling of regular fluid breaks during training (at 15–20min intervals) will likely prevent any excessive dehydration occurring.

Upon completion of pitch-based training, it is useful to also consume a further 20g of protein to facilitate a positive protein balance and thus promote training adaptation. For convenience and also speed of digestion, a liquid-based protein such as a ready-made milk-based or whey protein supplement is a logical choice. The provision of protein at this time is particularly important as lunch may be delayed by another 60 minutes or so due to other daily activities (e.g. massages, pool-based recovery sessions, physiotherapy treatment and other player appointments). Furthermore, if the pitch-based session is to be followed by a gym-based resistance training session, then there is an even greater requirement for protein intake at this time. Finally, if the training goal of the player in question is to increase lean muscle mass, this intake of protein should be accompanied by 40–60g of HGI carbohydrates (most likely in the form of a CHO-and-protein-based recovery drink) so as to provide further energy intake to facilitate muscle growth. Upon completion of both field- and gym-based training sessions, appropriate nutrition can likely be provided soon after by whole foods at lunch unless, of course, immediate access to lunch is delayed.

Lunch

In contrast to breakfast, there is usually a much greater variety of food choices available to players at lunch. From a practical perspective, it is of course important to ensure provision of key macro- and micronutrients, but also high-quality and varied food choices (to suit both the taste and cultural preferences of all the players) so as to encourage player uptake (an overview of suitable foods to consume at lunch is given in Table 13). To this end, the nutritionist must liaise closely with the club chef to initially ensure that all menu plans and actual food provision are of sufficient quality. For practical reasons (e.g. cost, time efficiency, ease of administration), lunch is usually served as a buffet with an array of food choices for starters, main meals and desserts. Due to the buffet-style service, careful attention should be given to educating players on portion size to prevent under- and overeating. This point is especially important for those players with training goals of increasing muscle mass or losing body fat, respectively. The development of visually attractive food labels to accompany each dish (although a somewhat time-consuming process) may be useful for educational purposes in this regard. Furthermore, it is useful to advise catering and food service staff of those players with special dietary goals so that they can help ensure that specific interventions are put in place. To encourage player uptake of the club's food provision, it is important that menu plans are appropriately recycled so that plenty of variety is apparent on a daily and weekly basis. Additionally, creating the right environment in terms of dining-room layout, lighting, ambience,

TABLE 13 Summary of good and poor/moderate food choices to consume at lunch

Good Choices	Poor/Moderate Choices (note that some of these HGI CHOs such as white breads could be considered suitable on CHO-loading days)
• Soups (ideally home-made)	• Pastry products
• Any fresh meats/poultry (not processed meats)	• Margarine
• Fish	• White bread, rolls, baguettes etc
• Salads	• White pasta (and creamy-based sauces)
• Vegetables	• Fizzy drinks
• Basmati rice	• Fried food
• Quinoa	• Cakes
• Sweet potato	• Biscuits
• Baked potato	• Ice cream
• Tortilla wraps	
• Greek yogurt and fresh fruit	
• Water/electrolyte drink, tea, coffee, fruit juice/smoothies	

relationships with peers and, of course, food presentation may seem trivial, but in reality these are major factors in influencing player perception of the quality of service provided.

Snacks

The provision of breakfast and lunch within the training ground is advantageous as sports science staff can carefully monitor (and possibly even control) the type, timing and quantity of nutrient intake in accordance with the specific training and performance goals. However, it is the players' nutrient intake throughout the remainder of the day (i.e. when they are away from the football club) that often consists of poor choices. This is perhaps best illustrated by choices of snacks that, if players are not educated appropriately, may largely consist of foodstuffs that are high in sugar and saturated fat (e.g. crisps, chocolate, fizzy drinks, pastries). Rather, snack choices for generic training days should typically be low-to-moderate GI based as well containing a moderate amount of protein and being low in saturated fat. In contrast, HGI-based snack choices may be more appropriate on the day(s) before and after games to facilitate muscle glycogen loading and re-synthesis respectively. A summary of suitable snack choices for these purposes is given in Table 14.

TABLE 14 Suitable snack choices for generic training days and CHO-loading/recovery days

Generic Training Days (note that these snacks generally emphasise high protein and moderate CHO and fat)	CHO-loading days (note that these snacks generally emphasise HGI CHO to promote CHO loading)
• Fresh fruit and Greek yogurt	• Energy bars/muesli bars/flapjacks
• Sushi	• Banana muffin
• Porridge and protein shake	• Smoothies
• Tuna salad with basmati rice	• Cereals
• Oat-based cereal bar and glass of milk	• Rice pudding
• Mixed nuts and seeds	• Paninis/sandwiches/bagels
• Biltong/jerky and oatcakes	• Bruschetta
• Olives, Parma ham, feta cheese and Ryvita	• Rice cakes
• Omelettes	• Pasta/paella pots
• Chicken/lamb skewers	• Milkshakes
• Avocado, prawns and couscous	
• Quinoa and salmon	

Dinner

Nutritional requirements for dinner are usually the same as for the lunch meal, though of course players are likely to consume this meal at home or in a restaurant. In this regard, it is useful to educate players on healthy 'eating out' choices as well as on basic cooking skills (especially young players) or to liaise with those responsible for cooking evening meals (e.g. parents/wives/girlfriends/partners/personal chefs) in order to ensure they are of sufficient quality and quantity. Indeed, this meal may be particularly challenging for the nutritionist as dinner is traditionally considered to be the largest meal of the day and, as such, there may be a tendency for players to overeat at this time. In addition to lacking portion-size control, players may also make the mistake of consuming the evening meal late at night (i.e. after 9 pm), which, if done regularly, may lead to an increase in body fat. Such an issue is particularly commonplace for foreign players whose culture involves late-night meal times that are often considered more of an occasion. To prevent issues arising with excessive body fat, it is beneficial to consume dinner earlier in the evening (certainly before 7 pm), and this meal should also contain less carbohydrate than that consumed at lunch (and should definitely emphasise LGI and MGI choices). In addition, dessert provision should be discouraged with this meal.

Bed-Time Nutrition

Given that sleep is effectively a period of prolonged fasting (i.e. usually 6–10 hours) that can induce protein breakdown, there is also a requirement to ingest a suitable quantity and type of protein prior to bed. In this regard, recent research demonstrates that ingestion of 40g of casein protein prior to sleep improves overnight protein balance compared with sleeping in a fasted state (Res *et al.*, 2012). In practice, ingestion of around 30–40g of a casein-based protein supplement (as casein is a slowly digested protein) would therefore be beneficial and is more appropriate than the traditional advice of drinking the rapidly digested whey-based protein. The requirement for protein at this time is particularly important for those players who wish to gain muscle mass and also for those who wish to maintain muscle mass when attempting to lose body fat.

CHALLENGES IN THE WORKING ENVIRONMENT

Translating the relevant scientific information into a practical performance nutrition programme should, in principle, be a relatively straightforward process. In practice, however, there are many cultural, organisational, financial and political factors that occur in the day-to-day running of a professional football club which greatly affect the extent and quality of the service provided. Indeed, unlike the controlled laboratory environment, the football world is dynamic, unpredictable and full of emotion. Such issues are further complicated by the magnitude of the task, considering that the sports nutritionist is typically only employed on a consultancy basis (e.g. one day per week) but is often required to provide a high-quality service to in excess of 100 players (i.e. from first-team to schoolboy level). Of all the sub-disciplines of sports science, nutrition is undoubtedly one of the key areas with genuine potential to influence performance and training adaptation, yet there remain many barriers to the uptake of good practice.

Implementation of a performance nutrition programme is perhaps initially complicated by the requirement to develop sound working relationships and communication processes with the many key individuals who make up the modern-day multidisciplinary sports science team. Given that all of us eat food daily as well as being surrounded by a multitude of contemporary sources of nutritional information (e.g. television, newspapers, magazines, social media) often informing us of the latest super-food or dietary craze, it is human nature to have some form of opinion on nutrition-related issues. Well-educated sports science and medical staff are also likely to have had some formal education on nutrition-related matters (though maybe limited to a few lectures during their undergraduate degree). It is therefore possible that the nutritional programme that is actually delivered day to day is a collective result of input from key backroom staff (and one that may or may not always be based on good practice) rather than being devised solely by the sports nutritionist. Nevertheless, it is essential that all relevant support staff are fully briefed on all of the strategies that are to be delivered on training and match days so that consistent service provision is delivered. After all, it is these individuals who are really on the front line on a day-to-day basis who are communicating and delivering the intended messages of the nutrition consultant, whose physical presence around the training ground is often limited. Similarly, assuming there are no confidentiality issues with players, it is crucial that any important pieces of information and any critical incidents that arise during player consultations are also fed back to relevant staff so that a truly multidisciplinary player development model can take shape. The optimal organisational and communication strategy to facilitate this information exchange will vary according to the situational dynamics of the football club, though regular group meetings and a suitable database to monitor and record key issues are obviously vital. However, in the unpredictable and highly reactive football environment, opportunities for focused and quality meetings perhaps do not occur as often as they should. Nevertheless (and as is true in any workplace), with the development of sound working relationships and organisational management structures (which may take multiple seasons to really develop), the quality of service provision can only get better, and slowly but surely (hopefully), the nutritionist can eventually implement a strategy that is perhaps more influenced by their own philosophy. It is important to note that this process will not occur overnight, and just when you consider progress is happening, the rapid turnover of management (that is inevitable in professional football) and associated backroom staff often brings a new set of philosophies and working values to which to adhere.

In addition to organisational issues, there are significant challenges involved in dealing with the attitudes and beliefs of the players themselves. Unlike other sports such as rugby or individual sports (e.g. running, cycling, boxing), the football culture is one in which nutrition is not often considered to be of paramount importance. Indeed, where, in the aforementioned sports, nutrition can induce measurable and visible changes in performance, optimal muscle glycogen stores or buffering of lactic acid does not immediately translate to more successful passes completed or matches won. In many ways, the nutritionist is therefore faced with the initial challenge of player (and, in some cases, staff) education, often returning to the basics of emphasising timing, type and quantity of food choices. The choice of language and the depth of information conveyed in this regard can also vary from player to player, given that the level of understanding can significantly vary within a playing squad. Indeed, several players (usually the senior professionals) may already be well informed on fitness and nutritional issues (possibly from their own experience and from working with other staff over many years) and are frequently looking for subtle differences to gain performance advantages. In contrast, younger players breaking into the first team perhaps do not fully appreciate that longevity as a professional footballer can often be due to the aggregation of many minor details that ultimately can culminate in performance enhancement.

Communication strategies with players can also vary considerably depending on their country of origin and their proficiency in the home language. Indeed, at its simplest level, if your message cannot be heard, then change will not take place. In such circumstances, having group consultations (with players and/or staff with a better command of the language) or conveying messages in more visual or written formats can prove effective. Over time, the successful practitioner is likely to develop a repertoire of communication strategies that are very much player specific.

With today's increased research knowledge base and intense fixture and training schedules, it is inevitable that sports supplements will play an increasingly important role within professional football. However, the development of an evidence-based supplement strategy is, in itself, a major challenge and is perhaps complicated most by the taste-driven culture inherent to football. The bottom line remains that if players do not like the taste of a particular product, then its uptake will be poor. As such, the quality of the supplement (e.g. in terms of its nutrient content) may often be compromised where a comparative product that may be less fit for purpose has a better taste. Furthermore, the taste preferences within a playing squad can also vary considerably and a sound supplement strategy should also take this into consideration. The list of supplement companies approaching clubs (and players directly) with the latest performance-enhancing supplement is endless, and this in itself can take up considerable time resources that could be better spent elsewhere.

Despite the significant capital invested in professional football, it might seem strange to the reader that financial constraints can also determine the extent of the nutrition service that can be provided. If we consider the example of daily fish oil supplementation, it may cost in the region of £15,000 to £20,000 (depending on the supplement provider) to supply an entire first-team playing squad over the course of a playing season. Sports supplement budgets will often be contained within the global medical and sports science department and, as such, the question remains as to whether such expenditure on a strategy that may not induce measurable change can be justified. Instead, such sums of money could go towards funding the salary of a junior sports scientist, which could prove to be a much more impactful use of resources in the long term. Similarly, the budget available to the club catering staff (though likely arising from a different funding stream) can also limit the quality and diversity of foods served within the training ground, as well as impacting the away-game strategy (i.e. a chef travelling to away games over the course of the entire season would also require a significant budget with which to work). Clearly, such issues are further exacerbated within clubs that have significantly less financial backing, such as those in the lower leagues of professional football.

REFERENCES AND FURTHER READING

Ali, A., Williams, C., Nicholas, C.W. and Foskett, A. 'The Influence of Carbohydrate-Electrolyte Ingestion on Soccer Skill Performance', *Medicine & Science in Sports & Exercise*, 39, no. 11 (2007), pp. 1969–1976. doi: 10.1249/mss.0b013e31814fb3e3.

Almond, C.S., Shin, A.Y., Fortescue, E.B., Mannix, R.C., Wypij, D., Binstadt, B.A., Duncan, N.C., Olson, D.P., Salerno, A.E., Newburger, J.W. and Greenes, D.S. 'Hyponatremia among Runners in the Boston Marathon', *New England Journal of Medicine*, 352, no. 15 (2005), pp. 1550–1556. doi: 352/15/1550 [pii].

Astrup, A., Dyerberg, J., Elwood, P., Hermansen, K., Hu, F.B., Jakobsen, M.U., Kok, F.J., Krauss, R.M., Lecerf, J.M., LeGrand, P., Nestel, P., Risérus, U., Sanders, T., Stender, S., Tholstrup, T. and Willett, W.C. 'The Role of Reducing Intakes of Saturated Fat in the Prevention of Cardiovascular Disease: Where Does the Evidence Stand in 2010?' *American Journal of Clinical Nutrition*, 93, no. 4 (2011), pp. 684–688. doi: 10.3945/ajcn.110.004622.

Atkinson, F.S., Foster-Powell, K. and Brand-Miller, J.C. 'International Tables of Glycemic Index and Glycemic Load Values: 2008', *Diabetes Care*, 31, no. 12 (2008), pp. 2281–2283. doi: dc08-1239 [pii].

Balsom, P.D., Wood, K., Olsson, P. and Ekblom, B. 'Carbohydrate Intake and Multiple Sprint Sports: With Special Reference to Football (Soccer)', *International Journal of Sports Medicine*, 20, no. 1 (1999), pp. 48–52. doi: 10.1055/s-2007-971091.

Bartlett, J.D., Hawley, J.A. and Morton, J.P. 'Carbohydrate Availability and Exercise Training Adaptation: Too Much of a Good Thing?' *European Journal of Sport Science*, 1–10 (2014). doi: 10.1080/17461391.2014.920926.

Beelen, M., Burke, L.M., Gibala, M.J. and van Loon, L.J. 'Nutritional Strategies to Promote Postexercise Recovery', *International Journal of Sport Nutrition and Exercise Metabolism*, 20, no. 6 (2010), pp. 515–532.

Bergeron, M.F. 'Heat Cramps: Fluid and Electrolyte Challenges during Tennis in the Heat', *Journal of Science and Medicine in Sport*, 6, no. 1 (2003), pp. 19–27.

Burke, L.M., Claassen, A., Hawley, J.A. and Noakes, T.D. 'Carbohydrate Intake during Prolonged Cycling Minimizes Effect of Glycemic Index of Preexercise Meal', *Journal of Applied Physiology*, 85, no. 6 (1998), pp. 2220–2226.

Burke, L.M., Collier, G.R. and Hargreaves, M. 'Muscle Glycogen Storage after Prolonged Exercise: Effect of the Glycemic Index of Carbohydrate Feedings', *Journal of Applied Physiology*, 75, no. 2 (1993), pp. 1019–1023.

Burke, L., Desbrow, B. and Spriet, L.L. *Caffeine for Sports Performance* (Human Kinetics, 2013).

Burke, L.M., Winter, J.A., Cameron-Smith, D., Enslen, M., Farnfield, M. and Decombaz, J. 'Effect of Intake of Different Dietary Protein Sources on Plasma

Amino Acid Profiles at Rest and After Exercise', *International Journal of Sport Nutrition and Exercise Metabolism* (2012). doi: 2011-0149 [pii].

Bussau, V.A., Fairchild, T.J., Rao, A., Steele, P. and Fournier, P.A. 'Carbohydrate Loading in Human Muscle: An Improved 1 Day Protocol', *European Journal of Applied Physiology*, 87, no. 3 (2002), pp. 290–295. doi: 10.1007/s00421-002-0621-5.

Clarkson, P.M. 'Minerals: Exercise Performance and Supplementation in Athletes', *Journal of Sports Sciences*, 9 Spec No. (1991), pp. 91–116. doi: 10.1080/02640419108729869.

Close, G.L., Ashton, T., Cable, T., Doran, D., Holloway, C., McArdle, F. and MacLaren, D.P. 'Ascorbic Acid Supplementation Does Not Attenuate Post-Exercise Muscle Soreness Following Muscle-Damaging Exercise But May Delay the Recovery Process', *British Journal of Nutrition*, 95, no. 5 (2006), pp. 976–981.

Close, G.L., Russell, J., Cobley, J.N., Owens, D.J., Wilson, G., Gregson, W., Fraser, W.D., Morton, J.P. 'Assessment of Vitamin D Concentration in Professional Athletes and Healthy Adults during the Winter Months in the UK: Implications for Skeletal Muscle Function', *Journal of Sports Sciences*, 34, no. 4 (2013), pp. 344–353.

Coffey, V.G. and Hawley, J.A. 'The Molecular Bases of Training Adaptation', *Sports Medicine*, 37, no. 9 (2007), pp. 737–763.

Cohen, M. and Bendich, A. 'Safety of Pyridoxine: A Review of Human and Animal Studies', *Toxicology Letters*, 34, nos. 2–3 (1986), pp. 129–139.

Costill, D.L., Pascoe, D.D., Fink, W.J., Roberts, R.A., Barr, S.I. and Pearson, D. 'Impaired Muscle Glycogen Resynthesis After Eccentric Exercise', *Journal of Applied Physiology*, 69, no. 1 (1990), pp. 46–50.

Decombaz, J., Jentjens, R., Ith, M., Scheurer, E., Buehler, T., Jeukendrup, A. and Boesch, C. 'Fructose and Galactose Enhance Post-Exercise Human Liver Glycogen Synthesis', *Medicine & Science in Sports & Exercise* (2011). doi: 10.1249/MSS.0b013e318218ca5a.

Drummond, M.J. and Rasmussen, B.B. 'Leucine-Enriched Nutrients and the Regulation of Mammalian Target of Rapamycin Signalling and Human Skeletal Muscle Protein Synthesis', *Current Opinion in Clinical Nutrition & Metabolic Care*, 11, no. 3 (2008), pp. 222–226. doi: 10.1097/MCO.0b013e3282fa17fb.

Foskett, A., Williams, C., Boobis, L. and Tsintzas, K. 'Carbohydrate Availability and Muscle Energy Metabolism during Intermittent Running', *Medicine & Science in Sports & Exercise*, 40, no.1 (2008), pp. 96–103. doi: 10.1249/mss.0b013e3181586b2c.

Gleeson, M. 'Immune Function in Sport and Exercise', *Journal of Applied Physiology*, 103, no. 2 (2007), pp. 693–699. doi: 00008.2007 [pii].

Gonzalez-Alonso, J. 'Hyperthermia Impairs Brain, Heart and Muscle Function in Exercising Humans', *Sports Medicine*, 37, nos. 4–5 (2007), pp. 371–373. doi: 37NaN25 [pii].

Gunnarsson, T.P., Bendiksen, M., Bischoff, R., Christensen, P.M., Lesivig, B., Madsen, K., Stephens, F., Greenhaff, P., Krustrup, P. and Bangsbo, J. 'Effect of Whey Protein- and Carbohydrate-Enriched Diet on Glycogen Resynthesis during the First 48 h after a Soccer Game', *Scandinavian Journal of Medicine & Science in Sports*, 23, no. 4 (2013), pp. 508–515. doi: 10.1111/j.1600-0838.2011.01418.x.

Howarth, K.R., Moreau, N.A., Phillips, S.M. and Gibala, M.J. 'Coingestion of Protein with Carbohydrate during Recovery from Endurance Exercise Stimulates Skeletal Muscle Protein Synthesis in Humans', *Journal of Applied Physiology*, 106, no. 4 (2009), pp. 1394–1402. doi: 90333.2008 [pii].

Hu, F.B. 'Are Refined Carbohydrates Worse Than Saturated Fat?' *American Journal of Clinical Nutrition*, 91, no. 6 (2010), pp. 1541–1542. doi: 10.3945/ajcn.2010.29622.

Hultman, E., Soderlund, K., Timmons, J.A., Cederblad, G. and Greenhaff, P.L. 'Muscle Creatine Loading in Men', *Journal of Applied Physiology* (1985), 81, no. 1 (1996), pp. 232–237.

Ivy, J.L., Katz, A.L., Cutler, C.L., Sherman, W.M. and Coyle, E.F. 'Muscle Glycogen Synthesis after Exercise: Effect of Time of Carbohydrate Ingestion', *Journal of Applied Physiology*, 64, no. 4 (1988), pp. 1480–1485.

Jackman, S.R., Witard, O.C., Jeukendrup, A.E. and Tipton, K.D. 'Branched-Chain Amino Acid Ingestion Can Ameliorate Soreness from Eccentric Exercise', *Medicine & Science in Sports & Exercise*, 42, no. 5 (2010), pp. 962–970. doi: 10.1249/MSS.0b013e3181c1b798.

Jeukendrup, A.E. 'Carbohydrate and Exercise Performance: The Role of Multiple Transportable Carbohydrates', *Current Opinion in Clinical Nutrition & Metabolic Care*, 13, no. 4 (2010), pp. 452–457. doi: 10.1097/MCO.0b013e328339de9f.

Jeukendrup, A.E. and Killer, S.C. 'The Myths Surrounding Pre-Exercise Carbohydrate Feeding', *Annals of Nutrition and Metabolism*, 57, Suppl. 2, (2010), pp. 18–25. doi: 000322698 [pii].

Krustrup, P., Mohr, M., Steensberg, A., Bencke, J., Kjaer, M. and Bangsbo, J. 'Muscle and Blood Metabolites during a Soccer Game: Implications for Sprint Performance', *Medicine & Science in Sports & Exercise*, 38, no. 6 (2006), pp. 1165–1174. doi: 10.1249/01.mss.0000222845.89262.cd. 00005768-200606000-00020 [pii].

Kurdak, S.S., Shirreffs, S.M., Maughan, R.J., Ozgunen, K.T., Zeren, C., Korkmaz, S., Yazici, Z., Ersöz, G., Binnet, M.S. and Dvorak, J. 'Hydration and Sweating Responses to Hot-Weather Football Competition', *Scandinavian Journal of Medicine & Science in Sports*, 20 Suppl. 3 (2010), pp. 133–139. doi: 10.1111/j.1600-0838.2010.01218.x.

Lee, J.K. and Shirreffs, S.M. 'The Influence of Drink Temperature on Thermoregulatory Responses during Prolonged Exercise in a Moderate Environment', *Journal of Sports Sciences*, 25, no. 9 (2007), pp. 975–985. doi: 778567937 [pii].

Levenhagen, D.K., Carr, C., Carlson, M.G., Maron, D.J., Borel, M.J. and Flakoll, P.J. 'Postexercise Protein Intake Enhances Whole-Body and Leg Protein Accretion in Humans', *Medicine & Science in Sports & Exercise*, 34(5) (2002), pp. 828–837.

Little, J.P., Chilibeck, P.D., Ciona, D., Forbes, S., Rees, H., Vandenberg, A. and Zello, G.A. 'Effect of Low- and High-Glycemic-Index Meals on Metabolism and Performance during High-Intensity, Intermittent Exercise', *International Journal of Sport Nutrition and Exercise Metabolism*, 20, no. 6 (2010), pp. 447–456.

Little, J.P., Chilibeck, P.D., Ciona, D., Vandenberg, A. and Zello, G.A. 'The Effects of Low- and High-Glycemic Index Foods on High-Intensity Intermittent Exercise', *International Journal of Sports Physiology and Performance*, 4, no. 3 (2009), pp. 367–380.

MacLaren, D.P.M. and Morton, J.P. *Biochemistry for Sport and Exercise Metabolism* (John Wiley & Sons, 2011).

Manore, M.M. 'Dietary Recommendations and Athletic Menstrual Dysfunction', *Sports Medicine*, 32, no. 14 (2002), pp. 887–901. doi: 321402 [pii].

Maughan, R.J., Watson, P., Evans, G.H., Broad, N. and Shirreffs, S.M. 'Water Balance and Salt Losses in Competitive Football', *International Journal of Sport Nutrition and Exercise Metabolism*, 17, no. 6 (2007), pp. 583–594.

McGregor, S.J., Nicholas, C.W., Lakomy, H.K. and Williams, C. 'The Influence of Intermittent High-Intensity Shuttle Running and Fluid Ingestion on the Performance of a Soccer Skill', *Journal of Sports Sciences*, 17, no. 11 (1999), pp. 895–903. doi: 10.1080/026404199365452.

Mettler, S., Mitchell, N. and Tipton, K.D. 'Increased Protein Intake Reduces Lean Body Mass Loss During Weight Loss in Athletes', *Medicine & Science in Sports & Exercise*, 42, no. 2 (2010), pp. 326–337. doi: 10.1249/MSS.0b013e3181b2ef8e.

Mohr, M., Krustrup, P. and Bangsbo, J. 'Match Performance of High-Standard Soccer Players with Special Reference to Development of Fatigue', *Journal of Sports Sciences*, 21, no. 7 (2003), pp. 519–528. doi: 10.1080/0264041031000071182.

Mohr, M., Krustrup, P., Nybo, L., Nielsen, J.J. and Bangsbo, J. 'Muscle Temperature and Sprint Performance during Soccer Matches: Beneficial Effect of Re-Warm-Up at Half-Time', *Scandinavian Journal of Medicine & Science in Sports*, 14, no. 3 (2004), pp. 156–162. doi: 10.1111/j.1600-0838.2004.00349.x. SMS349 [pii].

Mohr, M., Mujika, I., Santisteban, J., Randers, M.B., Bischoff, R., Solano, R., Hewitt, A., Zubillaga, A., Peltola, E. and Krustrup, P. 'Examination of Fatigue Development in Elite Soccer in a Hot Environment: A Multi-Experimental Approach', *Scandinavian Journal of Medicine & Science in Sports*, 20 Suppl. 3 (2010), pp. 125–132. doi: 10.1111/j.1600-0838.2010.01217.x.

Moore, D.R., Areta, J., Coffey, V.G., Stellingwerff, T., Phillips, S.M., Burke, L.M., Cléroux, M., Godin, J.P. and Hawley, J.A. 'Daytime Pattern of Post-Exercise

Protein Intake Affects Whole-Body Protein Turnover in Resistance-Trained Males', *Nutrition & Metabolism* (London), 9, no. 1 (2012), p. 91. doi: 1743-7075-9-91 [pii].

Moore, D.R., Phillips, S.M., Babraj, J.A., Smith, K. and Rennie, M.J. 'Myofibrillar and Collagen Protein Synthesis in Human Skeletal Muscle in Young Men after Maximal Shortening and Lengthening Contractions', *American Journal of Physiology – Endocrinology and Metabolism*, 288, no. 6 (2005), E1153–1159. doi: 10.1152/ajpendo.00387.2004.

Moore, D.R., Robinson, M.J., Fry, J.L., Tang, J.E., Glover, E.I., Wilkinson, S.B., Prior, T., Tarnopolsky, M.A. and Phillips, S.M. 'Ingested Protein Dose Response of Muscle and Albumin Protein Synthesis after Resistance Exercise in Young Men', *American Journal of Clinical Nutrition*, 89, no. 1 (2009), pp. 161–168. doi: ajcn.2008.26401 [pii].

Moore, D.R., Robinson, M.J., Fry, J.L., Tang, J.E., Glover, E.I., Wilkinson SB, Prior T, Tarnopolsky MA, Phillips SM. Morton, J.P. 'Supplements for Consideration in Football', *Sports Science Exchange*, 27, no. 130 (2014), pp. 1–8.

Mozaffarian, D., Katan, M.B., Ascherio, A., Stampfer, M.J. and Willett, W.C. 'Trans Fatty Acids and Cardiovascular Disease', *New England Journal of Medicine*, 354, no. 15 (2006), pp. 1601–1613. doi: 10.1056/NEJMra054035.

Nicholas, C.W., Williams, C., Lakomy, H.K., Phillips, G. and Nowitz, A. 'Influence of Ingesting a Carbohydrate-Electrolyte Solution on Endurance Capacity during Intermittent, High-Intensity Shuttle Running', *Journal of Sports Sciences*, 13, no. 4 (1995), pp. 283–290. doi: 10.1080/02640419508732241.

Noakes, T.D. 'Is Drinking to Thirst Optimum?' *Annals of Nutrition and Metabolism*, 57 Suppl. 2 (2010), pp. 9–17. doi: 10.1159/000322697.

Owens, D.J., Fraser, W.D. and Close, G.L. 'Vitamin D and the Athlete: Emerging Insights', *European Journal of Sport Science*, 1-12 (2014). doi: 10.1080/17461391.2014.944223.

Pfeiffer, B., Stellingwerff, T., Zaltas, E. and Jeukendrup, A.E. 'CHO Oxidation from a CHO Gel Compared with a Drink during Exercise', *Medicine & Science in Sports & Exercise*, 42, no. 11 (2010a), pp. 2038–2045. doi: 10.1249/MSS.0b013e3181e0efe6.

Pfeiffer, B., Stellingwerff, T., Zaltas, E. and Jeukendrup, A.E. 'Oxidation of Solid versus Liquid CHO Sources during Exercise', *Medicine & Science in Sports & Exercise*, 42, no. 11 (2010b), pp. 2030–2037. doi: 10.1249/MSS.0b013e3181e0efc9.

Phillips, S.M., Tang, J.E. and Moore, D.R. 'The Role of Milk- and Soy-Based Protein in Support of Muscle Protein Synthesis and Muscle Protein Accretion in Young and Elderly Persons', *Journal of the American College of Nutrition*, 28, no. 4 (2009), pp. 343–354. doi: 28/4/343 [pii].

Res, P.T., Groen, B., Pennings, B., Beelen, M., Wallis, G.A., Gijsen, A.P., Senden, J.M. and van Loon, L.J.C. 'Protein ingestion before sleep improves postexercise overnight recovery', *Medicine & Science in Sports & Exercise*, 44, no. 8 (2012), pp. 1560–1569. doi: 10.1249/MSS.0b013e31824cc363.

Robinson, T.M., Sewell, D.A., Hultman, E. and Greenhaff, P.L. 'Role of Submaximal Exercise in Promoting Creatine and Glycogen Accumulation in Human Skeletal Muscle', *Journal of Applied Physiology*, 87, no. 2 (1999), pp. 598–604.

Saltin, B. 'Metabolic Fundamentals in Exercise', *Medicine & Science in Sports & Exercise*, 5, no. 3 (1973), pp. 137–146.

Sawka, M.N., Burke, L.M., Eichner, E.R., Maughan, R.J., Montain, S.J. and Stachenfeld, N.S. 'American College of Sports Medicine Position Stand. Exercise and Fluid Replacement', *Medicine & Science in Sports & Exercise*, 39, no. 2 (2007), pp. 377–390. doi: 10.1249/mss.0b013e31802ca597. 00005768-200702000-00022 [pii].

Stellingwerff, T., Decombaz, J., Harris, R.C. and Boesch, C. 'Optimizing Human In Vivo Dosing and Delivery of Beta-Alanine Supplements for Muscle Carnosine Synthesis', *Amino Acids* (2012). doi: 10.1007/s00726-012-1245-7.

Tang, J.E., Moore, D.R., Kujbida, G.W., Tarnopolsky, M.A. and Phillips, S.M. 'Ingestion of Whey Hydrolysate, Casein, or Soy Protein Isolate: Effects on Mixed Muscle Protein Synthesis at Rest and Following Resistance Exercise in Young Men', *Journal of Applied Physiology*, 107, no. 3 (2009), pp. 987–992. doi: 00076.2009 [pii].

Tipton, K.D., Ferrando, A.A., Phillips, S.M., Doyle, D. Jr., and Wolfe, R.R. 'Postexercise Net Protein Synthesis in Human Muscle from Orally Administered Amino Acids', *American Journal of Physiology*, 276, no. 4, part 1 (1999), E628–E634.

Tipton, K.D., Rasmussen, B.B., Miller, S.L., Wolf, S.E., Owens-Stovall, S.K., Petrini, B.E. and Wolfe, R.R. 'Timing of Amino Acid-Carbohydrate Ingestion Alters Anabolic Response of Muscle to Resistance Exercise', *American Journal of Physiology – Endocrinology and Metabolism*, 281, no. 2 (2001), E197–E206.

Turnlund, J.R. 'Bioavailability of Dietary Minerals to Humans: The Stable Isotope Approach,' *Critical Reviews in Food Science and Nutrition*, 30, no. 4 (1991), pp. 387–396. doi: 10.1080/10408399109527549.

van Loon, L.J., Greenhaff, P.L., Constantin-Teodosiu, D., Saris, W.H. and Wagenmakers, A.J. 'The Effects of Increasing Exercise Intensity on Muscle Fuel Utilisation in Humans', *Journal of Physiology*, 536, part 1 (2001), pp. 295–304. doi: PHY_12382 [pii].

Vist, G.E. and Maughan, R.J. 'The Effect of Osmolality and Carbohydrate Content on the Rate of Gastric Emptying of Liquids in Man', *Journal of Physiology*, 486, part 2 (1995), pp. 523–531.

Wee, S.L., Williams, C., Tsintzas, K. and Boobis, L. 'Ingestion of a High-Glycemic Index Meal Increases Muscle Glycogen Storage at Rest But Augments its Utilization during Subsequent Exercise', *Journal of Applied Physiology*, 99, no 2 (2005), pp. 707–714. doi: 01261.2004 [pii].

Wylie, L.J., Mohr, M., Krustrup, P., Jackman, S.R., Ermidis, G., Kelly, J., Black, M.I., Bailey S.J., Vanhatalo, A. and Jones, A.M. 'Dietary Nitrate Supplementation Improves Team Sport-Specific Intense Intermittent Exercise Performance', *European Journal of Applied Physiology*, 113, no. 7 (2013), pp. 1673–1684. doi: 10.1007/s00421-013-2589-8.

Yeo, W.K., Carey, A.L., Burke, L., Spriet, L.L. and Hawley, J.A. 'Fat Adaptation in Well-Trained Athletes: Effects on Cell Metabolism', *Applied Physiology, Nutrition, and Metabolism*, 36, no. 1 (2011), pp. 12–22. doi: h10-089 [pii].

PART THREE

PART THREE

THE DEVELOPMENT OF PLAYERS: TRANSLATING SKILL ACQUISITION RESEARCH INTO PRACTICE

Dr Paul R. Ford[1], Martin Diggle[2], Chris Sulley[3] and Prof. A. Mark Williams[4]

Senior Lecturer, University of Brighton[1] Professional Game Youth Coach Development Head, The Football Association[2] Youth Coach Developer, The Football Association[3] Department of Health, Kinesiology, and Recreation, College of Health, University of Utah, USA[4]

The development of youth players into senior professionals is the primary goal of many coaches, support staff and clubs. Recent changes to the rules and regulations governing soccer clubs have highlighted the continued need to develop youth players into professionals. These changes include the Union of European Football Association's (UEFA's) Financial Fair Play regulations. UEFA's 'homegrown' player quota system rule requires 8 out of a squad of 25 players in European leagues to have been trained locally as youth players (UEFA, 2015). Moreover, the English Premier League's (EPL) Elite Player Performance Plan (EPPP) is focused specifically on enhancing youth development and player progression (Premier League, 2012). A key measure required by the EPPP in order to evaluate each club's performance in developing players is a 'Productivity Profile', which is a ratio of the number of players who progress from the youth development system of a club into the first-team squad. The Professional Footballers' Association (PFA, personal communication) highlighted the difficulty for clubs attempting to achieve a high ratio of progress of their youths to the professional team. In England, there are around 2,800 professionals, with around a third of these coming to the end of their contract each season. Approximately 350 of the players who are out of contract are offered new contracts at their existing clubs. The 500 or so remaining places are filled by other professionals who are out of contract, by foreign players, and by players graduating from the Youth Academies, of which there are around 750 each year. Around 85% of youth players and young professionals aged between 18 and 21 years of age are not awarded a professional contract each year.

There are many factors that contribute to the development, maintenance and improvement of expert performance in players. Scientists working in the field of skill acquisition and expert performance, as well as those working in related areas, including sports science, motor control, motor learning, psychology and neuroscience, have examined many of these factors. This research has led to a number of evidence-based principles that can help guide the development of players. Some of these principles focus on how various processes can be optimised to improve learning, including how sport-specific activity should be designed (e.g. Ford and Williams, 2012a), how coaches should provide instruction and feedback (e.g. Hendry *et al.*, 2015), how observational learning can be encouraged (e.g. Ong and Hodges, 2012) and how the learning of complex tasks occurs (e.g. Ericsson *et al.*, 1993). This research has led to a growth in the literature on expertise and skill learning both through traditional scientific outlets (e.g. Davids *et al.*, 2008; Williams and Hodges, 2012; Farrow *et al.*, 2013; Baker and Farrow, 2015; Baker, Cobley, Schorer and Wattie, 2017) and in popular books (e.g. Gladwell, 2008; Coyle, 2009; Syed, 2011).

Most people hold the knowledge derived from scientific research in high regard. A number of authors (e.g. Chalmers, 1999; Thomas *et al.*, 2010) detail why this scientific process of generating knowledge is more objective and controlled than knowledge derived from other sources. Other sources include intuition, authority and tradition, although these sources can also be important in some domains, such as coaching, when combined with knowledge derived from science. Many other domains use principles derived from research as the main source of knowledge guiding practice; these domains include medicine (Sackett and Rosenberg, 1995), education (Slavin, 2002) and business (Pfeffer and Sutton, 2006). In recent times, a number of articles have been published calling for the same evidence-based criteria to be used in the development of expert athletes (Ford *et al.*, 2010; Collins and Bailey, 2012; Ford and Williams, 2012a; Hendry *et al.*, 2015).

In soccer, it is the coach who is responsible for skill acquisition and development in players. However, a gap has been identified between researchers in this area generating or publishing evidence-based principles through the scientific process and coaches applying those principles in their day-to-day work (Farrow *et al.*, 2013). In other areas of sports science, such as physiology, the gap between research and practice has been closed by the employment of specialist support staff. However, there are no specialist skill acquisition support staff currently working in soccer and there is a general lack of such support across the sport (Williams and Ford, 2009). Some exceptions to this rule exist in the Australian Institute of Sport, which employs a number of individuals in this area (Button and Farrow, 2012), in the Scottish Institute of Sport, and at the Rugby Football Union (Williams, Ford *et al.*, 2012).

In the first section of this chapter, we provide a brief review of a key research topic in the area of skill acquisition and expert performance. The review focuses on how soccer-specific activity should be designed to optimise learning across different stages of player development. In part, this process involves a brief review of the activity engaged in and instruction received by players during coaching sessions. In this review, we provide practical examples, advice and proposed solutions to those responsible for delivering skill acquisition support to players. In the second section, we outline the challenges faced by those involved in trying to integrate evidence-based principles into clubs, coach education and other areas of soccer.

TRANSLATING THEORY INTO PRACTICE: THE SCIENTIFIC SUPPORT PROCESS

A number of evidence-based principles exist detailing how soccer-specific activity should be designed to optimise skill acquisition across the various stages of athlete development. In this section, we detail these evidence-based principles as they relate to the long-term development of soccer players from childhood through to adulthood. Figure 1 contains a summary of the key principles as a function of the age and each stage of player development.

Childhood Activity

During childhood, soccer players in most countries mainly engage in the sport through relatively high amounts of formal practice and competition (Ford *et al.*, 2012). The culture of formal or organised soccer activity for children in many countries contains adult-orientated goals that children may not be ready for or mature enough to experience, such as leagues, player of the match awards, a focus on winning a single match, an explicit focus on training to improve performance, and training that is regimented to the extent that players are not active decision makers during the activity. These adult-orientated goals are set and reinforced by coaches and significant others, such as parents. The negative effect of these adult-orientated goals for players can be to reduce enjoyment, motivation, experimentation and skill acquisition. Researchers have found some potentially negative consequences for athletes engaging in high amounts of formal practice and competition activity during childhood, such as reduced health, a greater incidence of overuse injuries, burnout, dropout and overtraining (Baker, 2003; Law *et al.*, 2007; Baker *et al.*, 2009). These problems are exacerbated in most developed countries because children in the 21st century engage in sport through these formal activities and no longer engage in *informal* and unstructured play activity (American Academy of Paediatrics, 2001).

FIGURE 1 Optimal developmental activities (and amounts) for soccer players from childhood to adulthood (Age, Yrs)

Age (Yrs)	5–12	13–16	17–21+
Stage	Childhood	Early adolescence	Late adolescence and adulthood
Activity (Hours):	Adult-orientated competition (Low) Deliberate play (High) Deliberate practice (Low)	Competition (from Med to High) Deliberate play (from Med to Low) Deliberate practice (from Med to High)	Competition (High) Deliberate play (Low) Deliberate practice (High)
Intention:	Fun and enjoyment	Improve performance	Win and improve performance
Other intentions:	Coach – implicitly improve player performance	Progression across stage to win and improve performance	
Some methods:	Create opportunities for informal deliberate play Create structured and 'smart' formal deliberate play 'Playing Form' activity (High) (e.g. small-sided games) Manipulate challenge point and task constraints	Individual and team goal-setting Practice designed around goal-setting Match used to improve performance Performance analysis and reflection	Match performance to win Preparation and reflection Individual and team goal-setting Performance analysis

Other researchers have raised concerns about the formal practice activities in which children engage. Ford *et al.* (2010; see also Partington and Cushion, 2011) examined the microstructure of 70 coaching sessions across 25 youth soccer coaches in England. A sub-set of the coaching sessions involved players who were under nine years of age and were at either elite, sub-elite or recreational skill levels. The activities across all the sessions were video-recorded and time-coded into two categories, termed 'Training Form' and 'Playing Form'. Training Form activity was defined as activities that did not have a game-play context, such as teammates/opponents, and that consisted of work on fitness, technique and skills drill practices. Playing Form activity was defined as activities that had game-related conditions containing teammates and opponents and that consisted of small-sided games, unidirectional games (e.g. 2 vs. 1), conditioned games and phase of play activities. Playing Form activity was judged to be more similar to the structure of competition match-play, and therefore the activity from which greater transfer of learning to match-play would occur compared with Training Form activity. Overall, the proportions of time spent in Training Form and Playing Form activity for the under-9 players were 69% and 31%, respectively, with little variation across skill groups. These findings raised concern as to whether coaches are providing child players with sufficient opportunity to engage in activities that lead to transfer of learning to a match situation. Players may have less opportunity to acquire key skills, such as decision making, anticipation and visual search, in Training Form than they have in Playing Form activity.

A key reason that Playing Form activities are under-employed by coaches during formal practice may be because they are viewed as being too demanding for young players. However, because Playing Form activity most likely provides greater transfer of learning to match-play than Training Form, coaches of child players should increase its use in practice and adapt activities to suit the skill level and age of their players. Researchers have identified a number of principles that can be applied by coaches to reduce the demands of Playing Form activity for learners. For example, Guadagnoli and Lee (2004) introduced the *challenge point framework*. In this framework, practice activities are viewed as presenting varying levels of difficulty depending on the skill level of the performer and the practice conditions. The optimal challenge point occurs around the point of task difficulty that a performer at a specific skill level would need in order to optimise learning. Practice tasks that are too easy or too difficult for a performer lead to either no learning or sub-optimal learning.

In a similar vein, the *constraints-led approach* detailed by Davids et al. (2008) provides a means for reducing the demands of Playing Form activity. The constraints-led approach (Davids *et al.*, 2008; see also Newell, 1986) views the task, environment and individual as having parts, boundaries and *constraints* that can be manipulated in order to bring about skill acquisition and learning. Although all three types of constraints can be manipulated, it is task constraints that are the easiest for a coach to manipulate, and many coaches already do this during practice to some degree. Davids *et al.* have usefully termed the manipulation of task constraints as 'bending the rules'. Practical methods to manipulate task constraints so as to reduce the demands or the 'challenge point' of the Playing Form activity, such as a small-sided game, include: increasing pitch size; reducing the number of players on each team; including extra players who play for whichever team is in possession of the ball during the game (i.e. 'floaters'); or ban tackling from the floor or ban tackling completely by only allowing interceptions of passes and pressure. Coaches can use these practical methods to ensure small-sided games contain an appropriate 'challenge point' for the skill level and age of the players.

Repetition of specific skills across extended time is a key part of their acquisition, but any repetition should involve the type of functional variability found in Playing Form activity, such as executing skills in differing conditions, situations and states, and at varying distances, speeds, angles etc (Davids *et al.*, 2008). Some other methods of manipulating task constraints in Playing Form activity to increase repetition and the acquisition of key skills and tactics can be seen in Figure 2. Figure 2a shows a small-sided game in which the two normal goals have been replaced by four smaller goals in each corner. This game constrains a player in possession of the ball to turn and switch-play more often than normal and to practise those key skills/tactics more often than normal so that the outcome is their acquisition. In this learning environment, constraints must be manipulated so that players regularly encounter the whole range of skills and tactics that constitute soccer performance. This type of learning environment has been termed 'guided discovery' because the coach or teacher sets a conducive environment for learners to 'discover' the solutions to problems themselves through playing. It is also similar to the 'Teaching Games for Understanding' (TGfU) methodology described widely elsewhere (Thorpe *et al*, 1986). By using small-sided games and other types of Playing Form activity that are adapted to an appropriate challenge point and that are designed to increase repetition of key skills and tactics, coaches can create an ideal learning environment for child players.

The potentially negative consequences of children engaging in high amounts of practice and competition activity have led researchers to consider alternative activities. Several researchers (e.g. Ford and Williams, 2012a) have recommended *soccer-specific play* as the optimal activity for child soccer players. Soccer-

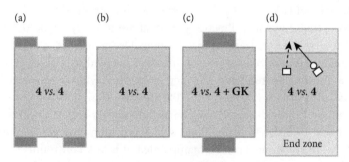

FIGURE 2 Methods of manipulating the task constraints of 4 *vs.* 4 small-sided games so as to bring about skill acquisition and learning of: (a) turning and switching play; (b) dribbling because players score by dribbling ball across end line; (c) shooting; and (d) forward running and forward passing.

specific play is usually informal activity engaged in with the intention of fun and enjoyment, usually led by the children themselves, and consisting of activities adapted from adult norms (Côté and Hay, 2002). Ford *et al.* (2012; see also Salmela *et al.*, 2004) showed that elite soccer players in the under-16 age category in Brazil accumulated very low amounts of time in formal soccer-specific practice and competition activity during their childhood. However, these players had accumulated a relatively high amount of time in informal soccer-specific play activity, such as beach and street soccer, as well as Futsal. The data from Brazil show that elite soccer players may not need to have engaged in high amounts of formal soccer-specific practice and competition during childhood if they engaged in relatively high amounts of deliberate play in the sport during that period. Similarly, high amounts of engagement in informal soccer-specific play activity during childhood are described in the biographies of eminent players, such as Wayne Rooney (Rooney, 2006), Cristiano Ronaldo (Ronaldo, 2007), Lionel Messi (Caioli, 2010) and Kaka (Jones, 2010).

Other researchers have shown that players who accumulate relatively high amounts of hours in informal soccer-specific play activity during childhood possess superior decision-making skills (Williams, Ward *et al.*, 2012) and reach higher levels of attainment (Ford *et al.*, 2009; Ford & Williams, 2012b) than those who accumulate fewer hours. Play activity may also lead to the acquisition of a larger implicit knowledge base, which has been shown to have some benefits for learning compared with knowledge that is acquired explicitly (Masters, 1992). More generally, play activity has been hypothesised to lead to several other benefits, such as increased motivation, self-determination, a 'love of the game' and commitment to engage further in an activity or domain, which are essential attributes required by young players to develop into senior professional players. The engagement in play activity might satisfy innate psychological needs for competence, autonomy and relatedness because learners design, lead and adapt the activity at a level of difficulty that is appropriate for them (Deci and Ryan, 2000). Furthermore, intrinsic motivational benefits for participants during play are thought to emanate from having the freedom to experiment and innovate without adult judgement (Côté *et al.*, 2007). Pellegrini and Smith (1998) believe that play activities that are led by the participants afford them the opportunity to develop fundamental problem-solving and reflective strategies. For example, in soccer these strategies may help players transfer principles of attack and defence across different problem/decision-making situations in the game. An engagement in play in soccer may provide opportunities for individuals to develop physical literacy, social skills, emotional development and physiological foundations that have both immediate and delayed benefits (Pellegrini and Smith, 1998).

A further concern is that in the majority of countries, children do not engage in as much informal soccer-specific deliberate play activity as previous generations did. Their lack of engagement may be due to a number of reasons, such as the perceived lack of safety for children playing without adult supervision, their engagement in other activities, and the inclement climate in some countries (American Academy of Paediatrics, 2001). Therefore, adults must provide more opportunities for children to engage in meaningful amounts of soccer-specific play due to its myriad benefits. Practical solutions include scheduling more soccer-specific play *during* formal practice sessions and physical education classes, creating school playgrounds/areas/parks that enable children to safely engage in soccer-specific play, and *changing* the formal match or games programme so that it becomes soccer-specific deliberate play. An advantage of creating play activity in formal settings as opposed to informal settings is that it has the potential to be cleverly designed so as to also lead to performance improvement and learning *without the players knowing this is the case*. However, children should engage in meaningful amounts of soccer-specific play activity each week, which probably cannot all be provided in formal settings alone. A key factor in adapting formal soccer activity is to ensure the intentions and behaviours of the coaches, players and significant others are compatible with a play environment. The coach usually leads in creating this *motivational climate* (Ames, 1992; Ntoumanis and Biddle, 1999).

Soccer coaches have been shown to provide relatively high amounts of instruction and feedback during coaching sessions with children (Ford *et al.*, 2010) and during competition or match-play (Smith & Cushion, 2006). Multiple researchers have identified a number of problems with high amounts of explicit instruction and feedback. First, explicit instruction and feedback leads to the accumulation of an explicit knowledge base about the skill or task, and researchers have shown that when learners who have been instructed in this explicit manner perform under conditions containing stress and pressure, their performance deteriorates, especially in comparison with learners who have acquired the skill or task by means of an implicit knowledge base (Masters, 1992; Masters and Poolton, 2012). Second, researchers have shown that when explicit instruction and feedback is directed to the movements of the learner it leads to a performance and learning decrement compared with that directed to the external effects of the movement (for a review, see Lohse *et al.*, 2012). Third, other researchers have shown that feedback directly following skill execution disrupts intrinsic and automatic feedback processes in comparison with delayed feedback, thereby leading to poorer learning (Swinnen *et al.*, 1990). Fourth, researchers have shown that instruction and feedback that is *positive* in nature leads to better learning than *negative* feedback (Lewthwaite and Wulf, 2012). Finally, when coaches provide high amounts of instruction and feedback during formal practice and match-play it usually creates a climate of 'authority and obedience', which may not be well-received by child players and may not be an appropriate way for them to experience the sport at this stage of their development (Cushion *et al.*, 2012).

One way a coach can begin to create a 'playful' climate and environment for child soccer players is to use a 'hands-off' approach to instruction (Williams and Hodges, 2005). This entails setting up the activity so that the players acquire skill from merely engaging in the activity without high amounts of verbal intervention by the coach. The amount of instruction and feedback provided is low and much of the time is spent silently observing play to ensure the activity is appropriate. Formal deliberate play requires a hands-off approach to instruction and feedback from coaches and significant others. Moreover, it requires a motivational climate in which the intentions and behaviours of the coaches, significant others and players are all directed towards creating a relaxed, informal environment in which the players are engaging in the activity for fun, and not for winning or for explicit performance improvement. Coaches can use Playing Form activities, particularly small-sided games (e.g. 3 vs. 3, 4 vs. 4) and unidirectional games (e.g. 2 vs. 1; 3 vs. 2) for this purpose. Such activity can be cleverly designed and adapted by coaches so as to manipulate the task constraints to increase the repetition of key skills/tactics and to adjust the challenge point to an appropriate level so that the players are also engaging in the activity for performance improvement and learning without them knowing that this is the case.

The Manchester United Youth Academy provides an example of how the formal games programme can be changed to 'formal deliberate play'. It has for a long time adopted a 4 vs. 4 scheme for its under-9 players (for a review, see Fenoglio, 2003) for home games, having opted out of the normal 8 vs. 8 match typically employed in Premier League youth academies. The coaches and significant others create a playful and relaxed environment for the players by observing from a distance, using a hands-off approach (Williams and Hodges, 2005) and letting the players referee the games themselves. Some of the task constraints of the 4 vs. 4 games have been adapted to bring about skill acquisition and learning of specific skills and tactics as highlighted in Figure 2. The Manchester United 4 vs. 4 scheme provides an excellent example of optimal formal soccer activity for child players, which we term 'formal deliberate play' or, because of the way the games are designed to bring about acquisition of certain skills, 'smart deliberate play'.

Adolescent and Adult Activity

Childhood activity likely provides the foundation from which expert performance can be developed in soccer players. Some of the principles outlined in the previous section on childhood activity also apply to older players, but some changes in activity types occur as players progress into adolescence and beyond. In the Ford et al. (2012) study, the developmental activities of elite under-16 soccer players during early adolescence in Brazil and in several other major soccer nations were characterised by a relatively large amount of engagement in formal practice activity. The players were engaging in around 10 hours per week or more of soccer-specific practice activity over a season during this period of their lives. The amount of soccer-specific play activity engaged in during adolescence gradually declined across this period. A key principle supporting these observations is the 'Power Law of Practice' (Newell and Rosenbloom, 1981), which holds that during the early stages of skill acquisition, performance improvement is rapid, whereas later in acquisition it slows and plateaus. It may be that deliberate play activity in childhood can lead to a rapid and optimal improvement in performance, but at some point later in the process this improvement slows and plateaus. Ericsson (2003, 2007) has used the phrase 'arrested development' to describe the plateau in performance that occurs later in the learning process. He states that expert performers are not satisfied with remaining at this performance plateau and, as a consequence, they plan and engage in a special type of activity termed 'deliberate practice' in an effort to improve performance beyond its current level. Their high levels of intrinsic motivation, dedication and persistence likely underpin this engagement in deliberate practice (Gould et al, 2002).

Deliberate practice activity is planned and designed to improve key aspects of current and future performance. It requires resources and effort and may not be inherently enjoyable. The motivation for performers is thought to come from its benefit for their future performance (Ericsson, 2003, 2007). The engagement in deliberate practice activity is thought to be one way players continue to improve their performance beyond its current level. It appears that early adolescent players should be engaging in increasing amounts of deliberate practice across this stage of their life so as to continually improve performance beyond its current level. The performance attributes that require improvement are skill based, physical, anthropometrical and psychological. The nature of that deliberate practice activity for adolescent players in terms of what exactly is focused on and what activity is engaged in appears to be specific to the individual or team. There is some skill acquisition research that can be used to guide this process during this period of a player's development, particularly that showing the importance of the acquisition of tactical knowledge for competition activity (for a review, see McPherson and Kernodle, 2003) and the benefits of using Playing Form activity, such as phases of play, during training with this age group (Ford et al., 2010).

The acquisition of tactical knowledge for competition activity has been shown to occur through a number of combined methods, including team meetings in which tactics are explicitly developed, physical practice or coaching sessions in which tactics are explicitly practised, competition, performance analysis and reflective practice (Richards et al., 2012). Tactics include how the team, the unit and the individual should play in the various phases and situations of the game, as well as how they should adapt their play for specific opponents. Phases of play, full matches, small-sided games and drills of scenarios from the match that are created so that the players are actively making decisions themselves can be used as the physical practice part of this process. However, match-play and its conditions are difficult to recreate in practice sessions, so from adolescence onwards match-play frequency should be relatively high and increasing to ensure specificity of skill acquisition. Some practical strategies that the authors have used for deliberate practice with elite adolescent youth players include using the matches themselves as deliberate practice, and scheduling deliberate practice activities based on what occurs in the match programme and on what would ideally occur. Goal-setting has been central to creating deliberate practice activity by using performance plans for individual players and teams to help motivate and focus attention on improving specific aspects of performance (Locke and Latham, 2002). Practice activity, match-play and instruction is then scheduled to improve these specific parts of player and team performance. Performance analysis is a valuable part of this deliberate practice, particularly when it is coupled with goal-setting that is specific, relevant and targeted as per that in deliberate practice. It can provide objective measurement of performance improvement (e.g. Harvey *et al.*, 2010) and feedback or feed-forward information for performance improvement (e.g. Richards *et al.*, 2012).

Performance in late adolescence and adulthood is measured through winning matches and trophies, as well as on the basis of the quality of performance. Adult and late-adolescent players should also engage in meaningful amounts of deliberate practice designed to improve or maintain their performance towards these goals (e.g. Ford *et al.*, 2012). The activity should seek to improve all of the skill-based, physical, anthropometrical and psychological attributes that comprise expert performance in the sport. In terms of skill acquisition, this practice will involve preparation for performance in the upcoming match/es, reflection on that performance, and the improvement of team and individual tactics/strategies. Practical strategies for this activity include on-field training sessions and off-field meetings, including meetings involving video footage (e.g. Richards *et al.*, 2012), as well as observation, visualisation and thought processes (Horrocks, 2012). Such activity leads to players acquiring increasingly complex memory representations to support their performance in the sport. These representations contain situation models that permit immediate access to knowledge of the situation and their situational options during performance, as well as to monitor, control and anticipate future events and actions in the situation (Ward *et al.*, 2011).

The content of deliberate practice activity for adolescent and adult players is likely to be dependent on the club's and the coaches' philosophy, values, knowledge, resources, medium-term vision, motivation and coaching style among other factors, as well as on the team/players' abilities, values, knowledge and motivation. Some general principles and processes to achieve the main goals do exist, including having a clear and unifying medium- and/or long-term vision supported by appropriate goals; a focus on winning soccer matches via detailed preparation for, engagement in and learning from them; a focus on improving performance through deliberate practice and other activity; and having clear behavioural and disciplinary rules. In terms of physical practice, it will consist of phases of play, games or matches, and drills of scenarios from the match, in all of which the players are active decision makers.

CHALLENGES IN THE WORKING ENVIRONMENT

A number of challenges exist in applying the evidence-based principles derived from scientific research in soccer. In this section, we provide a brief review of the challenges that individuals and organisations face in integrating evidence-based principles into practice. We also provide some tentative solutions to these challenges.

The majority of research is disseminated through peer-reviewed journals or academic conferences that coaches and support staff do not routinely access. The culture of academia leads researchers to work towards achieving traditional academic markers that benchmark their performance within the domain, such as publishing in academic journals with higher impact factors (Williams *et al.*, 2012). Moreover, in academia, translational research that attempts to bridge the gap between research and application is often viewed as being less worthy than traditional research. Therefore, some research lacks the ecological validity needed for the principles derived from it to be applicable to soccer. However, in recent times, some changes in the manner in which governments in the United Kingdom and other countries fund research has led to an increasing awareness in universities that their research must impact society by influencing public policy and behaviour. Given that the government prioritises funding to other areas of research, such as health and technology, it is likely that sports organisations interested in improving their own effectiveness will have to harness this increasing awareness around impact by funding research themselves and giving researchers access to elite players.

Coaches and the culture of soccer in some cases hinder the application of the evidence-based principles derived from scientific research. The culture of soccer and, in particular, the development of players through the programme of training and matches in a season leaves coaches with a lack of time to develop their own abilities. Researchers (Lynch and Mallett, 2006; Erickson *et al.*, 2007; Gilbert *et al.*, 2009; Young *et al.*, 2009) have shown that the amount of time spent by coaches on education courses is significantly lower than that spent coaching 'on the job'. As such, coaches' knowledge and skill is largely acquired through experiential learning gained while coaching, or through mentoring. This type of coach knowledge has been termed 'craft knowledge' (also known as 'tacit knowledge'), which is described as 'knowing-in-action' as it is the practical knowledge that guides the various steps and actions of the performance itself (Schön, 1983). While this practical knowledge is important for expert coaching performance, in soccer it appears that these experiences and observations have also led to a traditional and autocratic coaching style pervading the sport, which is handed down through the generations of coaches via these experiences (Cushion *et al.*, 2012).

Coach education courses tend to take the form of short and intense courses that are engaged in infrequently. However, coach education can play a role in the dissemination of the evidence-based principles derived from research in the areas of skill acquisition and expert performance. In England, the Football Association (FA) is currently working in conjunction with the Premier League and the Football League to provide ongoing elite coach development mentorship that affords the opportunity to disseminate ideas from research and the game to clubs and individual coaches. The FA's new youth coach education modular awards contain content about appropriate learning environments, practice activities and intervention approaches that will enhance skill acquisition and learning. These courses and the individual support structures that accompany them have been informed by a range of academic research, and materials have then been designed to help in their practical application, as well as to meet the needs of the coach. The ongoing challenge within coach education and development is to increase coaches' awareness of what they do and of the evidence-based principles from skill acquisition research that should underpin these practices.

A number of researchers (Ghaye, 2001; Gilbert and Trudel, 2001; Knowles *et al.*, 2001; Irwin *et al.*, 2004; Knowles *et al.*, 2014) have shown the importance of reflective practice in this process. There are different types of reflection available to coaches. Ghaye (2001) outlined three types: descriptive, creative, and critical. Descriptive reflection is retelling or rethinking past experience. Creative reflection is defined as rethinking past experience and formulating a new way or ways to act. Critical reflection is questioning and challenging current practice, habits, routines, values and beliefs. The ability to engage in critical and creative reflection by questioning and challenging current practice, habits, routines, values and beliefs (Ghaye, 2001) is a key process for a coach wishing to integrate new knowledge into their work and improve their effectiveness. The coach's epistemological beliefs about the nature and origin of knowledge (Schraw *et al.*, 2006) will play a major role in this process. Coaches are faced with various competing concepts underpinned by knowledge of a different nature and from different origins. For example, they may face knowledge from scientific research versus knowledge from intuition, observation, authority or tradition. Coaches require the ability to engage in critical and creative reflection so as to develop appropriate epistemological beliefs in order to be able to integrate the correct knowledge (e.g. craft, scientific) into their work and improve their effectiveness.

The goals of soccer clubs also sometimes hinder the application of evidence-based principles. Elite clubs have to balance the short-term need to produce a winning team with the medium-to-long-term aim of developing talent for their first team and the cost effectiveness of that process. Moreover, the focus of resources is often on the first team as the outcomes are more instant and tangible. However, with the changes introduced by UEFA and the EPPP, professional clubs in the UK have chosen to place themselves at a level that will provide more comprehensive resources for their youth development programmes. One of the fundamental challenges that an academy manager will face is in setting the vision, philosophy and processes of the youth programme in such a way as to align with the club's overall philosophy. Clubs also face challenges in ensuring that significant others who are central to the development of skill and expertise in players and who provide feedback to players, such as parents and agents, are educated to do so in an appropriate way to promote player learning.

An important challenge concerns how to objectively measure performance improvement, skill acquisition and learning in the game. Expert soccer performance during a match is multifaceted. Traditional academic methods of measuring learning by using delayed retention and transfer tests after a period of acquisition are less applicable in soccer. Soccer-specific tests of performance do not generally capture the complexity of the game, whereas the game itself can be too complex and variable to enable objective measurement. As described earlier in this chapter, performance analysis is a key tool that can be used to measure performance, its components and its improvement in the game. Some limitations in using performance analysis for this purpose exist because of variation in the opponents faced during matches with regard to their quality, tactics and personnel, and due to variations in other extraneous factors, such as time in the season and weather conditions.

SUMMARY

A number of individuals (Ford *et al.*, 2010; Collins and Bailey, 2012; Ford and Williams, 2012a; Hendry *et al.*, 2015) have called for evidence-based principles to underpin the skill acquisition process in soccer. However, a gap has been identified between the publication of scientific studies and the underlying principles being applied in practice (Farrow *et al.*, 2013). In this chapter, we have raised awareness of the evidence-based principles emanating from research in the areas of skill acquisition and motor learning. Further efforts are needed to ensure that coaching practice is underpinned by scientific principles where possible. We identified a number of challenges and barriers that individuals face in integrating these principles into soccer.

Coach education appears at present to be the main method for the principles to be disseminated and for those challenges to be met 'on the ground'. Coach educators have begun to, and must continue to, ensure that their courses and mentorship schemes highlight evidence-based principles and ways in which these may be integrated into practice. Coach educators are currently working with skill acquisition specialists to ensure that the correct information is provided on courses. There are currently no skill acquisition specialists working with soccer clubs or national associations. The role of a skill acquisition specialist is potentially more intertwined with that of the coach than other sports science disciplines – for example, both are interested in practices and instructional methods. However, the role of a skill acquisition specialist is simply to help coaches develop their understanding and application of the scientific principles, whereas the role of the coach is to work with the players. The recent rule changes governing youth development have given coaches, educators and skill acquisition specialists an impetus to work more closely together towards a shared goal. That goal is to provide optimal learning environments so that developing players have the best opportunity to realise their dream of being successful senior professional players.

REFERENCES

American Academy of Paediatrics. 'Organized Sports for Children and Preadolescents', *Paediatrics*, 107 (2001), pp. 1459–1462.

Ames, C. 'Achievement Goals and the Classroom', in D.H. Schunk and J.L. Meece (eds.), *Student Perceptions in the Classroom*, pp. 327–348 (Lawrence Erlbaum Associates, 1992).

Baker, J. 'Early Specialization in Youth Sport: A Requirement for Adult Expertise?' *High Ability Studies*, 14 (2003), pp. 85–94.

Baker, J., Cobley, S. and Fraser-Thomas, J. 'What Do We Know About Early Sport Specialization? Not Much!' *High Ability Studies*, 20 (2009), pp. 77–89.

Baker, J., Cobley, S., Schorer, J. and Wattie, N. *Handbook of Talent Identification and Development* (Routledge, 2017).

Baker, J. and Farrow, D. *The Handbook of Sport Expertise* (Routledge, 2015).

Button, C. and Farrow, D. 'Working in the Field (Southern Hemisphere)', in Williams, A.M. and Hodges, N.J. (eds.), *Skill Acquisition in Sport: Research, theory, and practice*, 2nd edn, pp. 367–380 (Routledge, 2012).

Caioli, L. *Messi: The Inside Story of the Boy who Became a Legend* (Icon, 2010).

Chalmers, A. *What Is This Thing Called Science?* (Open University Press, 1999).

Collins, D. and Bailey, R. '"Scienciness" and the Allure of Second Hand Strategy in Talent Identification and Development', *International Journal of Sport Policy and Politics*, 2012. Article first published online 23 May 2012. doi:10.1080/194 06940.2012.656682.

Côté, J., Baker, J. and Abernethy, B. 'Play and Practice in the Development of Sport Expertise', in Tenenbaum, G. and Eklund, R.C. (eds.), *Handbook of Sport Psychology*, 3rd edn, pp. 184–202 (Wiley, 2007).

Côté, J. & Hay, J. 'Children's Involvement in Sport: A Developmental Perspective', in Silva, J.M. & Stevens, D. (eds.), *Psychological Foundations of Sport*, pp. 484–502 (Allyn and Bacon, 2002).

Coyle, D. *The Talent Code* (Bantam, 2009).

Cushion, C., Ford, P.R. and Williams, A.M. 'Coach Behaviours and Practice Structures in Youth Soccer: Implications for Talent Development', *Journal of Sports Sciences*, 30 (2012), pp. 1631–1641.

Davids, K., Button, C. and Bennett, S. *Dynamics of Skill Acquisition: A Constraints-Led Approach* (Human Kinetics, 2008).

Deci, E.L. and Ryan, R.M. 'The "What" and "Why" of Goal Pursuits: Human Needs and the Self-Determination of Behavior', *Psychological Inquiry*, 11 (2000), 227–268.

Erickson, K., Côté, J. and Fraser-Thomas, J. 'Sport Experiences, Milestones, and Educational Activities Associated with High-Performance Coaches' Development', *The Sport Psychologist*, 21 (2007), pp. 302–331.

Ericsson, K.A. 'Deliberate Practice and the Modifiability of Body and Mind: Toward a Science of the Structure and Acquisition of Expert and Elite Performance', *International Journal of Sport Psychology*, 38 (2007), pp. 4–43.

Ericsson, K.A. 'The Development of Elite Performance and Deliberate Practice: An Update from the Perspective of the Expert-Performance Approach', in Starkes, J. and Ericsson, K.A. (eds.), *Expert Performance in Sport: Recent Advances in Research on Sport Expertise*, pp. 49–81 (Human Kinetics, 2003).

Ericsson, K.A., Krampe, R.T. and Tesch-Römer, C. 'The Role of Deliberate Practice in the Acquisition of Expert Performance', *Psychological Review*, 100 (1993), pp. 363–406.

Farrow, D., Baker, J. and MacMahon, C. *Developing Sport Expertise: Researchers and Coaches Put Theory into Practice*, 2nd edn (Routledge, 2013).

Fenoglio, R. 'The Manchester United 4 v 4 Pilot Scheme for U9s', *Insight: The FA Coaches Association Journal*, 6, no. 3 (2003), pp. 18–19.

Ford, P.R., Carling, C., Garces, M., Marques, M., Miguel, C., Farrant, A., Stenling, A., Moreno, J., Le Gall, F., Holmström, S., Salmela, J.H. and Williams, A.M. 'The Developmental Activities of Elite Soccer Players Aged Under-16 Years from Brazil, England, France, Ghana, Mexico, Portugal and Sweden', *Journal of Sports Sciences*, 30 (2012), pp. 1653–1663.

Ford, P.R., Ward, P., Hodges, N.J. and Williams, A.M. 'The Role of Deliberate Practice and Play in Career Progression in Sport: The Early Engagement Hypothesis', *High Ability Studies*, 20 (2009), pp. 65–75.

Ford, P.R. and Williams, A.M. 'The Acquisition of Skill and Expertise: The Role of Practice and Other Activities', in Williams, A.M. (ed.), *Science and Soccer III*, pp. 122–138 (Routledge, 2012a).

Ford, P.R. and Williams, A.M. 'The Developmental Activities Engaged in by Elite Youth Soccer Players Who Progressed to Professional Status Compared to Those Who Did Not', *Psychology of Sport and Exercise*, 13 (2012b), pp. 349–352.

Ford, P. R., Yates, I. and Williams, A. M. 'An Analysis of Practice Activities and Instructional Behaviours Used by Youth Soccer Coaches during Practice:

Exploring the Link between Science and Application', *Journal of Sports Sciences*, 28 (2010), pp. 483–495.

Ghaye, T. 'Reflective Practice', *Faster, Higher, Stronger*, 10 (2001), pp. 9–12.

Gilbert, W., Lichtenwaldt, L., Gilbert, J., Zelezny, L., and Côté, J. 'Developmental Profiles of Successful High School Coaches', *International Journal of Sports Science & Coaching*, 4 (2009), pp. 415–431.

Gilbert, W. and Trudel, P. 'Learning to Coach through Experience: Reflection in Model Youth Sport Coaches', *Journal of Teaching in Physical Education*, 21 (2001), pp. 16–34.

Gladwell, M. *Outliers* (Allen Lane, 2008).

Gould, D., Diffenbach, K. and Moffett, A. 'Psychological Characteristics and Their Development in Olympic Champions,' *Journal of Applied Sport Psychology*, 14 (2002), pp. 172–204.

Guadagnoli, M.A. and Lee, T.D. 'Challenge Point: A Framework for Conceptualizing the Effects of Various Practice Conditions in Motor Learning', *Journal of Motor Behavior*, 36 (2004), pp. 212–224.

Harvey, S., Cushion, C.J., Wegis, H.M. and Massa-Gonzalez, A.N. 'Teaching Games for Understanding in American High-School Soccer: A Quantitative Data Analysis Using the Game Performance Assessment Instrument', *Physical Education and Sport Pedagogy*, 15 (2010), pp. 29–54.

Hendry, D.T., Ford, P.R., Williams, A.M. and Hodges, N.J. 'Five Evidence-Based Principles of Effective Practice and Instruction', in Baker, J. and Farrow, D. (eds.), *The Handbook of Sport Expertise*, pp. 414–429 (Routledge, 2015).

Horrocks, D. 'Brains in Their Feet', *The Psychologist*, 25 (2012), pp. 550–551.

Irwin, G., Hanton, S. and Kerwin, D.G. 'Reflective Practice and the Origins of the Elite Coaching Knowledge', *Reflective Practice*, 5 (2004), pp. 425–442.

Jones, J. *Towards the Goal: The Kaka Story* (Zondervan, 2010).

Knowles, Z., Gilbourne, D., Borrie, A. and Neville, A. 'Developing the Reflective Sports Coach: A Study Exploring the Processes of Reflective Practice Within a Higher Education Coaching Programme', *Reflective Practice*, 2 (2001), pp. 185–207.

Knowles, Z., Gilbourne, D., Cropley, B. and Dugdill, L. *Reflective Practice in the Sport and Exercise Sciences: Contemporary Issues* (Routledge, 2014).

Law, M., Côté, J. and Ericsson, K.A. 'Characteristics of Expert Development in Rhythmic Gymnastics: A Retrospective Study', *International Journal of Sport and Exercise Psychology*, 5 (2007), pp. 82–103.

Lewthwaite, R. and Wulf, G. 'Motor Learning Through a Motivational Lens', in A.M. Williams & N.J. Hodges (eds.), *Skill Acquisition in Sport: Research, Theory, and Practice*, 2nd edn, pp. 173–191 (Routledge, 2012).

Locke, E.A. and Latham, G.P. 'Building a Practically Useful Theory of Goal Setting and Task Motivation: A 35-Year Odyssey', *American Psychologist*, 57 (2002), pp. 705–717.

Lohse, K.R., Wulf, G. and Lewthwaite, R. 'Attentional Focus Affects Movement Efficiency', in Williams, A.M. and Hodges, N.J. (eds.), *Skill Acquisition in Sport: Research, Theory, and Practice*, 2nd edn, pp. 40–58 (Routledge, 2012).

Lynch, M. and Mallett, C. Becoming a Successful High Performance Track and Field Coach', *Modern Athlete and Coach*, 44, no. 2 (2006), pp. 15–20.

Masters, R.S.W. 'Knowledge, (K)nerves and Know-How: The Role of Explicit versus Implicit Knowledge in the Breakdown of a Complex Motor Skill Under Pressure', *British Journal of Psychology*, 83 (1992), pp. 343–358.

Masters, R.S. and Poolton, J.M. 'Advances in Implicit Motor Learning', in Williams, A.M. and Hodges, N.J. (eds.), *Skill Acquisition in Sport: Research, Theory, and Practice*, 2nd edn, pp. 59–76 (Routledge, 2012).

McPherson, S.L. and Kernodle, M.W. 'Tactics, the Neglected Attribute of Expertise: Problem Representations and Performance Skills in Tennis', in Starkes, J. and Ericsson, K.A. (eds.), *Expert Performance in Sport: Recent Advances in Research on Sport Expertise*, pp. 137–168 (Human Kinetics, 2003).

Newell, K.M. 'Coordination, Control, and Skill', in Goodman, D., Wilberg, R.B. and Franks, I.M. (eds.), *Differing Perspectives in Motor Learning, Memory and Control*, pp. 295–317 (Elsevier, 1986).

Newell, A. and Rosenbloom, P.S. 'Mechanisms of Skill Acquisition and the Law of Practice', in Anderson, J.R. (ed.), *Cognitive Skills and Their Acquisition*, pp. 1–55 (Lawrence Erlbaum Associates, 1981).

Ntoumanis, N. and Biddle, S. 'A Review of Motivational Climate in Physical Activity', *Journal of Sports Sciences*, 17 (1999), pp. 643–665.

Ong, N.T. and Hodges, N.J. 'Mixing It Up a Little: How to Schedule Observational Practice', in Williams, A.M. and Hodges, N.J. (eds.), *Skill Acquisition in Sport: Research, Theory, and Practice*, 2nd edn, pp. 22–39 (Routledge, 2012).

Partington, M. and Cushion, C.J. 'An Investigation of the Practice Activities and Coaching Behaviours of Professional Top-Level Youth Soccer Coaches', *Scandinavian Journal of Medicine and Science in Sport* (2011). Article first published online 13 September 2011. doi: 10.1111/j.1600-0838.2011.01383.

Pellegrini, A.D. and Smith, P.K. 'Physical Activity Play: The Nature and Function of a Neglected Aspect of Play', *Child Development*, 69 (1998), pp. 577–598.

Pfeffer, J. and Sutton, R.I. 'Evidence-Based Management', *Harvard Business Review*, 84 (2006), pp. 62–74.

Premier League. *Youth Development Rules: Elite Player Performance Plan*. 2012, unpublished report.

Richards, P., Collins, D. and Mascarenhas, D.R.D. 'Developing Rapid High-Pressure Team Decision-Making Skills. The Integration of Slow Deliberate Reflective Learning within the Competitive Performance Environment: A Case Study of Elite Netball', *Reflective Practice*, 13 (2012), pp. 407–424.

Ronaldo, C. *Moments* (Macmillan, 2007).

Rooney, W. *My Story So Far* (HarperCollins, 2006).

Sackett, D.L. and Rosenberg, W.M.C. 'The Need for Evidence-Based Medicine', *Journal of the Royal Society of Medicine*, 88 (1995), pp. 620–624.

Salmela, J.H., Marques, M.P. and Machado, M. 'The Informal Structure of Football in Brazil', *Insight: The FA Coaches Association Journal*, 7, no. 1 (2004), pp. 17–19.

Schön, D.A. *The Reflective Practitioner: How Professionals Think in Action* (Temple Smith, 1983).

Schraw, G.S., Crippen, K.J. and Hartley, K. 'Promoting Self-Regulation in Science Education: Metacognition as Part of a Broader Perspective on Learning', *Research in Science Education*, 36 (2006), 111–139.

Slavin, R.E. 'Evidence-Based Education Policies: Transforming Educational Practice and Research', *Educational Researcher*, 31 (2002), pp. 15–21.

Smith, M. and Cushion, C.J. 'An Investigation of the In-Game Behaviours of Professional, Top-Level Youth Soccer Coaches', *Journal of Sport Sciences*, 24 (2006), 355–366.

Swinnen, S., Schmidt, R.A., Nicholson, D.E. and Shapiro, D.C. 'Information Feedback for Skill Acquisition: Instantaneous Knowledge of Results Degrades Performance', *Journal of Experimental Psychology: Learning, Memory and Cognition*, 16 (1990), pp. 706–716.

Syed, M. *Bounce: The Myth of Talent and the Power of Practice* (Fourth Estate, 2011).

Thomas, J.R., Nelson, J.K. and Silverman, S.J. *Research Methods in Physical Activity*, 6th edn (Human Kinetics, 2010).

Thorpe, R., Almond, L. and Bunker, D. (eds.) *Rethinking Games Teaching* (Loughborough University, 1986).

Union of European Football Associations. *Regulations of the UEFA Champions League 2015–18 Cycle* (UEFA, 2015). Unpublished report.

Ward, P., Suss, J., Eccles, D.W., Williams, A.M. and Harris, K.R. 'Skill-Based Differences in Option Generation in a Complex Task: A Verbal Protocol Analysis', *Cognitive Processing: International Quarterly of Cognitive Science*, 12 (2011), pp. 289–300.

Williams, A.M. and Ford, P.R. 'Promoting a Skills-Based Agenda in Olympic Sports: The Role of Skill-Acquisition Specialists', *Journal of Sports Sciences*, 27 (2009), pp. 1381–1392.

Williams, A.M., Ford, P.R., Causer, J., Logan, O. and Murray, S. 'Translating Theory into Practice: Working at the "Coal Face" in the UK!' in Williams, A.M. and Hodges, N.J. (eds.), *Skill Acquisition in Sport*, 2nd edn, pp. 353–366 (Routledge, 2012).

Williams, A.M. and Hodges, N.J. 'Practice, Instruction and Skill Acquisition: Challenging Tradition', *Journal of Sports Sciences*, 23 (2005), pp. 637–650.

Williams, A.M. and Hodges, N.J. *Skill Acquisition in Sport: Research, Theory and Practice*, 2nd edn (Routledge, 2012).

Williams, A.M., Ward, P., Bell-Walker, J. and Ford, P.R. 'Perceptual-Cognitive Expertise, Practice History Profiles and Recall Performance in Soccer', *British Journal of Psychology*, 103 (2012), pp. 393–411.

Young, B.W., Jemczyk, K., Brophy, K. and Côté, J. 'Discriminating Skilled Coaching Groups: Quantitative Examination of Developmental Experiences and Activities', *International Journal of Sports Science & Coaching*, 4 (2009), pp. 397–414.

CHAPTER 10

PERFORMANCE ANALYSIS IN PROFESSIONAL FOOTBALL

Dr Chris Carling[1], Jim Lawlor[2], Simon Wells[3]

Senior Lecturer in Coaching and Performance, Institute of Coaching and Performance, School of Sport and Wellbeing, University of Central Lancashire, UK[1]
Chief Scout, Manchester United FC, UK[2]
First Team Scout, Manchester United FC, UK[3]

INTRODUCTION

Over recent years, the analysis of football performance using match and motion analyses has grown in popularity especially among applied practitioners at elite standards of play. The progressive bridging of the gap between sports science and applied coaching practice has enabled a greater recognition of the need for and benefits of an objective systematic process for monitoring performance in training and competition. It is now widely accepted that the ongoing assessment of performance plays a critical part in helping to optimise daily training and preparation practices for competition by contributing to players' development and coaches' understanding of how their players perform. In the English Premier League (EPL), for example, the majority of clubs employ personnel to conduct performance analyses across all levels, including the first team, the reserve team and the youth academy.

In this chapter, we discuss the main steps of the performance analysis (PA) process specifically related to match-play. The first part looks at two components of the PA process: the rationale for analysing performance, and, as a brief overview, the technologies currently employed at elite standards. The second part discusses translating theory into practice, with recommendations on how to select an analysis system, and advice on what components of performance can be analysed and how the results generated are analysed, interpreted and presented. The final part examines the challenges facing PA in the professional football club setting by discussing the role of the contemporary performance analyst and the necessary craft skills. Insights into ensuring provision of a high-quality analysis service, based on the personal experiences of the authors, are presented. Practical advice is provided on meeting the challenges frequently encountered during each step of the process.

THE COMPONENTS OF THE CONTEMPORARY PERFORMANCE ANALYSIS PROCESS

Rationale for Analysing Match-Play

In contemporary professional soccer, it is now recognised that the laying of foundations for achieving success can be significantly enhanced by a more systematic, comprehensive and objective approach to coaching and practice. A greater understanding by contemporary coaching and fitness practitioners of the potential benefits of science and analytic processes has aided in bridging the gap between research and practice. Changes to coach education programmes by some of football's governing bodies to reflect modern advances in PA have also improved the understanding, acceptance and value of the discipline. In turn, this has led to the implementation and application of more scientific and evidence-based practice frameworks for optimising training, match preparation and recruitment. While there is increasing acceptance among coaching practitioners and managers of the use of objective data gathered from quantitative methods, the pragmatic approach to the game recognises that subjective or qualitative analyses of performance, often based on the personal experience and opinions of the coach, cannot be discarded. The craft knowledge of many coaches is developed through a combination of playing the game, observing matches, and successful mentoring by more experienced coaches. The personal knowledge and opinion of coaches is very helpful in developing an extensive library of information in relation to successful strategy and tactics. However, subjective analyses are potentially confounded by personal bias, expectations and needs, and by the limitations of human memory and observation. Thus, a combination of information collected from formal 'objective' and more subjective match analyses is a necessary basis for providing knowledge for understanding via provision of feedback.

As part of a scientific approach to understanding performance, PA provides a factual and permanent record of events underpinning both individual and team performance in competition (Carling and Court, 2013). The information generated aids the practitioner in making informed judgements on collective and individual contributions to performance. PA is necessary for identifying weaknesses that need

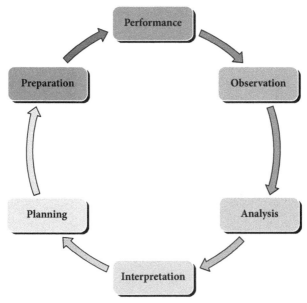

FIGURE 1 *Example of the coaching cycle highlighting the performance analysis stage*

to be addressed as well as strengths that can be built upon. Analyses of opposition teams and players help identify strengths and weaknesses that can be countered or exploited respectively. The feedback derived from analyses helps improve the decision-making process to aid the prescription of evidence-based practices for optimising the technical, tactical and physical requirements specific to soccer as well as impacting on team selection, choice of tactics and playing system/style (see Figure 1). This objective analysis focuses on collective performance as well as on that of individual players, with the information gained from it used to set short- and medium-term priorities, in conjunction with team members, for practice and instruction. Analysis of performance over a period of time is helpful in creating benchmarks against which future performance of the team and/or individual can be compared in order to identify positive and negative trends. A combination of information from video and statistical analyses and subjective scouting reports also enables more informed decisions to be made on player trading.

Techniques Used in Contemporary Performance Analysis

The use of many forms of technology, including digital video, computer software and electronic tracking devices to collect and analyse performance-related data in training and competition, is prominent in the contemporary professional football setting. A non-exhaustive list of match analysis technologies currently available is presented in Table 1. Professional clubs have adopted one or more forms of analysis technology to collect and analyse singly or in combination information

TABLE 1 Contemporary performance analysis systems for competition

Company/institu-tion (country)	System	System type	Website
Citech Holdings Pty Ltd (Australia)	Biotrainer	Electronic trans-mitter	http://www.citechholdings.com
Chukyo University (Japan)	Direct Linear Transformation	Automatic video tracking	
INMOTIO Object Tracking BV (Netherlands)	LPM Soccer 3D	Electronic trans-mitter	http://www.feedbacksport.com
GPSports (Australia)	SPI Elite	GPS tracking	http://www.gpsports.com
Hiroshima College of Sciences (Japan)	Direct Linear Transformation	Automatic video tracking	
National Defense Academy (Japan)	Triangular surveying	Triangular surveying	
Noldus (Netherlands)	Observer Pro	Manual video coding	http://www.noldus.com
Performance Group International (UK)	DatatraX	Automatic video tracking	http://www.datatrax.tv
ProZone Holdings Ltd (UK)	ProZone	Automatic video tracking	http://www.pzfootball.co.uk
RealTrackFootball (Spain)	Real Track Football	GPS tracking	http://www.realtrackfutbol.com
Sport-Universal Process SA (France)	AMISCO Pro	Automatic video tracking	http://www.sport-universal.com
Sportstec (Australia)	Trak Performance	Computer pen and tablet	http://www.sportstecinterna-tional.com
TRACAB (Sweden)	Tracab	Automatic video tracking	http://www.tracab.com
University of Campinus (Brazil)	Dvideo	Automatic video tracking	

on physical, technical and tactical play. Traditional hand notation and scouting techniques have progressively been phased out by a plethora of computerised analysis systems developed commercially.

Innovations in computer and digital video technology (software and hardware) have greatly streamlined the entire match analysis process. Live analysis is now a reality, allowing real-time monitoring of performance during and immediately after play. Some software mainly focuses on technical and tactical analyses of match performance (e.g. http://www.sportstec.com/; http://www.nacsport.com/). There are also touchscreen devices available, such as tablet computers and smartphones (see Statzpack and Platosport on http://itunes.apple.com/). The development in the 1990s of multiple camera systems provided non-intrusive mediums to track and collect data on player movements and actions over the entire course of competition (see http://www.pzfootball.co.uk). Data management systems currently exist, ranging from familiar computer database packages provided by Microsoft or Apple, to specific sports performance applications such as Edge10 (www.edge10.org/) and SportsData Hub (www. http://sportsdatahub.com/). Online commercial scouting databases of technical and tactical information (statistical data and video clips) are now routinely used by clubs to advise on player recruitment strategies. Solutions include: https://www.stats.com; http://info.scout7.com/; http://www.wyscout.com. For a detailed review of contemporary match-analysis technologies, see Carling (2016).

TRANSLATING THEORY INTO PRACTICE

Introduction

A large range of commercial PA technologies currently exists. Unfortunately, choosing a system to analyse performance and support coach decision-making is never straightforward. Technology is ever-evolving and the club must continuously review its information needs while attempting to fit its requirements in with the club's overall technological infrastructure and resources. Cost and quality of systems can vary quite dramatically and investments need to find the balance between needs and budget to ensure a return on investment. Only the very best in tailored and well-exploited match analysis systems can provide a sound basis to analyse performance and subsequently make an impact in daily training and competition.

Similarly, in addition to the type of system employed (and experience and skills of the analyst – see Challenges in the Working Environment), an effective performance analysis process relies on deciding what information should be recorded, for what purpose and how it is used to improve performance. Using sophisticated technology is one thing; it is, however, how the coach (with the support of an experienced analyst) uses the system to improve the game that really matters. Can it be used to aid understanding of performance and eventually be translated into practical applications to impact on training? There is a need to focus on areas of performance where results will have maximum impact and where advantages will be gained both in the short and the long term.

In this section, we attempt to translate theory into practice by providing advice on what to look for when choosing a system. We also discuss working with information generated from analyses, from the initial selection of game events and their analysis to potential issues when interpreting the information that will eventually be presented to players and coaching staff, and its subsequent practical utilisation. In many teams the Coach/Analyst and even technology relationship evolves in an organic and often trial and error fashion, and while this can afford progress to be made, there remains a need for a more strategic appraisal to control and cost this discipline.

Selecting a Performance Analysis System

There are three key issues that need to be balanced and taken into account before adopting a PA system – namely, *needs* versus *functionality* versus *cost*. When making a choice, it is important to set a balance between the information currently available and what will be needed, and not duplicate what already exists. Any system should be integrated according to current and (where possible) future strategic, tactical and operational needs. It should address clearly defined and measurable needs. In addition, if the system requires the athletes to wear any devices, it must comply with the rules of the sport. A health, safety and risk assessment should also be completed where necessary – for example, if equipping players with electronic devices. The implementation of any form of analysis technology necessitates clear responses to many practical and technical questions:

- Does the system provide data to answer the specific questions on and needs for performance of all coaching and fitness personnel?
- Can it help all teams or is it restricted to the senior team?
- Is it restricted to match-play or can it also, or only, be used in training?
- How often can and will it be used? (e.g. in both home and away matches?)
- Is it user-friendly, responsive and adaptable, and can it be tailored for different usage and changing needs? Can the coaching staff also easily use it to visualise output?
- Is it 'productive' in terms of time to code games and produce final output presentations? Is real-time analysis possible? If not, what is the delay to obtain results?

- What are the possibilities in terms of using the end-user software to statistically analyse, cross-tabulate and present data? Can data be easily exported for manipulation in other software?
- Does the system include a database for managing data and performing trend analysis, and can practitioners remotely access stored information?
- Does the system allow online and offline use? Does it always have to be connected to the internet?
- How much does it cost to purchase? Do we have to pay on a user-licence basis? Can we hire, or do we use, a service from an outside match analysis provider?
- Is there an after-sales support service, and will software and/or hardware upgrades be made available, and for what cost?
- Has it undergone adequate quality-control checks (algorithm and/or manual error correction of generated data, validity, reliability, accuracy) to ensure credibility of information? And what about storage and security?
- If a match analysis provider is used, do we agree with the definitions used by their operators to code match events or are these customisable?
- Will operator training and/or additional staff be required to use the system, and if so, what are the time and cost implications?

Selection of Performance Indicators

In some clubs, performance analysts can have considerable input into the selection of the key match events to be analysed, whereas in others this is considered the role of the coaching staff. Ultimately, the choice of events depends on the personal philosophy of the coaching staff, and notably on their pre-defined short- and medium-term objectives. All performance measures need to sit comfortably with the collective strategy and tactics used to attain the club's objectives. However, selection of information frequently evolves over the course of the season, mainly due to changes in current form and the constant need to take into consideration the broad range of tactics and playing styles of opponents. Specific needs will also vary across the different operational levels – for example, youth team, first team and reserve team – within a club.

Information relating to game performance and training can cover a large spectrum. Generally, it is collected on four individual but interrelated features of play, encompassing behavioural, technical, tactical and physical factors. Analysts and coaches tend to use a combination of statistical data and edited digital video compilations that will cover all four key factors. Behavioural elements of play are difficult to evaluate in a systematic unbiased way and are thus subjective in nature. Nevertheless, when scouting a potential future recruit, for example, the observers might provide a simple descriptive report backed up by selected video clips and match data. Recruitment analysts and scouts might attempt to analyse (individually and collectively) factors such as game understanding and intelligence, leadership, determination, discipline, aggression, the ability to perform under pressure, cohesion, and the willingness of players to work for the team. However, analysis of these and other behavioural aspects of play is beyond the scope of this chapter. In the following sections, we provide examples of key indicators of tactical/technical and physical performance.

Tactical and Technical Indicators

In tactical and technical analyses of play, a combination of both qualitative and quantitative techniques is generally employed. The former generally involves visualisation of selected game actions using digital video compilations. Where necessary, slow-motion playback and split-screen analyses of performance can be employed to clearly highlight important issues identified by coaching practitioners and/or analysts over the course of play. For quantitative analyses of tactical and technical performance, game events are coded to provide information on four key factors: the player involved, and the type, position and time of action. These four elements provide raw counts of important match events more commonly known as key performance indicators, or KPIs (Mackenzie and Cushion, 2013). The statistical information can then be pulled together with the corresponding video clips to enable synchronised visualisation and evaluation using both forms of analysis.

Generally, KPIs relate to the frequency of, efficiency of and/or success rates in outcome events such as turnovers, ball possession, passing, crossing, set plays, final third entries and goal attempts. These indicators can be used in an attacking and defending sense. For example, the total number of crosses conceded or ratio of final third entries achieved to goals scored, the percentage of duels won or lost, and the frequency of interceptions or turnovers made and free kicks won or conceded are of interest. Table 2 provides a non-exhaustive list of KPIs. However, KPIs only provide a rudimentary understanding of sports performance and give little information about techniques and behaviours underpinning the outcome measure. Information collected on which players regain possession, and where and how, for example, has important tactical implications for creating and preventing scoring occasions and goals. On regaining possession, coaches might want to examine their team's ability to keep the ball, control and vary the game tempo, enter into critical scoring areas and create scoring opportunities. Information on the decisive actions preceding occasions/goals is of interest. Knowing the origin of final actions is useful for identifying which areas teams are dangerous in and what type of actions they use (e.g. crosses, dribbles, set plays). Analysis of goal attempts can provide pertinent information on which players tend to shoot from distance or who regularly scores headers from crosses (back post, outswinging?), or on the area of the goal in which a player places penalties.

TABLE 2 Examples of key performance indicators

Key performance indicators: attacking/defending play
No. goals scored/conceded
No. goal attempts/occasions
% goal attempts on target
Strike rate for goal attempts: ratio goal attempts to goals
Expected goals ratio
Total shots ratio
No. set plays won
No. corners won
No. free kicks won
No. goal attempts and goals scored from set plays
Strike rate for set plays: ratio set plays to goals
% ball possession
% ball possession: opponents half/own half, final third
No. passes
% pass completion
% passes played forward/backwards/sideways
% forward pass completion
No. final third and/or penalty area entries
Strike rate for final third and/or penalty area entries: ratio to goals scored/goal attempts/occasions
No. crosses
% cross completion
Ratio: goal attempts or occasions to goals scored from crosses
Strike rate for crosses: ratio crosses to goals

Unfortunately, simple frequency counts might not tell the full story and can occasionally be misleading regarding how a team and/or player has performed both tactically and technically. Consideration should be given not only to 'how often' an action is performed but also to 'how well'. Further discussion on the analysis and interpretation of data is provided later in this chapter. Nevertheless, statistical information regarding attacking and defending actions should be completed (where possible) using qualitative analyses of play. These can include synchronised visualisation of edited video compilations mentioned earlier, heat map charts presenting zone coverage and 2D and 3D animations of actions. The latter are useful for presenting positional and movement information that might not be clear or even show up at all on the video footage. Features of attacking play that might not stand out in the statistical summary relate to width, penetration, support, improvisation and the capacity to change the game tempo, switch play and switch from defence to attack. Similarly, defending performance might include descriptive analyses of defensive organisation: marking and positioning, space reduction, depth, delay, concentration, support, control and the ability to turn over possession. Work is currently under way using sophisticated analytical techniques to automatically define teams' playing style and study dynamic interactions between players, taking into consideration their and the ball's position (see e.g. https://www.stats.com/webinars/playing-style-impacts-physical-demands-football/).

The employment of analysts purely to support recruitment is a recent development and the tools and products to support such work are relatively few. At present, the contemporary analyst therefore has a major opportunity to influence the parameter set used for recruitment analysis and also for presentation of the findings.

Physical Performance Indicators

In physical analyses of play, time-motion analyses techniques are frequently used as an indirect means of analysing the intensity of exercise and quantifying the physical efforts of players in match-play. Data derived from these processes permit the general and position-specific characteristics of physical performance to be quantified and enable more objective decision making in the structuring of conditioning elements for training and match preparation to replicate match-play needs. Data on the time spent or distance covered in predefined movement categories (based on running speed) are used to calculate exercise-to-rest ratios and notably high- to low-intensity activity ratios. This information can subsequently be used to tailor fitness training programmes to the demands that are specific to the playing position/individual. Time-motion variables frequently include:

- total distance run (global representation of the intensity of exercise);
- distance covered (or percentage of total distance or time spent) walking and in low-, moderate- and high-intensity (or cruising) and sprinting movement;
- ratio (in time or distance) of low- to high-intensity exercise;
- mean recovery time between consecutive high-intensity bouts or frequency of consecutive actions separated by very low recovery times (e.g. % of total actions performed after a recovery time <30s);
- nature of recovery activity between consecutive high-intensity actions (standing, walking, running…);
- repeated high-intensity running sequences (e.g. three or more consecutive high-intensity bouts with a mean recovery duration equal to or less than 20s between efforts);

- frequency and type of high-intensity bouts: 'explosive' action characterised by a fast acceleration or 'leading' action characterised by a gradual acceleration;
- frequency of other potentially physically taxing actions (short but intense accelerations and decelerations, turns, challenges, headers);
- distance covered and speeds when running with the ball.

The above information can also be interfaced (competition rules permitting) with other indicators of 'loading', including heart rate and GPS-derived indices. This leads to increased opportunities for monitoring and controlling the strain and workload inherent to the sport and potentially for reducing the risk of injury or ill health.

Working with Performance-Related Data

How Are Data Analysed?

Performance analysts must be familiar with the large range of performance-related data formats commonly derived from match and time-motion analyses. These include analysis and interpretation of output data regarding:

- time: e.g. total time spent in possession in opponents' half;
- distance: e.g. total distance covered at high intensities;
- speed: e.g. average running speed over the course of play;
- totals: e.g. total number of goal occasions achieved from corners;
- means: e.g. average number of uncompleted passes per game;
- percentages: e.g. percentage of total goal attempts on target;
- ratios: e.g. ratio of penalty-area entries to scoring occasions;
- rankings: e.g. league ranking for goals scored from set plays;
- scores/points: e.g. result, win/draw/loss.

Some formats have limitations and the analyst will frequently need to adapt their approach to ensure correct interpretation of data. For example, it is difficult to compare the cumulated or total number of shots between two teams if they have not played the same number of games. A mean value for shots performed per game or per 90 minutes might be better. Similarly, caution is required when using percentages to compare results as their interpretation can easily be distorted. For example, in a cup match played over two legs, a team managed 4 out of 5 shots on target (80%) in the first game, whereas 10 out of 15 (67%) were on target in the second game away from home. The coaching staff might judge that team performance was better in the second leg as a substantially higher overall number of shots were on target and the team created more scoring occasions. There may be more efficient ways of making certain data points stand out. For example, rather than presenting information on forward passes as a total number of actions, this may be presented as a percentage of the overall number of passes, providing an indication of a team's willingness to play the ball forward.

Selection and analysis of a number of key performance indicators for the team as a whole is a useful starting point. This can provide a quick snapshot of overall team performance. For consistency and ease of understanding, similar variables for both defensive and attacking play (e.g. goals scored/conceded, set plays won or conceded) can be used. Depending on the results observed in this first level of analysis, exploration of the data set can subsequently be fine-tuned to compare results across individuals or selected team units. For example, the overall time spent by an upcoming opponent in ball possession might be broken down into the percentage of this KPI spent in their opponents' half. The analysis of possession might then be further extended to determine which individual players spent the most time with the ball and who was the most efficient in converting possession into the creation of scoring occasions.

The coaching staff might ask the analyst to quantify the number of errors made by a player to explore a potential weakness – for example, it might be a player identified as having a low success rate in passing and shooting with his 'weaker' foot. Tactical instructions may ensue to force the player into playing the ball with his weaker foot. Practitioners might also want to judge the 'effectiveness' of a strategic change implemented in team preparation – for example, they might be interested in the effect of a modification in team tactics or playing formation on the total number of goals scored or conceded and scoring opportunities created or conceded, comparing the situation before the change with that following it. However, objectively quantifying what is a 'meaningful' or 'worthwhile' change in match performance remains a challenge, as does the question of which performance variables to use, and the process can be arbitrary. A coach might deem a 16% drop in the number of free kicks conceded less important than an 8% increase in attempts on goal. Analysts will also consider 'efficiency' measures, such as the ratio of goal attempts to goals scored by a striker or the ratio of crosses to scoring occasions from crosses for the team as a whole.

Potential relationships between variables can be examined using simple correlation coefficients. Practitioners might study, for example, the association between scores determined in fitness tests (e.g. repeated-sprint ability) and running performance in competition (frequency of high-intensity bouts). Frequently asked questions include the following: is a player with a lower fitness score in a test of intermittent endurance performance more susceptible to drop off in performance towards the end of match-play or, conversely, is an 'underperforming' player, albeit with a high fitness score in the test, not making the most of his physical ability?

The data set can also be broken down to identify key trends when winning or losing games (see Table 3). It might be useful to quantify how the team coped when

TABLE 3 Differences in a professional football team's key performance indicators according to match result (adapted from Carling *et al.*, 2015)

Attacking performance

Match Result	Goals scored	Goal attempts	On-target goal attempts	% On-target goal attempts	Final 1/3 Entries	Crosses	% Completed Crosses	Forward Passes	% Completed forward passes
Won	2.5 ± 1.1	16.0 ± 4.8	6.7 ± 2.8	42.5 ± 14.0	53.3 ± 13.7	24.0 ± 8.7	23.1 ± 9.8	333 ± 49	69.6 ± 7.2
Drawn	1.0 ± 0.8	14.4 ± 4.8	4.9 ± 2.5	34.1 ± 12.5	58.7 ± 13.9	25.1 ± 7.4	22.5 ± 8.1	342 ± 66	69.5 ± 7.4
Lost	0.7 ± 0.8	12.4 ± 4.3	4.4 ± 2.2	35.8 ± 14.3	56.6 ± 12.6	24.4 ± 8.5	20.5 ± 7.5	330 ± 56	68.3 ± 5.7

Defending performance (match events conceded)

Match Result	Goals Conc	Goal attempts	On-target goal attempts	% On-target goal attempts	Final 1/3 Entries	Crosses	% Completed Crosses	Forward Passes	% Completed forward passes
Won	0.6 ± 0.7	9.7 ± 4.1	3.1 ± 1.7	33.4 ± 16.3	39.4 ± 10.4	17.3 ± 6.0	20.7 ± 10.9	278 ± 43	62.8 ± 6.3
Drawn	1.0 ± 0.8	10.0 ± 4.1	3.7 ± 2.2	35.7 ± 16.9	42.5 ± 16.2	16.7 ± 6.7	23.6 ± 11.7	266 ± 45	60.7 ± 85
Lost	2.1 ±	11.4 ±	5.2 ± 2.6	46.5 ± 16.3	45.3 ±	15.8 ± 5.7	23.9 ± 10.4	266 ± 41	61.8 ± 7.0

losing a player (sending off, injury), when conceding a goal first, or when playing against certain team formations. The contributions of substitutes in comparison with those of the players they replace and those who remain on the pitch can be statistically evaluated. Similarly, a new player's performance compared with that of the peer they replaced and a comparison of a player's performance before and after a prolonged break due to injury are both pertinent. An assessment of a future recruit's match performance can provide comprehensive clues as to how the player might perform in relation to the club's current squad and style of play and/or in relation to the demands of playing in a new league, especially when recruiting a foreign player. Specific analysis of performance in games against top 6 teams or against peers in the relegation places can give an idea of a team's ability to 'raise their game' or 'grind out' results against teams fighting for survival, respectively.

Other practical analyses of statistical information might include quantification of the team's ability to adapt physically or tactically in away games versus home games or after conceding or scoring a goal. Quantification of performance in relation to team possession – in other words, during defensive or attacking play – can provide answers when a problem is highlighted by the coaching staff. Here, subjective analyses from video can sometimes be beneficial for physical analyses as the efforts of a player – for example, the willingness of a midfield player to support play or that of an attacker to track back defensively – are not always shown up realistically in the statistical picture. In some sports, longitudinal measures of the total distance run have made it possible to analyse the evolution of physical activity profiles over seasons. The overall physical requirements in Premier League match-play have notably increased (Barnes *et al.*, 2014). In turn, this information has had consequences for contemporary fitness training strategies. Similarly, PA can be used as a vehicle to promote excellence in young players by evaluating progress over time and, after accounting for individual contexts, it can even aid in setting age-group standards for certain key performance indicators.

Data can be explored to identify trends across match periods. Running performance, for example, is commonly analysed across halves or towards the end of games (e.g. final 15-minute interval) to aid in identifying whether a team or an individual within the collective unit is susceptible to accumulated fatigue. Similarly, the player's ability to cope with dense periods of high-intensity activity has been investigated by using the drop in the distance covered following a peak period of high-speed running. Analysis of the length of time spent in, and the type of recovery after, two or more consecutive intense efforts (of repeated-sprint activity) can give an indication of transient fatigue. Information can be used to assess a player's ability (or inability) to resist fatigue, and it has practical implications for countermeasures to fatigue such as fitness training regimens and recovery practices. Analysis of physical efforts in other match intervals, such as the first 5-minutes of play of the match and straight after the pause, can also give an idea of physical 'readiness' of players and has implications for the intensity and duration of warm-up routines.

The analyst might also track intra-seasonal changes in running-activity profiles or changes during periods of fixture congestion to try to identify players who are coping and those who are failing to maintain performance. Analysis of changes in running activity might be associated with tactical or technical measures to identify any concomitant variations in skill-related activities or proficiency. It is also useful to analyse results in relation to past performance – for example, comparing running efforts in a player over the first 10 games in the present season and the previous season, or before and after international duty. Some managers/coaches like to divide the season into thirds or halves, or into blocks of games, and benchmark progress to each of these milestones. The analysis of data might attempt to quantify variations or, conversely, look for consistency or improvements in certain areas of performance over a number of matches. Simple standard deviations and/or percentage coefficients of variation can give a useful idea of variations in performance over the course of a season. It can be interesting to isolate and then compare data from games that fell near to average performance with those that were far from average. Ranges or maximum or minimum values can also give an idea of 'ideal' or 'worst' performance.

Interpreting Results – Considerations

The interpretation part of the analysis process should also be the moment when the analyst takes into account extrinsic and intrinsic factors that potentially influenced the match-to-match results and benchmarking of data. Simple statistical analyses may not always be a fair reflection of how a player performs, as factors such as opposition standard, team formation and playing style all play a part in determining performance. Running activity, for example, might be less affected in games against top 5 opposition teams than it is in games against the bottom 5, whereas the inverse could occur for tactical and technical aspects of play. Contextual issues that must be accounted for include changes in staff or player personnel, current form, whether the match is home or away or a local derby (fixture lists), progression in some competitions and exit in others, as well as environmental conditions (e.g. wind, pitch quality). Uncontrollable events can also impact the data – for example, the associated travel/logistics issues, training regimes and competition schedules resulting from players' national team obligations. While clubs frequently encounter difficulties accessing information about these trips, they must take the effects into account as potentially there will be some impact – minimal in some players, but significant in others. These points are further emphasised when using a third-party data provider as important aspects of qualitative contextual information relating to KPIs might be lost in the data collection process.

The constant interaction between physical, technical, tactical and psychosocial factors over the course of play can lead to errors when interpreting data. Match data are often 'noisy' in nature and are affected by the random and natural variations across games, so that multiple measures are necessary to provide a more accurate understanding of what has happened even in a single match. A forward player's underperformance both physically and tactically in attacking play (e.g. less distance covered in high-intensity exercise, lower number of ball touches) might simply be linked to the tactical demands inherent in his or her team's playing style, or perhaps to a current lack of confidence affecting his or her contribution. A substantial drop in physical performance towards the end of a game in a holding midfielder might be found to be related to team ball possession or even to the amount of time the ball was in play. Consideration of the player's psychological status, physiological make-up and preparation, technical execution, tactical understanding, decision-making abilities and contextual factors is necessary, but unfortunately this is not always possible.

Statistical data might not always accurately represent the bigger performance 'picture'. Occasionally a team might have 'statistically' outperformed their opponent but lost the game, and vice versa. Statistics can potentially lead to a false idea of how well a player or team performed. A player who has a high success rate in passing (e.g. 90%) might tend to play a less risky game based on short sideways and backwards passes. Similarly, a low proficiency rate in passing by an attacking midfield player might be linked to a lack of off-the-ball movement by teammates. Caution is also required if an overall ranking index is used, as low performance in one aspect of play by a team against a team of a higher standard might be countered (and thus hidden) by extremely high levels of performance in another. The bringing together of quantitative and qualitative methods again provides a greater understanding than either approach can achieve alone.

Data Presentation Formats

Once data have been collected, some players or coaching personnel will want immediate feedback – for example, on completion of a match. The immediacy of feedback and its on-demand provision and presentation are crucial for gaining acceptance of the process. Where training is concerned, basic information presented orally or visually immediately after play is generally acceptable for most players or coaches, and they will then be happy to allow time to be taken to produce a more detailed analysis that will follow. While the largest part of the match-analysis process generally involves data collection, analysis and output, analysts frequently provide visual and verbal presentations of findings collectively and/or individually to coaches and players. These interventions are commonly given during team talks over the course of the build-up to the next match and/or the day after the game itself while performance is still fresh in the memory. Advice for analysts on these presentations is provided below in the section Challenges in the Working Environment. Nevertheless, crucial decisions on the format in which information is presented are necessary. Ultimately, coaching staff and players will judge the utility of match analyses on the output they see. It is important that the analyst starts from the point of view that coaches will use the final output to affect the decisions they make and their subsequent choice of preparation strategies.

Most coaches and players are familiar with breaking down match performance using edited video recordings of match-play during team talk presentations. Nevertheless, as mentioned earlier, a balance of both quantitative and qualitative information feedback may prove most beneficial and may remove any doubts that there might be from using the results of only one type of analysis. In addition, the feedback content should be examined by the coach/manager to ensure a balance in both positive and negative elements of performance. Attention should be paid to the methods of reporting and to how and how much these can and should be customised according to ever-evolving needs, especially as reports can be results-dependent. Consensus is essential to provide result templates that are appropriate to coaching and fitness personnel and that will help inform and guide decisions to eventually impact upon match performance. The reporting formats must be discussed thoroughly between staff and analysts and agreed on, and they must undergo regular review to avoid amassing oceans of poorly presented data that will ultimately be rejected.

Report templates commonly used in professional soccer club settings generally include graphical representations, tables and descriptive text. Irrespective of presentation, the chosen format should capture the attention of the viewer, be informative and leave no doubt regarding interpretation of information (see Tableau software for pertinent examples: http://www.tableau.com/). Additional formats, such as zone coverage charts or spatial pitch maps (e.g. showing where attacking channels are displayed) and 2D/3D animated match reconstructions, can also provide pertinent qualitative information related to tactical aspects. Report templates, where possible, should be associated with corresponding video clips and completed with annotations and comments relating to the match objectives and coaching points. In general the analyst must 'know' his or her key technical staffs in depth, as presenting data and prompting questions are key responsibilities. It is for the analyst to ask questions and for the coach to answer them. The growth in social media platforms, portable tablets and smartphones offers a valuable channel to distribute information, but this must be carefully considered in the context of elite football.

Practical Applications of Data

The information collected from game analyses is the foundation for providing objective feedback on individual and team performance. In turn, it has scope for informing practitioner-led interventions within training and preparation for competition. Indeed, a measure of success of match analyses and the outcomes generated by them is their implementation in the training process – hence the importance of collecting data with practical implications. The challenge remains one of how to effectively integrate into practice the evidence base that has been generated, and how to evaluate its eventual impact in the competition setting.

In general, performance analysts have little or no input in the coaching interventions conducted by coaching and fitness personnel. The analyst can, however, play an important role in evaluating whether there is evidence of progress (or not) in the competitive setting – for example, by comparing data collected before and after the intervention. While care is necessary when considering the magnitude of any change in performance, drops or improvements in some outcome scores (notably tactical and technical KPIs) are fairly easy to interpret. For example, a reduction in the number of goal attempts conceded per game (20 vs. 15 = 25% drop) from the first to the second half of the season would generally be considered positive by analyst and practitioner. In contrast, determining whether physical output is dropping during a prolonged period of fixture congestion or whether there has been a 'positive' change in performance following a fitness or recovery intervention is more difficult due to the random and natural variations in running performance inherent in football competition (Gregson et al., 2010).

CHALLENGES IN THE WORKING ENVIRONMENT

Role of the Contemporary Performance Analyst

Over recent years, the position of the 'performance analyst' or 'match analyst' has slowly gained acceptance as one of several viable sports science professions within contemporary professional football. The performance analyst is now universally considered to be an integral and indispensable part of an interdisciplinary sports science support team, frequently liaising with strength and conditioning and science personnel. However, as time has moved on and departments have grown, the separation of technical and physical analysis, notably in English Premier League clubs, has meant there is now frequently a split in the analysis of technical/tactical and physical performance data (see Figure 2).

Staffing structures within football clubs differ the world over and indeed differ even across Europe and the UK. The size, resources and level of competition all have an effect on what can be done. Generally, and thankfully, the historical trend where every new manager made wholesale changes is no longer the norm. Like large-scale organisations in other business sectors, this enables clubs to retain important staff, knowledge and experience often acquired over a number of seasons, which has been integral in allowing the club to gain a competitive

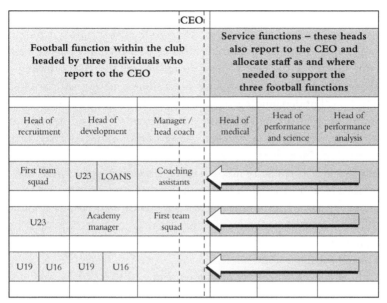

			CEO			
Football function within the club headed by three individuals who report to the CEO				**Service functions – these heads also report to the CEO and allocate staff as and where needed to support the three football functions**		
Head of recruitment	Head of development		Manager / head coach	Head of medical	Head of performance and science	Head of performance analysis
First team squad	U23	LOANS	Coaching assistants			
U23		Academy manager	First team squad			
U19	U16	U19	U16			

FIGURE 2 Example of organisational structure in a Premier League football club

edge. Club owners quite rightly want managers to focus on the task of ensuring the senior team perform and allow the other fundamental structures, staffing and knowledge base to be retained and incrementally improved from within. What we present here in Figure 2 is not a common model, which exists in many clubs. It is a representation of what our collective experience and knowledge to date show is a model more capable of being successful and of being managed.

It is divided into two elements, a Football Function, represented on the left and Service Functions, represented on the right. The manager, or more commonly the head coach, may have one or two assistants who they themselves bring to the club, but not more than this. The three service function managers then select and provide the most appropriate staff from their command to support the first team column on an ongoing basis (to be reviewed annually). They also distribute staff to the other functions of development and recruitment on the same basis. The strength of the structure (which is essentially of matrix type) is that there is a professional career path for everyone in the model managed by the head of the service functions, who on an annual basis reviews who should go where to optimise the performance of the units and to keep the model fresh and satisfy the personal and professional ambitions of their staff teams. In addition, it facilitates clarification of the roles and responsibilities of the medical and performance teams. For example, if a player has a medical issue, the initial responsibility for the care and support and accountability for that player lies with the medical department. At the appropriate time in the return to play continuum, the athlete will then be managed predominantly by the performance and science stream as they undergo the final stages of rehabilitation before resuming team training. Communication between both parties is essential throughout the return to play process to ensure smooth transitioning of the player through the key stages. Medical practitioners in general may not have detailed technical understanding/training in the detail of physiology or physical conditioning for football, and likewise sports scientists are not trained to treat illness or injury, but there have been many occasions where they stray into each other's domain with mixed and often suboptimum results. The Head of Performance Analysis is a more modern role but becoming more necessary in the move by clubs to more analytical tools and the requirement to store and process huge volumes of data. This person will not only select, manage and maintain the hardware, software tools and infrastructure needs of all these functions but will also recruit, train, mentor and position staff across this model to provide the best support for all the football functions.

The CEO would have only six people reporting to them. The model does not suggest an equal level of status or remuneration among these six but rather the structure ensures the right individual is able to be fully capable and accountable for their staff and performance of that function. Horizontally, they are able to integrate across the football functions and vertically they are able to manage the staff and resources within their command. Obviously, a fully staffed structure of this nature would only exist at the bigger clubs who have the resources, volume and need to implement it. The functions would be scalable to smaller operations as long as the key fundamentals of the roles and responsibilities remain and this is the key objective for owners/CEOs.

In an ideal set-up, the performance (or 'technical') analyst should perhaps only focus on liaising with the technical coaching staff, leaving physical analyses to strength and conditioning staff and sports scientists. Analysis requires feedback with a directed approach, and this can only be given if the analyst is qualified to give it. The fact that an analyst has a degree in sports science does not mean that he or she is qualified to direct top-level players in physical performance. If possible, this should be left to experts in the sports science/performance department. The performance analyst can then focus on providing statistical accounts and video-based feedback to the coaching staff/players on technical and tactical performance. However, in some clubs this is not always possible due to limited human resources and an unwillingness to provide funding.

Some analysts can perform several key roles within a football club, whereas others focus on a single area. The analyst may only be minimally involved in some of the phases in the coaching process outlined earlier in Figure 1 but is often expected to support the outcomes (i.e. interpretation/identify areas to work on/feedback to the players). The coaches/manager drive most of the phases but expect support from the analyst as and when needed. Many

Premier League clubs have now moved away from having a single analyst and have built a team of technical analysts each covering specific areas. Their roles might be providing video analyses of tactical training sessions or evaluating data on a future recruit. An analyst might perform real-time technical and tactical analyses during competition, ensuring that coaching staff combine their subjective opinions with objective statistical data to make key split-second decisions. Another might be assigned to monitoring direct opposition or identifying trends in play in other top-flight clubs both at home and abroad to aid short/medium-term planning decisions. Specialised scouting analysts are frequently employed as a bridge between the craft knowledge, experience and intuition of field scouts and managers and a more scientific approach to player recruitment using video and statistics. It is also common for analysts to aid in youth development schemes through the provision of video compilations to academy or reserve-team players.

Many clubs now have a 'head' or 'lead' performance analyst. As well as performing many of the usual tasks mentioned earlier, the head performance analyst will also have a managerial-type role. This can entail recruiting and managing PA personnel and looking after budgets and project expenditure while organising, developing and ensuring the future of the PA process within the club. To ensure the smooth running of the department, there must be a strong link between the technical department, especially via the head analyst, and the coaching staff/manager. The lead analyst needs to ensure that all analysts have received the necessary training to respond adequately to the club's needs when filming and monitoring performance. He or she must also ensure that the coding of match-play is always impartial, reliable and accurate. Internally, all analysts must be familiar with and respect the definitions agreed upon in their club to code game events, and thus consensus with coaching and fitness staff on event definitions is essential. If working with a third-party data provider, the analyst should know who to contact in case clarifications of the definitions used to code game events are necessary. For example, a defensive clearance directly into touch might be considered by some clubs a successful clearance, whereas some analysts might quantify it as a lost possession, and thus an unsuccessful action. A standard and universally accepted framework, especially on technical parameters and definitions used in football, would enhance consistency and clarity, leading to more valuable comparison of data sets between clubs and countries (McKenzie and Cushion, 2013).

The lead analyst must consider the integration of a database service to ensure that as data collection is repeated, storage and trend analysis of information can be used to answer key performance-related questions. It can take time to collect sufficient data to discern and detect trends in play. Top clubs participate in many competitions, sometimes five per season, and with tour and pre-season games, this can push the total up towards 70 games. The volume of data this results in can be vast, and disciplined selection, prioritisation and management of information is crucial and requires significant financial and time commitment.

It is also the role of the lead analyst to consider the integration of a backup service to ensure there is no loss or corruption of data. Similarly, ensuring the protection of information – in other words, who can access it and what they can do with it and how this can be done – is critical. Considering the significant financial and time investment involved in the creation of the data set, as well as the high level of intellectual property and the confidentiality and sensitivity of the information, appropriate steps must be taken from the outset. Other key functional departments within the club (finance and IT) also need to play their part in contributing to the support and resourcing of a vital service to the team and coaches. Performance data is not an 'add-on' to be accommodated; it is a key and core data set which directly supports the coaches and manager in their decision making.

Craft Skills of the Contemporary Performance Analyst

For anyone wishing to pursue a career in the field, a background in PA via educational and/or professional training courses is evidently essential. Prior experience can be acquired over the course of a degree in sports science and/ or football coaching awards. A sports science degree is extremely useful as this will provide pertinent scientific knowledge in many other interrelated aspects of the game that potentially influence performance (e.g. physiology, biomechanics, socio-psychological aspects). PA accreditation schemes exist and include those offered by the International Society of Performance Analysis of Sport (www.ispas.org) and the British Association of Sport and Exercise Sciences (http://www.bases.org.uk/). Professional training courses, such as those led by Prozone, are also available (https://www.stats.com). Numerous football science conferences are held almost every year (see http://www.wcss. org.uk/ and http://www.scienceandfootball.com/). Recently numerous blogs have appeared providing pertinent information on football analysis, see for example northyardanalytics.com and statsbomb.com. Clubs frequently advertise internships, which are a valuable means of gaining applied experience and enhancing the skills gained from a degree in sports science, although they are frequently unpaid. Finally, while coaching experience is currently not essential, a recognised award can significantly aid the analyst in understanding some of the concepts, prerequisites and philosophies that are part of coaching and managing the contemporary soccer player. Knowledge of 'the game' is crucially important and this expertise may be obtained in many ways, as a former player, coach or student of the game. An absence of this knowledge will severely inhibit progress in the role and the credibility/effectiveness of the individual analyst.

The craft skills required to contribute to a high-quality PA service within a professional football club are numerous. The analyst must generally be able to work in a non-stop, high-pressure, results-orientated yet highly confidential environment. An analyst must work within two competing dynamics – planned tasks which happen frequently and must be completed, and ad hoc requests which become top priority and require a swift response. This balance of workload is a key task which the analyst must learn to anticipate and achieve. The capacity to organise and manage multiple tasks efficiently and use a range of technologies and information sources is essential. Operational activity is mainly day to day and week to week, sometimes leaving little room for medium- or long-term planning. A typical Monday morning might entail preparing a detailed statistical account of the weekend's first-team match for the coaching staff and compiling individual videos for downloading and visualisation by players on their personal mobile viewing device. Afternoon work might include coding and editing videos of the upcoming opposition's performance to identify strengths and weaknesses, followed by the setting up of video equipment to film an early-evening academy training session. He or she will frequently use a battery of equipment and software, some developed in-house and some acquired; thus, being at ease with many forms of PA technology is important.

Analysts must be trained and prepared to deal with potential logistical and technical issues that occur with hardware when filming training or competition. Computer hardware and software problems can occur and the analyst must have a contingency plan (e.g. who to contact, data backup facility, alternative solutions) and the skills to deal with such situations. Indeed, a smooth data-collection process is essential as the service may come under threat if the players and coaching staff fail to commit to the method due to operational problems. This point stresses the importance of selecting the most appropriate system for the environment. A discreet presence is also necessary when filming or monitoring training so as not to disturb the session and because performance might be affected if players are aware of the presence of the observer. Top clubs have gone so far as to build observation facilities into their training grounds, covered and protected from the elements, with power supplies and indeed networked IT services built into the unit. This positive step allows real-time feedback to be generated and provides a professional environment in which to analyse performance. The analyst must have the skills to deal with and provide solutions for potential logistical and technical problems when delivering presentations to staff/players. This can be the case notably when travelling with the team to away games as the audiovisual equipment and hotel-room facilities might be restricted.

A proactive attitude generally is highly important, especially in anticipating the questions and requests of coaching and fitness personnel, particularly in relation to past and present form, and subsequently in providing quick and pertinent responses. Analysts need to be able to plan their work (often unsupervised) in order to be able to anticipate, based on their knowledge of working closely with the coaching staff, additional demands and queries. Despite a frequent shortage of time, the analyst should not just look to deliver their usual reports, but should innovate and look beyond the simple game-to-game analysis cycle. Analysts must have strong analytical skills to efficiently explore and synthesise data and formulate solid conclusions on the basis of the evidence. They should always remain objective in their approach to data collection, analysis and presentation of findings – in other words, they should not simply provide what the coaching staff might want to see or hear! Analysts should be able to give subjective opinions as well as the objective opinion they have formed through the collection and analysis of data. Some coaches, indeed, might seek an 'opinion' after the presentation of data and key findings.

High-level interpersonal skills and the ability to integrate into a 'football club culture' are essential for success and progress in the role. Analysts need to be 'in tune' with the cultural subtleties of the football environment and this is a key skill often in no way 'teachable'. The ability to communicate and interact with coaches and players on both a one-to-one and a collective basis is a key part of the role. At the same time, analysts must have an understanding of the football environment. They must speak the same language as coaching colleagues they directly work with and avoid industry jargon ('metrics' and 'analytics', for example!). It is important that the statistics relate to the terminology traditionally used by coaches. This skill is important to ensure that the analyst can efficiently and confidently transform the masses of information they collect into clear and meaningful messages and presentations to enhance understanding and assimilation in coaches and players.

There are many sociological and learning complexities involved in employing video-based coaching practice. Performance-related feedback must be summative but always developmental in nature. Collaborations can be with academy players, international first-team players, foreign coaches who are possibly coming to grips with a new language, and new managers with a different global vision of the game. In general, the analyst (and the PA model they employ) must be able to adapt their approach to suit different learning styles, philosophies and environments common to professional football. Having not been schooled in the science of sport, some contemporary sports practitioners are sceptical of the relevance to the game of quantitative analyses of playing performance.

When presenting information to players, the content should be agreed beforehand with the coaching staff. Information needs to be conveyed in a clear, concise, logical and direct manner. The data may be clear to the analyst but not to others, and must be set out in an unambiguous manner for ease of understanding by the audience. Many EPL players are not native English speakers and this must be considered, often the careful use of visual information can help convey a message more clearly than verbal/textual information. Presentations should be based around transmission of the major messages derived from the analyses, while having additional detail to hand as required. As mentioned earlier, a combination of video and statistical information summarised in bullet-point format can be an efficient means of transmitting observations and take-home messages. The latter must always have value in terms of objectives and results and be placed in the current playing context. The analyst will frequently have to cater for different learning speeds and styles and cope with varying attitudes to their work from coaches and players. Players' prior experiences, thoughts and perceptions of match analysis can greatly affect how they receive feedback. Some players can have a positive approach to match analysis and might even take ownership of their own performance. In contrast, others are sensitive to criticism even if the feedback is presented 'constructively'. In this case, care is needed not to alienate the player, and a coach-led intervention or one-to-one presentations with the analyst may be preferable. The session should always finish where possible on a positive reinforcing note – that is, by presenting instances of successful performance or bringing attention to the effective implementation of a play practised in training.

Finally, it is important to mention that maintaining motivation and energy levels is difficult as analysts are commonly faced with working long hours and frequently at weekends (even more so if they travel with the first team). Work rate, desire and passion, terms commonly associated with a world-class player, are vital if an analyst is to succeed, and if their passion for the game is questionable, they will get 'found out' very quickly – especially at the highest levels of the game. While recognition of the value of their role is improving, salaries unfortunately do not always reflect the difficulties and pressures inherent in the role. Collectively analysts need to work to change this issue. One step in this direction has been the creation of an official membership organisation for sports scientists by the Football Medical Association in English professional football (see www.footballmedic.co.uk). Recently, there has been a trend for analysts to move with respective managers from club to club. This demonstrates the value and benefits this role has been shown to deliver, while further cementing its importance and helping to secure better salaries and terms and conditions for staff.

SUMMARY

Over the last decade or so, sports science and associated technological advances have had a major impact on practice within the contemporary professional football club environment. In clubs there are now fully financed and resourced PA departments which provide services and support to all teams in the club.

The relationship between analyst and coach was traditionally seen as a give-and-take affair. However, this has changed and the analyst is now seen as a key member of the technical team and sports science staff. While coaches and managers have taken on board a greater understanding of systems and data, analysts have probably made more progress in the other direction, deepening their knowledge of the game and the key factors that are important to managers, coaches and players. While there is still progress needed in terms of resourcing and recognition and reward with respect to the performance analysis profession, the body of staff in clubs is helping to change this, and highly qualified and motivated professional analysts joining their ranks in the future will greatly help this evolving process continue.

Refinements in the size, convenience, precision and reliability of measurement devices have notably opened new doors for analysts in terms of monitoring performance in players in training and competition. Emerging developments currently include smart clothes and footwear in which unobtrusive electronic monitoring sensors are embedded. Future technological advances will likely involve real-time acquisition of data from multiple sources. In addition to customary information such as time-motion data and heart-rate profiling, the concomitant monitoring of biochemical and brainwave responses to exercise is now emerging, as are analyses of muscle activity patterns, joint speeds and contact forces. The increased range and quantity of data generated by performance technologies will be processed, analysed and to some extent interpreted by intelligent systems to support the feedback and decision-making processes. The hallmark of a progressive PA department will be that it stays at the forefront of these developments while constantly making the best use of the knowledge base generated.

REFERENCES

Barnes, C., Archer, D.T, Hogg, B., Bush, M. and Bradley, P.S. 'The Evolution of Physical and Technical Performance Parameters in the English Premier League', *International Journal of Sports Medicine*, 35 (2014), pp. 1095–1100.

Carling, C. 'Match Evaluation: Systems and Tools', in Strudwick, T. (Ed), *Soccer Science* (Human Kinetics, 2016).

Carling, C. and Court, M. 'Match & Motion Analysis of Soccer', in Williams, M. (ed.), *Science and Soccer: Developing Elite Performers*, pp. 173–198 (Routledge, 2013).

Carling, C., Le Gall, F., McCall, A., Nédélec, M. and Dupont, G. 'Squad Management, Injury and Match Performance in a Professional Soccer Team Over a Championship-Winning Season', *European Journal of Sports Sciences*,15, no. 7 (2015), pp. 573–582.

Gregson, W., Drust, B., Atkinson, G. and Salvo Di, V.D. 'Match-to-match variability of high-speed activities in Premier League soccer', *International Journal of Sports Medicine*, 31 (2010), pp. 237–242.

Mackenzie, R. and Cushion, C. 'Performance Analysis in Football: A Critical Review and Implications for Future Research', *Journal of Sports Sciences*, 31 (2013), pp. 639–676.

PART FOUR

PART FOUR

CHAPTER 11

PRACTITIONER REFLECTIONS FROM INDUSTRY

Dr Alec Scott, Dr James Malone, Dr Victoria Tomlinson, Dr Robert Naughton, David Flower and Lewis Charnock

Football Exchange, Research Institute for Sport & Exercise Sciences, Liverpool John Moores University, UK

This chapter aims to present a series of graduate case studies from individuals who currently work (or have done so formerly) in the football industry after graduating with a sport and exercise science-related degree from a higher education university. The intention is to provide a series of practitioner reflections on a number of important questions and topics that we feel future graduates need to consider if their aspiration is to work in professional football at both academy and first-team level. Importantly, we feel that future practitioners need to be aware of the subtle, and often idiosyncratic, craft skills and qualities that are required to work in professional football. The accounts reflect the individuals' personal thoughts on the following questions:

1. What is your role and personal background?
2. What are the key educational, personal and professional competencies that you feel are required to progress into your role (or associated roles) and how did you develop these?
3. How would you describe your approach and philosophy to practice within your role?
4. How have you dealt with and/or how do you deal with the range of challenges within the applied environment (personal, cultural, organisational) and how has this changed over time with experience?
5. What developments (e.g. processes, technology, science etc) do you think will serve to enhance the support of elite players in the future within your role?

ALEC SCOTT: PERFORMANCE ANALYST

Role and Personal Background

I graduated from Liverpool John Moores University (LJMU) with a 1st class BSc (Hons) after studying Science and Football between 2007–2010. The course provided me with a real insight into many of the scientific disciplines that support professional football teams, such as nutrition, physiology, psychology, and performance analysis. The programme really helped form my decision to want to work in professional football through the content of the course, lectures from applied practitioners in the field, whilst also providing opportunities to work in the football environment at Tranmere Rovers Centre of Excellence, Everton FC Academy and the Liverpool FC Community Department.

After graduating, I was fortunate to have the opportunity to work with Liverpool FC 1st team, in a full-time internship role working in both the Performance Analysis and Sport Science departments, alongside studying for a PhD at LJMU. The unique nature of the internship meant I was able to further develop my theoretical understanding through the thesis, that allowed me to explore the physical and technical demands of elite soccer performance using different analytical methods (i.e. Prozone and GPS tracking technology). What made the internship so special was the ability to apply the theoretical knowledge to an elite environment and assist in opposition scouting, match performance analysis and player monitoring, whilst learning from leading applied practitioners.

At the end of my internship with LFC, I was successful in my application to work with the England senior football team as an assistant Performance Analyst and have been in the role since May 2013. During my time with England, I've assisted in the preparation and delivery of analysis to the senior team at the 2014 World Cup in Brazil and the qualification stages for the 2016 European Championships in France. This coming summer (2015) I will (hopefully) have also completed my PhD after my viva examination in July!

Key Educational, Personal and Professional Competencies
Educational
The collaboration between my working environment at LFC and continuation of my education as a PhD student at LJMU helped significantly in my development as an applied practitioner. To have the opportunity to learn and experience the professional environment first hand meant that I was able to develop an ability to interpret research or information in a much more meaningful way that considers the potential impact within the professional environment.

Personal

A very important personal quality that I feel can sometimes be overlooked is the ability to be able to communicate information to the varying staff within a club. It was important for me to learn that the coaches, players and backroom staff within an organisation do not all come from the same academic background and that your knowledge or understanding of a particular subject is only as informative, or as influential, as your ability to be able to communicate that information to your audience.

Professional

The key professional competency that I believe any student or practitioner requires to work in sport is experience of the professional world. There is only so much academic literature or research that can help an individual to interpret or prepare for the environment without experiencing the day-to-day working life, the personalities, the challenges, and the emotions that professional sport teams offer. I've been very fortunate to work at Liverpool FC and England with elite athletes, coaches and practitioners who strive for excellence and continuous development and I consider these as defining professional experiences in my own development.

Philosophical Approach to Practice

In the five years that I have worked in professional football, I have experienced working for three different managers who have each brought different coaches and backroom staff. Each one of these different staff members brought a myriad of experiences, success, footballing and working philosophies, which have all provided me with invaluable insight into sports science and performance analysis roles. From these experiences, my personal approach to practice is to strive for continuous improvement and personal development. I believe it is vital for any student or practitioner that wants to better themselves, to be accepting of new challenges, ideas and concepts; as fundamentally it is helping you develop and evolve as a practitioner.

Dealing with Challenges in the Applied Environment

The environment of a football club has a very special culture and identity, and is something that is unlike many other working environments. During my internship at Liverpool FC I experienced a number of challenges and found the working environment difficult to adjust to. Initially, I found it difficult to adapt to the intensity of a 6–7 day working week, particularly through the congested winter fixture period. Working as a performance analyst I find one of the biggest challenges that I have faced, and still at times find difficult, are the time demands associated to the position. The nature of the role requires you to focus a lot of energy and time to the preparation and post game analysis to ensure you're giving the players and coaches every opportunity to be successful. In order to provide this, there is the need to sacrifice more time to the role and this was something I have learnt to come to terms with. In spite of these demands, there is a great sense of achievement when the hard work in the preparation for a match can help towards a winning performance on the pitch.

Developments to Enhance the Support of Elite Players in the Future

The technologies that we use in our working processes at England are essential to ensure we're providing players with the tools to enhance their understanding and preparation for matches, as well as to reflect after the event. The developments in tablet technology and applications are providing new ways to enhance player interaction and educate them on tactical information, such as England's playing philosophy. Such forms of technology have the potential to maximise learning opportunities, particularly when there are limited training sessions during short in-season international camps. Additionally, the development in Global Positioning Systems (GPS) technology could also play a huge part in the way tracking analysis and physical data can interact with video footage to provide a greater insight into performance during live competitive matches. To have the ability to provide the coaches with physical, technical and tactical information on individual players, positional units, or the team, can help hugely in supporting important decision-making processes during matches (i.e. substitutions, analysing player work rates and team shape).

Finishing note

I have always believed that I was going to follow a career path that I was passionate about and enjoyed. Working in professional football has allowed me to do just that, and experience so many incredible things that I did not believe were possible when I first began. Working as a member of the England World Cup backroom staff last year was one of the proudest moments I ever wished to achieve, and believe that the hard work, dedication and sacrifice necessary to work in professional football is worth it.

JAMES MALONE: SPORTS SCIENTIST

Role and Personal Background

I worked as a Sports Scientist for Catapult Sports covering the European region. Catapult Sports provide athlete-tracking technology that is currently used across multiple sports and teams, such as Borussia Dortmund and Ajax, to monitor physical and tactical performance. My role specifically involved direct interaction with both existing and potential clients around product demonstration, first line support and sports science consultancy. The role provided an excellent opportunity to work with people from different cultures and sporting backgrounds within the elite setting.

I achieved both a BSc. (2.1) in Sports Science and MSc (1ˢᵗ class) in Sports Physiology from Liverpool John Moores University (LJMU) from 2006–2010. Following this period, I underwent and completed a 3-year PhD project between LJMU and Liverpool Football Club, investigating the training load practices in elite soccer. During this time I worked both full-time with the Liverpool first team squad and also enrolled on a full-time PhD degree. Following the completion of my PhD project, I entered my current employment in which I have been involved for the past 2 years. Whilst at LJMU, I also completed part-time internships at Everton Football Club (2009–2010), Nike SPARQ (2010) and the LJMU scholarship programme providing physiological support (2009–2010).

Key Educational, Personal and Professional Competencies

Whilst it is crucial that students undergo the correct academic pathway to achieve the required qualifications, a significant part of the competencies I have acquired (and are still working on) have come from working out in the field. The BSc degree provided a great insight into exercise physiology with high-level academic leaders in various fields. However, I felt the degree was quite broad at times and didn't quite shape you into leaving after 3 years with a clear pathway to work within sport. Hence I underwent the taught MSc degree programme where I further developed my theoretical knowledge around physiology. It was during this year that I also gained significant experience through various internship programmes that enabled me to then progress my career.

Whilst having a high level of academic knowledge is clearly a desirable target for students, I believe that to work within elite sport (particularly in soccer), you certainly also require the right mindset and personality. No matter how many journals you read or essays you write, nothing can prepare you fully for the experience of working in the applied world. It has taken me the best part of 5 years to get to a stage where I'm confident enough to work in elite sport and feel like I can positively contribute. The key competency for this has been hard work and dedication – whilst completing my MSc I worked 7 days a week with 10–12 hour days to fit everything in!

Philosophical Approach to Practice

My natural personality is to be quite humorous and make light of situations. For the majority of instances this has been a positive trait to have, whilst other times not so much. My approach to work is that of utmost dedication and preparation. I feel one of my main skills is the ability to organise and follow up on promises or agreed actions – both key components of my former role. When working with clients I try to gain an understanding of their perspective and what they require, as we are often guilty (myself included) of just telling people our own opinion without listening to others.

Dealing with Challenges in the Applied Environment

During my 3-year PhD programme working full-time at Liverpool FC, I faced many challenges whilst working in an applied environment on a daily basis. When I first worked at the club I was often star-struck and felt inferior to other members of staff. It took the majority of those 3 years to build up to a level of confidence with both players and staff where I felt comfortable in the working environment and was able to voice my opinions. This improvement came about through reflection (both individually and with others) and experience of difficult situations from which I learnt greatly.

Developments to Enhance the Support of Elite Players in the Future

In terms of my former role, there has been a rule change that allowed teams to wear athlete-tracking devices within competitive matches. Whilst this has been adopted by some clubs, the majority in the top European leagues declined this opportunity. This may be due to current contractual situations with technology partners, or a lack of co-operation from the players. The challenge will be to progress with the recent rule changes to help match the training and match demands together using the same tracking technology. This will help to better shape our training regimens and improve the management of the players.

Finishing Note

Whilst at times it has been a difficult journey to progress from my initial studies to my current position, the opportunities and experiences generated have made the hard work worthwhile. The key message for future graduates would be perseverance in what you do. As long as you have a professional attitude and are willing to work hard, then the opportunities will arise. Gaining hands-on experience working in the field enabled me to learn skills that I may not have acquired through just textbooks – so I would encourage you to be proactive with your approach and career planning.

VICTORIA TOMLINSON: SPORTS PSYCHOLOGY PRACTITIONER, PRIVATE PRACTICE

Role and Personal Background

With over a decade of experience in the professional sport industry, I have gained invaluable insight, knowledge and understanding into the culture of professional and high performance environments. Within my role as a British Psychological Society (BPS) Chartered Psychologist and former Head of Education and Welfare at an English professional football club, my objective has been to manage psychological well-being and to promote working practices within the performance environment. The key aims to support well-being have been to facilitate autonomy and personal growth, to develop and maintain positive relations with others, and to achieve a sense of mastery and competence in managing performance and the environment. Working as part of a collaborative multidisciplinary team, I have been able to work in conjunction with various practitioners (coaches, sports scientists and medical practitioners), along with many different types of individuals and age groups.

I completed my undergraduate degree in mainstream Psychology and Biology, and postgraduate training in Sports Psychology at Liverpool John Moores University. I established contact with a professional football club academy, and from there I carried out my BASES Supervised Experience (SE) placement, over a 6-month period. This experience provided invaluable insight into the environment and culture of a professional football club, and led to my first opportunity of employment as a training sports psychology practitioner within a professional football club academy. Following this, I completed three years applied training and supervised experience in order to gain successful BASES accreditation and BPS chartered certification. I am also qualified as an AASP Certified Consultant in the USA.

Key Educational, Personal and Professional Competencies

I gained experience in conducting research in applied settings during the completion of my doctoral research in psychological well-being (PWB) and qualitative research methods, which utilised both mainstream theory and an exploration of culture and practice. Within my research, I worked closely with athletes in one-to-one and group situations, and alongside coaches and medical practitioners within a collaborative multidisciplinary team. Practitioner collaboration, engagement and commitment to participatory action research encouraged and facilitated significant changes to everyday practice within the environment. As a result, I gained extensive experience in qualitative research methods, in-depth qualitative research interviewing, data management, analysis and report writing.

Within my research, the study of PWB as a concept helped shape the practitioner that I am today. I developed through the process and it added to my career and skill set. The process of reflection occurred on a daily basis, as the cyclical process of action research itself provided a platform for staged, layered and shared reflection to take place, but also as a reactive form of reflection in and on action (as it happened). Reflective practice has been fundamental to my progress as a practitioner, and is a process that I continue to use and develop, to drive improvement and change in day-to-day practice.

With extensive education, training and experience, I also acquired professional knowledge and understanding in teaching and applied practice. Previous roles included teaching in Higher Education at Liverpool John Moores University, teaching on sports psychology modules, and evaluating teaching and learning practice at all levels. Within my teaching and research role at the university, I was able to stay abreast with current research in sports science and football. As a result, this aided and enhanced my professional knowledge in the applied field. Furthermore, the teaching experience I had gained supported my career progression into the role as Head of Education and Welfare, of which my responsibilities included leading and contributing to our in-house academy education programme, module development and curriculum review, working with colleagues to support a strong academic programme identity, and producing teaching materials informed by current research to motivate and inspire student learning.

My teaching and research experiences furthered my career progression, and complemented my applied practice and experience in professional football, with particular reference to psychological well-being, youth development and coaching practice.

Philosophical Approach to Practice

As a dedicated chartered psychologist and offering over 11 years of experience in the applied field of professional sport, my moral view to practice is to care about what I do. My personal philosophy to practice is a person-centred and holistic approach, with core values seeking to build trust and rapport, strong relationships, co-operation and engagement, to work collaboratively with people, and to understand the culture of the environment.

In practice, my objective is to work alongside athletes and practitioners in a mentoring, supporting and challenging role to monitor and optimise their effectiveness in delivering. I aim to promote best practice, to establish, develop and manage key relationships using appropriate interpersonal skills and communication methods. From my own experiences, I've learnt that in the applied field you're judged on how you apply yourself in the environment, around practitioners and athletes, working well with people, being effective and facilitating best practice, and that most importantly, you've got to care about what you do.

Dealing with Challenges in the Applied Environment

I have experienced a range of challenges within the applied environment that have changed over time. Initial challenges that I faced when first starting out involved gaining acceptance into the environment, and earning the respect and credibility from players and practitioners as a young training sports psychology practitioner, a role that would be new to the academy programme. In addition, I also needed to gain acceptance into the environment as a female working in a predominantly male-oriented environment.

As a result of immersing myself in the football environment, I felt after six months I gained a level of acceptance with players and practitioners. Surprisingly, over time, I felt my gender brought advantages to my role. I felt there were fewer barriers when it came to accessing emotions. For example, once I had established rapport with the players they appeared comfortable to open up and reflect on their feelings and emotions. I began to realise that the disadvantages of being female in such a male-oriented environment were mainly initial barriers, barriers to be overcome at the beginning, when attempting to gain acceptance. Certain challenges forced me to ask questions of myself, that I found challenging from both a personal and professional perspective. For example, at times, I questioned the academy environment, an environment that was often hostile, and sometimes, I suspected, purposefully. The rationale, or at least the rationale as I understood it, was that this was a way of being, prepared players for the 1st team environment. I often questioned whether providing such an environment realistically facilitated or hindered player development? That said, I recognised there was scope to support players and help increase their ability to receive challenging feedback in order to better prepare them to become accustomed with the academy and/or the 1st team environment. On reflection, and with hindsight, the range of challenges I have faced within the applied environment have been significant to my learning and development as a practitioner.

Finishing Note

It's a challenging and exciting environment, and my learning and development is ongoing! I have found relationships and interactions to be key, building strong working relationships with players and practitioners (coaches, sports scientists, and medical practitioners). Having the opportunity to learn from their craft/professional knowledge and experience has been invaluable to my journey.

ROBERT NAUGHTON: PERFORMANCE NUTRITIONIST

Role and Personal Background

I graduated from Liverpool John Moores University with an honours degree in Sports Science (Physiology) in June 2011. Whilst in my final year of my undergraduate degree, my interest in Sports Science really developed into a huge passion. I found myself consistently looking to develop my knowledge through academic application (journal reading and testing mainly) and voluntary work. After graduation I knew I wanted to continue in academia and this led to me wanting to continue further study, and I was able to enrol on an MSc in Sports Physiology.

During my MSc I managed to secure a year placement as an intern at an academy of a Premier League club. This was a difficult year as I had the task of balancing my studies, my internship, my paid work and my voluntary work. However, on reflection, although it was difficult at the time, I got to work with and know a lot of great people, and learnt a huge amount in a relatively short period of time. Following the completion of my MSc I knew I wanted to do a PhD, so much so that I chose 'filler' jobs after I first left LJMU, deciding not to start a career in something.

After the best part of a year of working in a job I hated, and a number of failed PhD applications, I was successful for a PhD back at LJMU investigating nutrition in youth football. Along with this, I am currently working as an intern at a Premier League academy as a Performance Nutritionist, which allows me to gain vital first-hand experience whilst collecting my PhD data.

Key Educational, Personal and Professional Competencies
Educational

You have to know what you're talking about. I feel it's vital to have a depth of knowledge within your specialty (in my case nutrition), but it's also important to have knowledge of the specialties surrounding you (i.e. Strength & Conditioning). My degrees have played a huge role in this as they have provided me with my foundation of knowledge. I've also been fortunate enough to have been taught, and continue to be taught, by world leaders in their field. Keeping up-to-date with current research is important, however, there are lots of things that you can't learn from a textbook or journal, only first-hand experience can teach you some lessons. I think coming into my role with previous experience of playing and working in sport has helped me, and also general experience of working in the real world, dealing with real people and problems.

Personal

I think it's vitally important to simply be a good people person. Within sport you meet so many different kinds of people, and I think it's important to be able to adapt to different kinds of people, whilst not trying to be something you're not. I think remaining humble and never thinking you're 'a somebody' is another key skill. It's a cliché, but I think you should treat people how you would wish to be treated, know their name, be polite (manners make a huge difference!), and be respectful. The flip side of that is this, understand that some people will treat you poorly, be rude to you and not give you the time of day. This happens in all walks of life, but it's how you deal with it and learn from it that's been important for me.

Professional

Similar to educational and personal, I think you have to know your profession and how to deal with different types of people. From my own experience, I also think it's important to always be looking on improving yourself and this can be across the board. Improving your knowledge, qualifications, experience, practices, communication skills etc. I've met some people who do have great jobs in sport and academics, but have since then switched off and are no longer looking to better themselves.

Philosophical Approach to Practice

My approach to my applied role is to try to educate and inform those I work with (players, staff, parents etc.), with the aim of them being able to understand the consequences of the choices they make and how that affects their performance. I'm quite laid back in that I won't 'have a go' at a player who's eating badly, nor will I stand over them and force feed them 'good' food (although some people think I should). I think football needs a slight cultural shift in its approach to nutrition, and I think that shift is currently happening. More and more players are taking the initiative, rather than having to be consistently told what and when to eat. As I've mentioned I think to educate and 'empower' the player is a better approach for long term development.

My philosophy to practice is something that I'm still learning myself and will most likely continue to develop over time. However, I do believe in the importance of having a good team, pushing each other on, supporting each other, all working towards a common goal and feeling valued. Just like on the pitch, to have a good team you need good leadership from the top and the team working towards a common goal.

Dealing with Challenges in the Applied Environment

I think trying to establish myself – firstly within my department, then with the players and staff – was a big challenge. When I started working within the sports science department I was aware I was working with people at the top end of their field, and they wouldn't blindly follow everything I suggested. However, this was great as it meant I would ensure my suggestions were evidence based and worth attempting. At first, the players could be stand-offish with me, as I was new and they hadn't had much nutrition guidance previously. Yet, after being around them I was able to build relationships and work with them openly and honestly – the relationships I have with the players have helped me hugely develop my practitioner skills.

Having work sprung on you that has to have a quick turn-around and outcome is another challenge. However, I believe this has had a positive effect on me. Stress, and how you deal with it, is a huge factor within professional sport, therefore it is something that you learn to deal with. Academic experience sets you up for this in some ways, the stress (or perceived stress) of deadlines, meeting new people, getting good marks etc.

Developments to Enhance the Support of Elite Players in the Future

In terms of processes, I'm unsure, as this is something I'm trying to correct and improve now in my current role. Generally speaking, for nutrition I would have to say development of player education and understanding is vital. In terms of technology, I think phone apps could play an important role. I think the technology is currently there; it's more a question of designing the right one that is user friendly and will help the players engage. Of course, it would also be highly beneficial if a practical and accurate piece of kit could measure energy expenditure, perhaps one day this will be available.

For science and research, I am extremely fortunate to be involved in the club I am currently with, as the 1st team and academy sports science staff are all partaking in research. I am one of five PhD students at the club I'm involved in, and the sports science department as a whole has a large number of papers already published and under development. That said, I do think if football was more accepting to sports science, some groundbreaking research could be pursued. Bridging the gap between science and practice is a difficult challenge, but an important one for any graduate looking to work in sport, particularly a skill-based sport such as football. Perhaps if we can conduct research within elite football we will discover ways that we can guarantee improved performance through different nutritional protocols.

Finishing Note

As I'm still studying, a common question is where do I see myself in 5–10 years? In all honesty, I never give it a huge amount of thought, as I've grown to view the journey as more important than the destination. I think I would like to be an academic, conducting research and teaching, whilst also working in the field. Growing up, I was *always told to do something you enjoy and it wasn't till I was 19 that I realised what I wanted to do. When I first arrived as an undergraduate at LJMU, I was probably guilty of thinking I'd reached my destination, which obviously in reality was just the start for me. With how I feel currently, I hope I never feel like I've arrived at the destination, but rather that I'm on a new path continuing my journey within Sports Science, physiology and nutrition. My journey is still ongoing and so far it's been fantastic, as mentioned I been able to learn from the best, I've worked in some amazing environments, and more importantly, met a lot of good people along the way. I'd advise anyone who is keen to get into Sports Science, or any profession for that matter, to not just worry about the end outcome but to savour the journey they set out upon. In my opinion, only by doing this will you get the most out of the experience and be able to seize opportunities that come along the way.*

One final thing is that every experience, good or bad, can be learnt from and used positively in the future. As an undergraduate, I used to think that reflective practice was not required, but I've found it extremely beneficial during my post-graduate work. What I failed to understand is that reflective practice isn't necessarily working through Gibbs' model, it's also occurring when you're out on a run, in the car, having a coffee with a friend or colleague discussing experiences. I've found that as I've got older and further into my career, I'm better at being honest with myself and those around me who I trust, and that has helped me further develop.

DAVID FLOWER: FITNESS COACH

Role and Personal Background

I'm currently the first team Fitness Coach at Everton Football Club, but this section reflects my previous role as the U23 fitness coach. My role was to oversee and manage the development of all aspects of physical performance for the U23s squad, in addition to assisting with First Team programmes and helping with the transition of players from U18s to U23s. I completed a BSc (Hons) Science and Football and an MSc Sports Physiology at Liverpool John Moores University. I have previously completed Sports Science internships at Everton FC and West Bromwich Albion FC, working across First Team and Academy age groups. I then worked with Everton Ladies FC, working closely with the Head Coach to oversee all aspects of performance across Academy and Senior age groups, before accepting my current position.

Key Educational, Personal and Professional Competencies

I think ultimately a sound theoretical and scientific understanding of physiological and biomechanical principles is essential for my work. This knowledge, developed primarily through my university education, helps to underpin my practical work and forms the basis for the rationale of my work. Whilst the foundation of this knowledge was gained through undergraduate and post-graduate education, I feel as though this is something that has evolved since I completed these qualifications and is always something I am continually looking to develop further.

To be personally competent in my role, I think this essentially relates to being able to form and maintain effective working relationships with the people around me. This relates highly to immediate staff, such as the U23s Head Coach, First Team Fitness Coach, Head of Performance and Head of Medicine, in addition to other physiotherapists and coaching staff. Also, and importantly, the players! I feel I have developed this ability over time working with these people; however, I have been able to draw on previous applied experiences to help build relationships quicker and also maintain them in potentially difficult situations.

Philosophical Approach to Practice

I feel this is an area that I am still trying to understand fully and am in the early stages of defining my own 'philosophy of practice'. I think I try to always be honest and have clear and simple communication with staff and players. With regards to my practical work, often on the field or in the gym, I like to keep this fairly simple and cover the basics of physical development, always being able to relate back to a sound scientific rationale.

Dealing with Challenges in the Applied Environment

Personally, I feel as though I naturally lean towards a more introverted personality, which can be challenging in an environment that expects and encourages extroverts. I think initially this is something I struggled with in my role, especially due to the full-time, day-to-day nature of the role. However, I feel that over time, I have become more comfortable in the environment. I also feel that I have used the personal challenges that I have experienced to reflect and understand myself as a practitioner better. I think a lot of the challenges I face are related to organisational issues as a result of cultural influences. The environment is often fluid and fast moving, with plans (or sometimes lack of planning) often changing; sometimes minute-to-minute. Through self-reflection, I have realised that to work at my best I need a structure or framework from which to work. Clearly in a football environment that is constantly changing, a rigid working structure is challenging to work from. I think with experience I have learnt to ride with the changes and develop a personal framework and structure that I am comfortable to work in, yet that is dynamic enough to adapt.

Developments to Enhance the Support of Elite Players in the Future

Better application of monitoring systems in management of training load (alongside evolution of monitoring tools such as GPS). Individualised recovery protocols based *on specific competition stress. A better understanding, and ultimately application, of learning processes and how (especially) young players learn, process and apply information.*

LEWIS CHARNOCK: PERFORMANCE PSYCHOLOGIST

Role and Personal Background

My initial dream, like many other young boys, was to be a professional footballer. I played football for a professional academy from the age of 7, however was released at youth team level when my club went into liquidation. I then decided to enrol at Liverpool John Moores University (LJMU) to study Sport & Exercise Science and graduated with an honours degree in June 2014. The degree covered all aspects of sports performance: physiology, nutrition, strength & conditioning and psychology. This confirmed to me that the next best thing to playing at an elite level would be, to hopefully one day, work with elite level athletes. It was only in my final year of my undergraduate degree that my interest in sports psychology was ignited; reading and being taught sports psychology material uncovered performance issues that I actually had experienced as a youth footballer trying to make my way in the game. I decided halfway through my final undergraduate year to apply for the MSc Sports Psychology course at LJMU. I enrolled on the course in September 2014 and within a few weeks I wanted to experience the applied world and began the professional pathway of British Association of Sport & Exercise Sciences (BASES) Supervised Experience in the discipline of psychology. I managed to secure voluntary work in the sports of cricket, rowing and boxing alongside my applied placement at a Premier League Football Club's Academy as a Sports Science (Psychology) support student. The placement has now developed into my current role at the club's Academy in which I am a Performance Psychologist. The role mainly centres around supporting coaches and staff to help them develop psychological skills in youth football players and conducting group workshops on psychology to players, parents and coaches for the age groups Under 9s to Under 16s.

Key Educational, Personal and Professional Competencies

The key educational competency that I feel is required in my role is being comfortable with and having a comprehensive knowledge base of different approaches to sports psychology support. I think you have to have an understanding of different philosophies and frameworks; whether that is psychodynamic, behavioural, cognitive or humanistic. I think not only do I have to have a good understanding of the approaches, but also it is vital that I am able to apply these to the real world in sporting performance. I doubt many elite sport coaches want to know about Pavlov's dog and classical conditioning and how this theory may influence why players behave in certain ways! I also feel it is important that in terms of personal qualities, I am able to 'fit in' to a sporting organisation's culture. In elite level sport, especially professional football, I think you have to possess good interpersonal skills and be able to build relationships quickly with all individuals in an organisation (from the receptionist to coaches to the kit man). Another early lesson that I have learned in my fledgling career as a probationary sport and exercise scientist (psychology) is that you also need to be competent with other disciplines of sports sciences. There have been many occasions already that coaches or performers have consulted me on other disciplines such as physiology, biomechanics or nutrition. I feel that it is important that you are comfortable in talking and appreciate other sports science staff's roles and that all staff contribute to successful sport performance.

Philosophical Approach to Practice

My philosophy of practice is a humanistic, person-centred approach to psychological support. I tend to focus on the self-development of the coach and athlete and consider factors not only from their chosen sport, but also in wider life that may influence their ability to perform at their best. In my view, the most important aspect of my approach to practice is to initially gain the trust and build a rapport with the client, whether that is a player, coach or staff. That is central to my approach, I feel that the client is only able to fully open up to a sports psychology consultant if they firmly believe that you are always acting in their best interests and their confidentiality will not be broken, unless they want it to be. I do believe that mental skills training such as relaxation, imagery and deep breathing have a place in providing sports psychology support and it may be of benefit to provide symptom relief in certain situations. Nevertheless, I currently work from a Socratic approach to identify the deep, underlying cause of performance and hope to help the athlete gain greater self-knowledge, to recognise their strengths and gain realisation that they have the choice to act in the 'here and now'.

Dealing with Challenges in the Applied Environment

Sometimes I feel that there is still a stigma in sport, especially in football, in that if an athlete seeks psychological support, they are considered 'weak' or something is wrong with them. Due to this overhanging stigma of being 'weak', I feel that some performers do not feel comfortable to speak to their coaches in the fear of de-selection or, at worst, being deemed surplus to requirements in the organisation. In this early stage of my career I have already gained the impression that psychological support is sometimes only wanted when something is not going well; the approach to psychology is reactive and not proactive. I deal with this issue by trying to educate coaches and athletes alike that it is, in fact, ok to talk and fine to question themselves, not only when things go wrong, but also after good performances or results. This is an aspect of my role that is continuous; I have to educate, and to some extent, campaign for psychology to be acknowledged as a considerable factor that influences performance, much like technical or tactical aspects that are already widely accepted.

Another challenge I feel that has presented itself in my early career is when you join a new organisation it is vitally important that you have clarity and nail down your role within the organisation. People have to know what you do, what you are there to offer and ultimately, who you are. I learned this was a great challenge in my initial applied experiences; I didn't really work with the client or organisation to gain clarity on my role. This resulted in other staff and people in my early experiences not really knowing who I was, or what I offer, and this could lead to me, at times, feeling undervalued. I now deal with this challenge with a forthright approach – as soon as there is any prospect of me providing psychological support with key discussions with the athlete or club. As soon as I gain entry into the organisation I try to determine what my role will look like. In terms of psychological support, I have discussions and ask questions such as what do they want from me? What do I think they need? What do I think will work? I feel that this has greatly assisted me in gaining clarity in my role so everyone knows what I do, and who I am!

Developments to Enhance the Support of Elite Players in the Future

In the future, I feel that the development that will best serve to enhance the support that I am able to provide is that the Applied Sports Psychologist will become a widely accepted role in elite sport. I believe that there is 'muddy water' when it comes to sports psychology; some sports and clubs buy into sports psychology, others completely dismiss sports psychology; it is currently their prerogative. I feel as though the discipline of sports psychology has made great strides in the last decade; however, there is still a way to go. I believe that processes such as there being requirements to have a qualified member of staff that provides sports psychology support would greatly assist in enhancing the support in the future.

Take Home Message

My early experiences of my role in sports psychology support have been fascinating and have reinforced that I made the right decision to embark upon this career. There is a definite and pivotal role for psychology support in elite sport, not as an isolated medium, but fully blended with and fully integrated with other performance enhancing disciplines such as physiology, nutrition and biomechanics. The common denominator is that they all contribute to athletes realising their potential and being the best that they can be.

FINISHING POINTS

This range of graduate narratives has provided us with an insight into the personal and highly unique experiences that they have faced in their journey into professional football. It is clear that the football industry, at both academy and first-team levels, provides unique challenges that practitioners will have to deal with. While many of these are connected to the respective scientific disciplines, it is evident that future practitioners will also need to navigate a range of cultural and contextual challenges that are framed around occupational working practices. All graduates have mentioned the importance of 'experience' prior to commencing work in the football industry, and it is clear that understanding your own practitioner identity is critical in shaping your approach to professional practice. In addition, personal qualities of the individual are perhaps the distinguishing features of effective practice, which points towards the importance of engaging in personal and shared reflection to make sense of yourself and the world.

We're sure that every practitioner working in the world of professional football, young or old, inexperienced or vastly experienced, has a 'tale to tell' that has defined his or her journey and current existence. However, it is hoped that these graduate case studies have prompted you to consider your current personal values, skills and competencies that will enable you to be an effective and competent applied practitioner and scientist.

THE NEXT STEPS

Prof. Valter Di Salvo

Director, Football Performance and Science Department, Aspire Academy and Qatar FA

I am honoured to contribute to a text on behalf of someone who helped to change the game of football from a performance and science perspective. The game is about intensity and it is this aspect that Tom Reilly began to analyse and improve over 40 years ago. Tom introduced many new concepts to the game but a key aspect was his early approach to match analysis, the most important element. His article in 1976 on the positional demands of the game inspired my approach to training methodology throughout my career. Without the benefit of the technology that we have available today, his manual approach to analysing the positional demands of the game was a brilliant idea and one that influenced my decision to use new technology to go deeper into the analysis of the game's demands. Despite the importance of this area, I am still surprised today that it is not applied as it should be. Plenty of research articles have confirmed the large positional differences in match demands first identified by Tom in 1976 – for example, if we compare central defenders with wide midfielders, we see almost a doubling of the high-intensity demands in the latter – yet even today we still see examples of players in different positions training in the same way. It is not acceptable that, more than 40 years after Tom first showed us these differences, this fundamental aspect of training methodology is still ignored.

Tom's contribution goes way beyond analysing the demands of the game; he also helped to develop people who are now working around the world, supporting coaches as strength and conditioning coaches and sports scientists. In the end, it is the coach who takes the decisions – he is the director of the orchestra – but all the other components are so important in allowing the coach to do the right job, to make the right decisions, to analyse what the opposition do. Today when we talk about performance, we still have some coaches who do not like to talk about sports scientists because they still feel they are too far away from the pitch. Sometimes this is true and we need to get closer to the coach. The coach may prefer the term 'performance' to 'sports scientist' as he better understands this concept. Today in the world of football there are positions as performance directors who manage the performance team. This is an important development and I think it is essential that we both define and manage this area correctly. Under this person we now have nutritionists, psychologists, sports scientists and strength and conditioning coaches, who work together to develop the players in accordance with the demands of the game. This is the correct way in which a performance or sports science team can impact the game.

Another way in which we can help the players is to try to speak their language. This is now completely different – social media is the language of the new generation of player, and we have to take this into consideration. Their world is images, video etc; therefore, we have to adopt these tools to communicate with them. We need to create live feedback during training, not just for the technical and tactical aspects, which has been happening for a few years, but for all the different types of training, be it strength training in the gym or speed training on the pitch. They should see what they have done well and what they have done poorly, and these approaches can help us to make them more aware of how they need to improve. This should be a key consideration for us going forward. Another important development in the future concerns data. Traditionally, the owners and users of the data have been the coaches and the performance staff. However, the owners of the data should be the players. They should receive this information. This will also facilitate their awareness of what they are doing well and what they are not doing well; in this way, the drive to improve comes from them seeing what is required. So data needs to be managed in a very clear way that integrates all the different areas and which is available to the player.

The next big challenge for the performance team is to speak the language of the player, to provide live feedback during his training and to provide integrated feedback on all the components that affect their performance. I am quite sure that as Tom Reilly did over 40 years ago, to analyse the game in order to go deeper into what the player needs to do to perform, moving forward we need to continue to analyse the player in an integrated way and to ensure we maximise our impact on both the coach and the player.

INDEX